Why Pray for Israel?

Why Pray for Israel?

Ken Burnett

Sovereign World

Sovereign World Ltd
PO Box 784
Ellel
Lancaster LA1 9DA
England

www.sovereignworld.com

ISBN: 978-1-85240-505-2

The publishers aim to produce books which will help to extend and build up the
Kingdom of God. We do not necessarily agree with every view expressed by
the authors, or with every interpretation of Scripture expressed. We expect readers to
make their own judgment in the light of their understanding of God's Word and in an
attitude of Christian love and fellowship.

Cover Design by Andrew Mark, ThirteenFour Design
Typeset by Hurix Systems Pvt. Limited
Printed in the United Kingdom

CONTENTS

Foreword

It is with great pleasure that I write this foreword to the expanded version of Ken Burnett's book *Why Pray for Israel?* For some thirty-five years I have known Ken and worked with him. Throughout those years I can bear witness to the fact that a fire has burned within him and has never dimmed or been quenched. That "fire within his bones" has been a consuming burden for Israel and the Jewish people. He is a living illustration of the words found in the book of Exodus:

> Behold the bush burned with fire, and the bush was not consumed.
>
> (Exodus 3:2 KJV)

The truth exemplified in that statement was true of Moses and also of Israel, then and now. It was also as true of the apostle Paul as it has been of the true Church until today! Ken has now reached his ninety-first year and still that fire burns within him as powerfully and brightly as ever. The old thorn bush has not been consumed but has become the continuous fuel for that continuous flame. Would to God that there were thousands more like him!

It is the same spirit burning within Ken Burnett as was in the apostle Paul, expressed so powerfully and movingly in those words:

> I have great sorrow and unceasing anguish in my heart ... I could wish that I myself were cursed and cut off from Christ for the sake of my brothers, those of my own race.
>
> (Romans 9:2 NIV)

7

Throughout the book which he has written, we touch this burden and this fire. It encapsulates a lifetime of ever-deepening experience and understanding of the mystery of Israel. The rich and divinely given insights contained within it can only add to a reader's understanding.

Such an understanding is vital if a true and balanced picture is to be gained of what the Lord is doing in these days. The apostle Paul wrote:

> I do not want you to be ignorant of this mystery, brothers, so that you may not be conceited: Israel has experienced a hardening in part *until* the full number of the Gentiles has come in.
>
> (Romans 11:25 NIV, emphasis added)

The word "until" implies a time limit to the hardening in part which the Jewish people have experienced. If the conclusion of that time is approaching, we should expect the Holy Spirit to be freshly emphasizing these truths. We would also expect the powers of darkness to be confusing the issues by creating excesses amongst its proponents and by inspiring bitter and bigoted recrimination amongst its antagonists. It should not, therefore, be a cause for surprise that there is confusion over this subject, or that it has become the focal point of much controversy and conflict. Even the apostle refers to it as "this mystery," signifying a secret which has to be revealed. The fact is that in the same manner in which the Lord has to reveal to us the mystery of the gospel and the mystery of Christ – whether the mystery of His person, His indwelling, or His Body, the Church – the mystery of Israel has also to be revealed to us.

It is a secret which He alone is able to make clear, but which He is more than ready to unveil to those who belong to Him and who will humbly seek Him in childlike trust and simplicity. May He use this book to bring such an understanding!

We shall always be thankful for Ken and for the truth that has burned so brightly within him and is so clearly expressed in this book. What makes it so unusual is the fact that it is not just an emphasis on the fulfillment of divine prophecy, adding to our Biblical knowledge, but is a challenge to be involved and to become intercessors and prayer warriors for Israel. We thank the Lord for the years during which He has enabled Ken not only to establish but also to lead prayer for Israel, until his retirement a few years ago. He has not only borne testimony to the truth concerning Israel but has inspired so much genuine intercession and travail for her. May this book be used to expand and further equip the army of genuine intercessors for Israel that God has already raised up through Ken's leadership, and that of others.

Lance Lambert
Jerusalem, July 2009

Preface

Whilst it is certainly a long time since the first writing of this book in 1983, that first imperative, that calling to pray for Israel, has much multiplied and has in no way diminished.

The term "Jewish feasts" has always been a misnomer. The actual Biblical term, "The LORD's appointed times" (Leviticus 23:2 NASB), itself points to the fact that, in their relevance and importance, these feasts or festivals go way beyond even Israel and the Jewish people. Every one of the seven festivals holds a message for the Church, for Christian believers. Some of these have been revealed and fulfilled, but those that remain are shortly to be "uncovered" – *with vast effect upon the earth.*

Some of this is touched upon within this updated version of what I wrote long ago. I believe that new readers plus re-readers will, with great personal reward, grasp the fact that *God really does have an appointed time!* This is for each of us, and for our respective nations, but *especially* for the nation through which He chose to initially send forth the gospel: Israel. This book unravels something of her near future – inscribed in the unchanging Word of God.

Psalm 102 should lead us to the prayer of faith, because the very return of the Lord to this earth, and His coming enthronement in Jerusalem, hinge upon this:

> It is time to be gracious to her [Israel],
> *For the appointed time has come.*
>
> (Psalm 102:13 NASB, emphasis added)

Ken Burnett
July 2009

CHAPTER 1

Why Pray for Israel?

Asking this very question today, the slightest change in the intonation of voice will bring with it a flood of widely differing responses.

For example, with the sincere but uninformed, the forehead might pucker, and the head be tilted, but the ear would listen: "Why *pray* for Israel?"

With the incredulous, the eyebrows could rise, the arms be flung back, and the mind could already be stacking up its own answers: "*Why* pray for Israel?"

Or, again, with the more firmly set, the lips might even curl, the temperature rise, and the face could redden! "Why pray for *Israel*? Land-snatchers! Aggressors! Murderers! The spark for a third World War!"

To all three attitudes, and any others, the author brings this arresting thought from Scripture:

> His [God's] way is in the whirlwind and the storm,
>> and clouds are the dust of his feet.
>
> (Nahum 1:3 NIV)

In other words, God's ways are not our ways; God's thoughts are not our thoughts. He is to be found in the most unlikely circumstances. Why *not* pray for Israel? God's answer to your query and mine is there in His placing before us yet another question. This was raised and put to Queen Esther, the monarch's wife of that time, as she faced the threatened annihilation of the Jewish people:

> Who knows whether you have come to the kingdom for such a time as this?
>
> (Esther 4:14 NKJV)

To put it another way: Haven't you come to this very point in time – for this *very* purpose – to pray for this tiny but beleaguered nation?

The time

The two timings are similar: Esther's influence with her king, Ahasuerus, at the time of Haman's intended destruction of the Jews; and the potential prayer power of the Christian and the Church, at this time of escalating hatred of Israel.

> You will be hated by all nations because of me.
>
> (Matthew 24:9 NIV)

Were this not the answer, we may well ask *why*, of all the books of the Bible, is the book of Esther preserved? There is no direct mention of God in it but, instead, a synopsis of the fate of Haman and others who are found plotting the destruction of the Jewish people. The verse from Esther and its context indicate that *our relationship with God at this time carries with it a specific responsibility* related to the current threat (through Israel's neighbors) to destroy Israel.

Queen Vashti, who had preceded Esther (each being a type of the Church), lost her position through disobedience, because she did not like the channels used to call her – the king's eunuchs and attendants (Esther 1:10, 12). Esther herself, an orphan and outcast, was eventually chosen by the king to replace the deposed Queen Vashti. (There is a hidden prophetic warning within this passage – amplified in Romans 11:21–22.)

Let us bear in mind at this point that, geographically, only one place is mentioned in the Bible for specific prayer – *Jerusalem!* Why? As this book unfolds, we shall get a glimpse of God's purposes for and through that city, with insight as to where we, as Bible-believing Christians, fit in. Many Christians today are in total ignorance (as was the author of this book at one time) as to why God would choose such a place. Yet, as long ago as the time of Moses, some twenty-six veiled references to Jerusalem were made in the book of Deuteronomy (e.g. Deuteronomy 12:5). *And Jerusalem's history did not by any means end with the crucifixion!*

If there is any doubt that God has called us, the Christian Church, to such prayer, to such a position at this very hour, let us be reminded that God's holy Word is entrusted to *us*, not to politicians. Jeremiah's inspired exhortation:

> *Hear* the word of the LORD, O nations,
>   And *declare* in the coastlands afar off:
>   And say, "He who scattered Israel will gather him ..."
> (Jeremiah 31:10 NASB, emphasis added)

is for *us*, Bible-believing Christians, to hear and to vocalize. It is for us to proclaim, to pray over! God's will, God's strategy, God's purposes are revealed to us through His Word. *Even a passive belief in this portion of the Word of God is quite insufficient.*

Let us also remember that the term "nations" above refers to *Gentiles,* non-Jewish people (Hebrew: *goyim*), and the term "the coast-lands" especially includes Britain (see Chapter 8).

Our own welfare

At the heart of the matter, Esther is warned that she cannot just opt out of concern for the Jewish people (Esther 4:13). Similarly, the question is, can we opt out today?

> For if you keep silence at this time, relief and deliverance for the Jews will arise from another place, but you and your father's family will perish.
> (Esther 4:14 NIV)

Because of the massive political overtones, the doctrinal confusion, and the controversy that Satan has managed to weave within the Church on the subject of Israel, many well-meaning Christians totally shy away from this matter, *which is the very key to understanding God's end-time purposes for the Church.* This, in spite of the fact that Israel itself is mentioned 2,567 times in the Bible which, coupled with such terms as Jerusalem, Zion, Jacob, Judah and Ephraim, give a total of almost 5,000 references related directly to Israel. (The person reading their Bible through once a year thus reads daily an average of almost fourteen references to Israel.) Is not the Lord virtually saying, "Haven't you come to my Kingdom for this very hour and purpose? Am I not soon to confound all nations with the sight of my holiness, power and faithfulness? Will this not be demonstrated through my tiny servant nation – Israel – before the eyes of the whole world?" (See Ezekiel 36:23; 38:23.)

Is there not a clear link between God's dire warning in Romans 11:22 to the wild (Gentile) branches being cut off, and that warning addressed to Esther that "you and your father's house will perish" (Esther 4:14 NASB)? Our own well-being *is* involved. The gallows that Haman had built for Mordecai's destruction proved to be his own undoing and departure point. Robbing Israel as we do of all the Biblical promises made to her in the Word of God equates to putting Israel on the gallows! But the truth is that even in her present unbelief, the "insignificant" nation of Israel has by no means ceased to be God's servant nation.

You, O Israel, my servant,
  Jacob, whom I have chosen,
  you descendants of Abraham my friend,
I took you from the ends of the earth,
  from its farthest corners I called you.
I said, "You *are* my servant";
  I have chosen you and have not rejected you.
So do not fear, *for I am with you;*
  do not be dismayed, for I *am* your God.
I will strengthen you and help you;
  I will uphold you with my righteous right hand.
                                    (Isaiah 41:8–10 NIV, emphasis added)

Whether we like it or not, our attitude to Israel is our attitude to God. God affirms of Zion: "He who touches you touches the apple of His eye"(Zechariah 2:8 NKJV). The eye is the most sensitive part of the whole body, and Zion thus pictured to us is a simple but vivid exhortation to love and to care – and it is a warning.

The human eye is protected in five ways – by constant washing, and by the eye socket, the eyelid, the eyelash and the eyebrow! It is also worth noting that a valid reading of the same passage is as follows: "He that toucheth you toucheth the apple of his [own] eye" (KJV)! Our attitude to Zion will definitely affect the nature and accuracy of our *own* Christian vision as a whole.

We are virtually told here that Zion is God's window on the world! So, the question arises as to whether or not the present regathering of the Jewish people to their original land is just a political accident – or the work of the One who is repeatedly called the God of Abraham, Isaac and Jacob.

Vigilance

One third of Matthew 24, the "spinal chord of biblical prophecy, into which all other such passages must fit,"[1] is taken up with warnings to the Church on readiness in the last days (Matthew 24:32–51). In the parallel chapters of Mark 13 and Luke 21, one quarter of the verses apply in the same way – all aptly summed up in:

> Keep on the alert at all times, praying that you may have strength to escape all these things that are about to take place, and to stand before the Son of Man.
>
> (Luke 21:36 NASB)

The very first words in our Lord's response to His disciples' question about his return (Matthew 24:3) were "Take heed that no man deceive you" (Matthew 24:4 KJV)! This is a clarion, personal call repeated many times and in many ways in the Bible.

The Christian *can* be led astray and *can* lead others astray. We *can* fail to maintain a spiritual alertness to situations around us. Jesus' repeated warning was to "Watch – keep awake, be vigilant." While thankful to God for the renewing by His Spirit today of much of the Church, all too few of us are aware of the importance and relevance of the restoration of Israel.

The exhortation, "Awake, thou that sleepest, and arise from the dead, and Christ shall give thee light" (Ephesians 5:14 KJV), is addressed to Spirit-filled believers (verse 18)! *How can we purposefully, informedly and with God's enlightenment, pray for Israel? May these chapters really be a help to you.*

In recent years, much prophetic teaching on the rapture has provided an easy "escape route" for the Church – with Israel left behind to "face the music"! This helps to put us to sleep and blinds us to the delay that is clearly referred to in the coming of the Bridegroom (Matthew 24:48; 25:5; Mark 13:36). But the future of what is called "the Church" (also called "the commonwealth of Israel" in some versions in Ephesians 2:12) is inextricably bound up with the *spiritual* restoration of Israel. This is of key importance.

Firstly, this must involve a physically restored Israel. (Listen to any daily news broadcast!) God has set her aside for a coming work of the Holy Spirit. She is the *focal point* of what God is doing, and what He *will* do in these last days – hence the ceaseless efforts by her enemies to wipe her off the map. It is the Bible, more often than not in its literal meaning, which will give us answers, not the news media: "The entrance of thy words giveth light" (Psalm 119:130 KJV).

God's sorrow and anguish

If, as we affirm, we really believe that *"All* Scripture is inspired by God and profitable for teaching, for reproof, for correction, for training" (2 Timothy 3:16 NASB, emphasis added) then let us consider a passage written by a Hebrew who had ample reason to turn against his own kinsmen, but who, by the Holy Spirit, made this five-fold, soul-searing declaration:

> I speak the truth in [Messiah] – I am not lying, my conscience confirms it in the Holy Spirit – I have great sorrow and unceasing anguish in my heart ... for the sake of my brothers, those of my own race, the people of Israel.
>
> (Romans 9:1–4 NIV)

The writer, of course, is none other than the apostle Paul. With such a five-fold reminder of divine inspiration, can we doubt that Paul does anything but reveal the very heart of God? Is not *all* Scripture inspired? Did the Lord's sorrow end when Jesus wept over Jerusalem?

> O Jerusalem, Jerusalem ... how often I have longed to gather your children together, as a hen gathers her chicks under her wings, but you were not willing.
>
> (Matthew 23:37 NIV)

Don't you catch, through Paul's words, the tears and yearnings of Jesus over Israel and Jerusalem *to this very moment?* Paul's sorrow was not simply a twinge of remorse. It was *great* sorrow ... enough to cause him to offer himself, were it possible, as a *substitutionary* sacrifice for his fellow Israelites! Note here that Paul is not simply concerned with fellow Jews but with *fellow Israelites*. He realized that Israel as a *nation* had a future, although, of course, that would embrace individual Jews.

Also, note that it is *unceasing* anguish. Anguish is described in the Collins dictionary as "acute pain of body or mind." Whose experience in Gethsemane does this remind us of? This attitude is not expounded in Bible teaching today, nor something we experience in our daily Christian walk – *unceasing* anguish! *Genuine tears, of Holy Spirit origin, would so wash away from us the complacency and apathy of the Western Church today!*

Paul goes on to add in Romans 9:2 that this is in his heart, in his innermost being, at the center of his thinking, mind and will. If, like

others, you have prayed that beautiful, expressive prayer of Paul's in
Philippians 3:10:

> that I may know Him [Jesus – the Messiah] and the power of His resurrec-
> tion, and the fellowship of His sufferings, being conformed to His death ...
> (NKJV)

have you ever thought that His sufferings *include* an identifying with
the needs of His people Israel *now* – today?

The Jewishness of our Savior

Jesus did not cease to be Jewish at His death. The "one mediator
between God and men, the man [Messiah] Jesus" *is* Jewish. Moreover,
He is concerned not simply for His fellow Jews, His kinsmen, but for
the nation, *His* nation, which they represent – *Israel*. What you and I
do, or do not do, to them is done, or not done, to Jesus!

> 'Whatever you did for one of the least of these brothers of mine, you
> did for me ... whatever you did not do for one of the least of these,
> you did not do for me.
> (Matthew 25:40, 45 NIV)

The least and the most we can do is to *pray for Israel*, although we must
also move into the practical realm to aid this oppressed nation. Paul
himself later added, "My heart's desire and prayer to God for them
[Israel] is for their salvation" (Romans 10:1 NASB). Again, not a theological treatise, but a "heart's desire" – the earthly place to which God's
angels are tuned in – far more than are our hearts, or even our heads!

Are you ignorant, unconcerned or even hostile to Israel?

If, like myself at one time, you have not the faintest concern for
Israel – don't give up! Seek the Lord diligently and persistently, until,
little by little, line upon line from his Word, or perhaps even more
quickly in some other way, he writes these things on your heart.

It is God which worketh in you both to will and to do of his good pleasure.

(Philippians 2:13 KJV)

and

If any man will do his will, he shall know of the doctrine ...

(John 7:17 KJV)

Then, from the Spirit's prompting within you, you will begin to pray and maybe to travail for His land, His people.

So, under the Lord's hand, you should become like Aaron, the priest of God, who was *commanded* to bless Israel with the indelible, unforgettable words that *had* to be vocalized, not simply read or written:

"Thus you shall bless the people of Israel [a commandment].
You shall say to them:
The LORD bless you, and keep you;
The LORD make His face shine on you,
    And be gracious to you;
The LORD lift up His countenance on you,
    And give you peace."
So they shall invoke My name on the sons of Israel,
and I *then* will bless them.

(Numbers 6:23–27 NASB, emphasis added)

Note that this is in the imperative: "Thus you *shall* bless the people of Israel," and the Lord's closing words show that, by the priest's obedience, God *would* bless Israel. Any priestly failure implies the withholding of that blessing. Yet, for centuries, right up to this very point in time, the Church has almost entirely failed to see its priestly role on behalf of Israel. This is basic; the initial exhortation is in Genesis – the book of Beginnings. We deny ourselves the accompanying blessing that the Lord promises: "I will bless them that bless thee" (Genesis 12:3 KJV).

Significantly, the same priest, Aaron, was bidden to *carry* the names of each of the twelve tribes of Israel on a "breastpiece of judgment" (a place of decisions by the heart). *Each* name was expressed by a precious stone, not simply by a name or a symbol, but by something indestructible, and individually representative and precious for each tribe. Precious stones usually increase in value as time goes on – and God's love for Israel has certainly not diminished. Aaron was to bear these twelve names upon his heart *whenever* he went into the Holy Place, "for a continual remembrance before the LORD" (Exodus 28:21, 29–30 NRSV).

Jesus went to great depths to retrieve and redeem those stones. One day they will be polished and sparkling, to manifest the Messiah's glory. The twelve gates of the heavenly city in Revelation 21 bear the names of the twelve tribes of Israel, and the wall's twelve foundations bear the names of the twelve apostles. For what reason? Because they have a central role in God's eternal purposes!

Is not that in itself sufficient to answer our opening question: Why pray for Israel?

God's command

In reality, praying for Israel is not an optional extra for Christians. Although some will obviously have prior calls to other regions, none can escape the twice-repeated and emphasized command to pray for the very heart of Israel, which is, of course, Jerusalem.

> 1. Pray for the peace of Jerusalem: they shall prosper that love thee.
> (Psalm 122:6 KJV)

If this were merely some ethereal Jerusalem where there will be no more war or strife, no terrorists, no suicide bombers, no Muslim claim for governmental dominance, no claim for the Holy City and the Temple site, and no concentration or clash of every kind of false and superficial Christianity – *why pray for its peace?* In such a heavenly realm, peace would surely be assured!

One of the root causes of centuries of darkness within Christendom has been our failure to place a *literal* interpretation here. While prior to 1948 and the re-establishment of the State of Israel we could have excused this, today we cannot. With such a Jerusalem and such a nation as Israel *visible* before our eyes, there can be no excuse for refusing to seek the Lord, *even if only to express a willingness to receive new revelation from the Holy Spirit.*

Although the Church in Britain has slept through most of the centuries (though there was an awakening during the Puritan age) in regard to praying for Israel and Jerusalem, God has certainly not slept. He clearly states that "He who keeps Israel will neither slumber nor sleep" (Psalm 121:4 NRSV).

> 2. For Zion's sake I will not keep silent, and for Jerusalem's sake I will not rest, until her vindication shines out like the dawn ...
>
> (Isaiah 62:1 NRSV)

While uttered by the prophet Isaiah, these great words are undoubtedly the Lord Himself speaking, as the rest of the chapter progressively reveals. God's second command to us to pray is along those lines – to be *unresting.* And it is addressed to *every* Christian:

> You who call on the LORD,
>   give yourselves no rest,
> and give him no rest till he establishes Jerusalem
>   and makes her the praise of the earth.
>
> (Isaiah 62:6–7 NIV)

Nowhere else in Scripture is there such a call to relentless, specific prayer! Although the Lord tells us *He* will take no rest, paradoxically He puts the ball into our court in bidding *us* to give Him no rest, and not to take any for ourselves! Why? Because there is some vital purpose in God's heart in and through Jerusalem to bless the whole earth! It is not simply that God loves the Jews, Jerusalem or Israel (which He truly does), but that He also loves the world and the Arabs and has covenanted to bless the whole world through His elect people (Romans 11:12, 15). That covenant has been only partially fulfilled. Much, much more has yet to come.

O God of Heaven, to Thee we raise our prayer
For all Thine Ancient People now our care,
That Thou wouldst win them home again to Thee
With love eternal, and with pardon free.

O Gracious Father, who in love dost yearn
That Jew and Gentile unto Thee may turn –
Redeemed in Christ, of Thine own wondrous grace
We plead with Thee for Israel's chosen race.

O Loving Saviour, Shepherd of the sheep,
Who dost Thy ransomed flock in safety keep,
We plead with Thee to bring Thy lost ones home;
"Scattered and peeled," oh, let them cease to roam.

O Holy Spirit, Comforter and Guide,
Breathe on us now and in Thy power abide,
Speed on Thy message from the worlds above,
And flood dark souls with holy light and love.

O God the Father, Son and Holy Ghost,
This boon from Triune God we covet most,
We pray Thee, hear Thy servants' suppliant cry
For Jews far off – that all may be brought nigh.[2]

Notes

1. Quoted by Derek Prince.
2. Composed by Rev. Leonard T. Pearson.

CHAPTER 2

Insights into Israel

I am concerned for you and will look on you with favor; you will be
plowed and sown ... I will ... make you prosper more than before.

(Ezekiel 36:9, 11 NIV)

Ezekiel chapter 36 contains twenty-six specific promises of God:
twenty-six forms of encouragement, preceded throughout by God's
"I will ... I will ... I will ..."

Even before these are listed, the Lord interposes: "Behold, I
am *for* you" (Ezekiel 36:9 KJV). To "behold" anything is a matter of
sight – whether physical or spiritual – and we are thus bidden to actually see and witness that God today is *for* Israel – His "appointed time"
to "favor" her has come. By "Behold!" God means us to "stop, to discern, and to take good heed". It is far more than just "Look!" In other
words, the fact that God is *for* Israel is of primary importance for both
the Jew and the Bible believer to grasp.

References in this chapter (Ezekiel 36) to the *land* of Israel move
through the following terms (emphasis added):

My land (verse 5)
His land (verse 20)
Your *own* land (verse 24)

The land that *I gave* to your fathers (verse 28 NKJV)
This land that was desolate has become like the *garden of Eden*
(verse 35 NKJV)

We are seeing God's "I will's" in the process of fulfillment today, e.g.
fulfillment of the *explicit* promise of the land being tilled and sown. (It
had lain forsaken and desolate for centuries – Ezekiel 36:34–35) We are
seeing the faithfulness, the handiwork and the heart-throb of God in a
quite unmistakable way. Few Christians return from their pilgrimage
there with anything less than superlatives: "Thrilling, unforgettable,
life-changing, indescribable!"

It is not hard to fall in love with the land of Israel. In fact, it is
almost impossible not to do so! There is a vibrancy and life, a color and
fertility, a fragrance and atmosphere which cannot be missed. Who
would want to miss it? Is it not *His* land? Has God not said, "Behold
[take notice], I am for you"? It is good for God's children to be in tune
with Him, and also to be *for* His land and His people.

It was one thing for the Lord to take a ragged band of slaves from
Pharaoh and the furnaces of Egypt in order to weld them into a great
nation. *But how much greater* to bring Jews of almost 100 different languages from the four corners of the earth, *at His appointed time*, and
to return them anew to what God calls, initially and possessively,
"*My* land":

Again I will build you, and you shall be rebuilt, O virgin of Israel!
(Jeremiah 31:4 NKJV)

Formerly denuded of tree and forest, centuries of neglect, desolation
and destruction were the fruit of previous occupants, with farms turned
into swamps. Now we are seeing rich soil, wooded slopes, mile after
mile after mile of beautiful citrus groves and olive groves, mile after
mile of cotton fields, vineyards, hosts of fish farms, acres and acres of
wheat and barley, banana plantations, date palms and so on – all with a
color or a greenery that emulate the Garden of Eden. All the stronger is
our conviction that these are but a physical picture and the forerunner

of a *spiritual abundance* that is going to flow out for the *blessing of the whole world.*

> If their ... loss [i.e. decay] means riches for the Gentiles, how much greater riches will their fullness bring!
>
> (Romans 11:12 NIV)

Through a further blessing, still yet to come, Ezekiel confirms this confidence:

> "I will not hide My face from them anymore; for I shall have poured out My Spirit on the house of Israel," says the Lord God.
>
> (Ezekiel 39:29 NKJV)

Elsewhere in Ezekiel (sixty-five times in different ways) we ecstatically read: "Then they [the nations] will know I am the Lord." The transformation within the land of Israel is yet to be even more visible evidence of God at work, and a somber reminder of his Lordship.

However, leaving the "romance" of the country, let us consider more practical aspects of this transformation and, in a little more detail, all that contributes to the total picture already described.

Eretz Yisrael (The land of Israel)

Its size

If you have not studied a world map you may be surprised, after all the controversy surrounding her (and the Israeli fruit that your store might sell), to find that Israel itself is, in fact, a very tiny country, no bigger than Wales. It is an area of but 8,000 square miles (excluding the Sinai desert) or approximately 10,260 square miles including the disputed territories.

So tiny is its land area that one might wonder why there is all the fuss and commotion when Israel's opposing and surrounding Arab neighbors total a land area of 5,280,000 square miles – 636 times that of little Israel! In fact, even when standing close to a large map of the world, it is not at all easy to pick out Israel – it is so small. Amos doubly reminds us of this:

How can Jacob survive? He is so small!

(Amos 7:2, 5 NIV)

On almost all maps, the name "Israel" is written in the Mediterranean Sea, the land area being too small to contain it. The area originally allocated before the Arab attack of 1948 was only about 4,000 square miles.

Location and description

Israel stands at the junction of three continents: Europe, Africa and Asia. *It is a natural land-bridge* between the latter two and between the Mediterranean and Red seas.

The land features vary from the snowy peaks of Mount Hermon in the north, where winter skiers sport, to the subtropical waters (teeming with fish and corals) of Eilat – a major holiday resort and scuba-diving center. Mount Hermon towers to 9,230 feet, overlooking the Golan Heights in the northeast, which, in their turn, look down upon the fertile Hula and Jordan valleys. Mount Hermon – with its heavy rain, snow and blizzards – is vital to the life of Israel. Both the snow and rain are vital in filling Lake Kinneret (Lake Galilee) from which so much is constantly pumped to water the desert regions in the south.

Lake Galilee is a major source of water and of fish for the whole country. Eilat (population over 27,000) in the extreme south is a deep-sea port on the Red Sea, and is a sun-drenched beach resort – Israel's outlet to Africa and Asia and the terminal of the land-bridge. Solomon's galleys once anchored here; to the north are the copper mines of Timna that he utilized almost 3,000 years ago.

In between these two extremes of climate, location and topography, we have further variety:

The coastal plain

This houses nearly two thirds of the country's population along its narrow strip of land. It is intensely cultivated, with its fertility yielding a wealth of orange, lemon and grapefruit groves that go a long way towards fulfilling Isaiah's words:

> In days to come Jacob shall take root,
> Israel will blossom and sprout,
> And they will fill the whole world with fruit.
>
> (Isaiah 27:6 NASB)

On the coast, we find beautiful Nahariya in the north, the Crusader port of Acre (Acco), the heavy industry area and port of Haifa (city center population: 265,100), the popular seaside resort of Natanya, and the former Roman port and amphitheater of Caesarea, to which the apostle Peter traveled 1,900 years ago to meet the Roman centurion Cornelius (Acts 10). Here also Paul made his defense to Felix, Festus and Agrippa, later sailing to meet Caesar (Acts 23–27). Further south lies the citrus-growing area of the Sharon Plain.

Tel Aviv, built upon the sand dunes and non-existent at the beginning of the twentieth century, is a sprawling modern city of some 1,300,000 people (center of the city – population: 392,000), embracing numerous adjoining towns. It is the "Wall Street" of Israel, where the nation's business economy and major banking and shopping centers are found. Its short seafront holds many towering hotel blocks, and close by is Ben Gurion Airport at Lod – the main hub of Israel's air traffic. Just south of Tel Aviv we find the port of Jaffa, where Peter had the vision of a great sheet let down from heaven containing all kinds of animals, reptiles and birds (Acts 10:9–12).

Upper Galilee in the north sees 4,000-feet high mountains, good winter rainfall and fertile valleys, with fruit, olives and cotton, and with carp in artificial ponds. Lower Galilee in the south rises in places to about

2,000 feet – an ideal farming area. Within its hills and plains, its main crops are wheat, beet, groundnuts, cotton, melons, bananas and grapes.

Samaria and Judea stand between the coastal plain on the west and the Jordan Valley and Dead Sea Basin on the east. Nearly half of the 680,000 inhabitants are farmers. Nablus, Jerusalem and Hebron stand high on its central spine.

The colorful beauty of the Judean hills turns to the unusual, awe-inspiring splendor of the Judean desert as they descend eastwards to the Dead Sea. Where the two meet in the south, we find Qumran, the cave area where, significantly, the Dead Sea Scrolls were recovered immediately prior to Israel's rebirth. Here, where the Negev desert begins, one may suddenly see a tomato plantation or a field of crops surrounded by desert ... pioneering projects galore!

The northern part of the Negev desert takes in Beersheba, city of the patriarchs, whose population has expanded from 5,000 in 1948 to almost 200,000 today. Dimona stands nearby with its textile plants, nuclear research center, and mineral processing factories that tap the seemingly inexhaustible wealth of the Dead Sea.

The Dead Sea, taking in fresh water from the Jordan for thousands of years (but only doing so now in a very limited way), yet with no outlet, contains an incredible wealth of minerals (running into a value of trillions of pounds). It includes potassium chloride, magnesium bromide, sodium chloride, magnesium chloride and calcium chloride, all of which are processed at Sodom. Along its shores we find visitors from across the world seeking cures to skin and other conditions that have not found relief elsewhere ... Geographically, this is the lowest spot on earth – 1,312 feet below sea level – yet simultaneously it is by far the wealthiest. What hidden spiritual lesson is contained within this apparent paradox?

Valleys

The Hula Valley, the most northern valley, was one of the major malaria-ridden swamps, drained and transformed by pioneering Jews – often at the cost of precious lives. In the early days of Israel's transformation, it was converted into an extremely fertile area, bearing luscious fruit orchards, cotton fields and fish ponds. But the subsequent ill effect on the wildlife of the area has resulted in a reversion that favors the latter. It is an absolutely amazing stopover place for tens of thousands of migratory birds each year.

A sense of history and achievement hangs in the air as we view this valley from the Golan Heights, mindful of those self-sacrificing early pioneers, and those also who, as farmers, lost their lives under the Syrian guns prior to the 1967 war.

The spectacular Jezreel Valley covers some 140 square miles and is again a reclaimed malaria-swamp area – a tribute to the many who gave their lives to see fulfilled their beloved Isaiah scripture:

> Thou shalt no more be termed Forsaken; neither shall thy land any more be termed Desolate: but thou shalt be called Hep-hzi-bah, and thy land Beu-lah: for the LORD delighteth in thee, and thy land shall be married.
>
> (Isaiah 62:4 KJV)

Israel's devotion to her land is termed a "marriage" in God's sight, because it is God-originated, and God-kept. The implications of this are endless and provide a major reason for the writing of this book! Is it the Lord who places "Next year in Jerusalem!" on the lips and in the hearts of Jews in the Diaspora – or is it merely a whim of their own choice?

Jezreel is Israel's major granary, and also a further cotton-producing area. The huge white bales of gathered cotton, dotting the countryside in the fall, mark the industriousness of a people where the plant was practically unknown some sixty years ago. Today, cotton is the second major agricultural export. But Jezreel will also be the area of one of the huge end-time battles over Israel (Joel 3).

The Jordan Valley, through which the Jordan River winds its way to the Dead Sea, is unique both in its depth below sea level and in its continually contrasting arid and fertile regions. Green orchards and fruitful fields alternate with dry and sandy wastes ... the nearby boundary of barbwire reminding us of less-than-friendly neighbors a few miles to the east.

Rainfall

It is important to note that, since the return of the Jewish people to their homeland (Israel), there has been a marked increase in the average rainfall – in this country *where water is absolute life!* Figures in 1974, compared with the 1931–60 period, showed an average increase in rainfall across the country of 45 percent.

While this increase tailed off during the 1990s – significantly so with the drought in 2007 and 2008 – on the whole the extra rain has led to much higher agricultural yield and the provision of water for the ever-increasing population. Many of us believe that the drought affliction is God's call to prayer by the country as a whole. We hardly need reminding of God's word in 2 Chronicles 7:14.

However, it is also important to realize that a major cause of this welcome improvement in rainfall has been the planting of trees throughout Israel. Since trees in the Bible so often symbolize believers (Isaiah 55:12; 1 Chronicles 16:33), we can blend the practical in with the spiritual! Few trees survived the 400 years of Turkish rule (up to 1917), during which time the trees were subject to a special tax. Most people cut down their trees rather than meet the costs involved.

But from 1948 to 2008 over 240 million trees were planted in over 250,000 acres, producing many luscious belts of green! Those trees have helped to oxygenate the air and promote the rain. There is actually an implication in Leviticus 19:23 of planting trees when one enters the land of Israel! Those of us who have led tour groups to Israel have often specifically followed this guideline from God's Word, gaining the joy not only of literally planting a tree, but also of allowing it to symbolize our prayers for the citizens around, that they might come to a saving faith – "like a palm tree ... planted in the house of the LORD" (Psalm 92:12–13 NIV).

Flora and fauna

The flora of Israel are amongst the most prolific in the world. There are 3,000 species compared with 1,700 in Britain and 1,335 in Norway. The "rose of Sharon" is said to be a tulip, native to the Sharon Valley, and the "lily of the valley" is really a narcissus which grows in great abundance in the lowlands of Israel. Surprisingly, over 1,000 species survive in the Negev and Sinai deserts. The flora of Israel's Bible days may be seen and studied at several "Gardens of Israel" including *Neot Kedumin*, near Kyriat Ono in the Tel Aviv area.

The fauna of Israel take in thousands of species from several other geographical areas. These include the leopard, hyena, polecat, wolf, jackal, coney, ibex, porcupine, antelope and wild boar, while others like the bear, the lion and the elephant disappeared with the forests. Three hundred and fifty species of birds are known of, some of them transmigratory from Europe to Africa. It is forbidden to hunt most of them. Eagles, ospreys and vultures nest in the mountain crags.

The return – past, present and future

The population has risen from 800,000 in 1948 to about 7,411,000 by 2009 (exclusive of the areas – called the West Bank by some – of parts of Judea and Samaria, and also exclusive now of Gaza).

Tens of thousands of destitute refugees from the Nazi crematoria came to find a home and build a new life in Israel. But hundreds of thousands also streamed in as refugees from Arab lands round about. Others have come from the free world, drawn by an "instinct" that no one can truly plumb.

It is well known that over one million have flooded in from Russia, following the collapse of communism in 1991. While this has necessitated painful adjustments for both the returning Russian Jews and the existing Israelis, these from the north have nonetheless also brought great blessing with them. *The writer has reason to believe that there are at least a further six million Jews scattered throughout Russia, the Ukraine and Siberia.*

In spite of strong anti-Israel forces that prevail throughout the world, it is encouraging to note a marked rise in the numbers making "Aliyah" from 2006 to 2008 from the West – i.e. North and South America, Britain and Europe. *It seems that thousands more will voluntarily stream back to their native land, before being otherwise forced to do so by the rising tide of world anti-Semitism.* Many Jews in the former Soviet Union have been suffering (through their neighbors) for their desire and efforts to migrate, but sometimes for their faith.

Of the 7,411,000 total population, some 5,593,000 are Jewish, 1,498,000 are Israeli Arabs, and the remainder (320,00) are mixed – mainly Bedouin and Druze. The variety of cultures, backgrounds, languages, and even forms of worship of the different Jewish people is not without its problems where practical resettlement is the family or personal need. But much has been and is being done to meet and overcome the stresses involved. *This is all as much a spiritual battle as anything* – especially in the learning of the basic language: Hebrew! Therefore, prayer of the right kind for the learning of Hebrew is a *key* to the greater unifying of the nation.

Can you imagine the differences between the reserved and gentle Yemenite Jew, small and lean with a culture almost unchanged in 3,000 years, and the broad, big-built and bold Jew from (say) New York – complete with his own sophisticated modern-day culture? The one never having seen an airplane prior to the Operation "Magic Carpet" airlift of 1949, and yet gripped by a Messianic fervor, the other, the New Yorker, sauntering nonchalantly from the skyscrapers and Cadillacs of New York (via a US airline) also to the land of his forefathers ... there to meet with his long-lost relative – the Yemenite!

These are some of the ingredients that God has been mixing together to recreate Israel. One Israeli has called it, "Israeli soup"! All this is buried within the simple promise:

> "For behold, days are coming," declares the Lord,
> "when I will *restore* the fortunes of My people Israel and Judah."
> (Jeremiah 30:3 NASB, emphasis added)

A large proportion of the Jewish population is under fourteen years of age and a good percentage are over sixty-five.

In March 1950, the Iraqi government passed a law permitting Jewish emigration, provided all property was left behind. Of the 130,000 Jews there, 121,500 did not hesitate and, over a period of eight months, Operations Ezra and Nehemiah brought them to their homeland. These intermingled with Jews from Bulgaria, Libya, Poland and Romania, together with Jewish internees from Cyprus, and Jews from displaced persons' camps in Italy, Germany and Austria. Behind all of this lies the merciful, faithful hand of the God of Israel (Jeremiah 31:23).

Almost 700,000 of the refugees in the early years were from Arab countries – most coming devoid of all they possessed. Despite all the difficulties, these were settled in Israel. One has to ask why the Arab "refugees" who ignored the appeal of the Jewish authorities in 1947–48 to remain (instead of fleeing at the bidding of the Arab League) have not *even now* been resettled by those who control the oil wealth of the world.

Further migration of Jews to Israel is needed, to add stamina in facing the pressures of the pioneering life there. Israel's economy and stability are under constant threat from its neighbors. Even so, it remains the Land of Promise not only to the eye but also to the heart – in the way that those who have trodden its soil have hearkened (often unwittingly) to the voice of the God of Israel. "'Something' is drawing me back!" has been the frequent and emotive testimony of those returning to their own land.

> I … will look on you with favor; you will be plowed and sown …
> I will … make you prosper more than before.
>
> (Ezekiel 36:9, 11 NIV)

This is a promise not only to a land, but also to the individual who, in response to God, lovingly treads the soil of Israel with a desire to do God's will. The tilling and sowing are spiritual aspects of growth that the Holy Spirit is achieving in the hearts of many who turn to Him today, particularly as Christians extend their hand of love and help to Israel. Pray for the return of Jewish people both to their homeland *and* to their God: "the Holy One of Israel, your Savior."

> I give Egypt for your ransom … you are precious … in my sight, and
> … I love you.
>
> (Isaiah 43:3–4 NIV)

I have called you by name; you are Mine!

(Isaiah 43:1 NASB)

We should be praying that Jewish people, wherever they are, will be *prepared* for their call and that they will respond. How much better that they be *drawn* to Israel rather than being *driven* here. The Lord in Jeremiah 16:16 makes a clear distinction between fishing and hunting. This is the difference between one *wanting* to travel in a certain direction, as opposed to being hunted and *forced through fear* to eventually go the same way. *Anti-Semitism is growing fast throughout the world today.*

The Arabs of Israel

Non-Jews, mainly Arab, numbering 156,000 in 1949, have grown rapidly as a result of natural increases and immigration. The birth rate of Israel's Arab (Muslim) community is amongst the highest in the world, reaching a peak in 1964 of 4.5 percent annual growth. In 1975, the growth rate was 4.1 percent compared with 1.8 percent in the Jewish sector. As shown above, the total non-Jewish population is currently over 1,500,000.

A large concentration of non-Jews – mainly Arab – is in the Haifa and northern region. But the largest is in the Jerusalem area where some 35 percent are Arabs – and about 2 percent of these are Christian. Another 40,000 non-Jews comprise the twenty-three Bedouin tribes of the Negev.

The Arabic-speaking Christian population has much decreased in recent years, due to great pressures from the Muslims Arabs. In Bethlehem, the Christian percentage has dropped from 80 percent in 1975 to less than 20 percent in 2009. Some of these are fine believers and certainly warrant our prayer. But elsewhere (especially in Jerusalem) denominationally there is a blending of Greek Catholics, Greek Orthodox, Maronites (linked with Lebanon), Latins, Protestants and Anglicans.

Israeli Arabs enjoy full equality before the law and are free to maintain their own culture, religion, tradition and language. Arabic is the second language of the state and taught in all schools. Because of the tension in the land, military service is not imposed upon the Arab citizens, but hundreds of Christian and Muslim volunteers do, in fact, serve in the Voluntary Services. Were the tensions not fostered from elements abroad, there is little doubt that a real harmony would flourish between Israeli Arabs and Israeli Jews. Arab women are beginning to play a more active role in society. Their status has greatly improved since Israel's social legislation which abolished polygamy and child marriage, granted women full voting rights and instituted free and compulsory education for girls.

The Druze people

The Druze people number about 117,000 and are a self-governing religious community. They stem from an eleventh-century breakaway sect from Islam. At their own request they have been doing compulsory service in the Israel Defense Forces since 1957.

The Arabs and the Druze play an active role in the political life of Israel with a voter participation rate of over 80 percent in all elections to date. Representatives of both communities have served and continue to serve as members of Israel's parliament, the Knesset, and as deputy ministers. In general, the Arabs behave as loyal citizens of the land, partaking of the country's political and economic fabric.

The kibbutz

The *kibbutz* is a communal settlement or village in which all the property is in common ownership by its members. There are some 267 *kibbutzim* in Israel, varying in size from 100 or so people to over 2,000. An average size is about 380 persons, and an elected committee democratically runs the settlement. Goods are distributed according to need; there is no money used in its internal dealings. With excellent community dining halls, members enjoy a fair standard of living, and work diligently. For married couples, there is family accommodation. Cultural, sports, educational and holiday interests are provided by the kibbutz. Only about 2.8 percent of the population live in these

communal settlements. Kibbutzim wield less influence today on the
social, economic, political and cultural life of the nation. Previously
they used to provide a high proportion of the officers and men in the
elite sections of the Israel Defense Forces, paratroops, naval comman-
dos and air force, and also in the Knesset and Cabinet. This has waned
since the 1980s.

Nonetheless, while originally being solely agricultural, kibbutzim today have developed individual industries on their respective
camps – factories making anything from furniture to plastics, from
electronic parts to boots and precision tools. The farming itself is
highly mechanized, and farm produce and manufactured goods are
exported in quantity.

The moshav

The *moshav* is a co-operative "village," usually agricultural, though
some run an industry also. Features embrace both private and collec-
tive farming, all owning a share of the enterprise. Family life is more
pronounced, there being no communal dining hall. Although each family farms and manages its own plot, the moshav owns and maintains all
the heavy machinery, markets all produce and collectively purchases
all seed, fodder and other supplies. There are now some 440 *moshavim*
as opposed to only 78 in 1948. The moshavim population totals about
156,700 compared with approximately 103,000 of the 267 kibbutzim.

Localized and world benefits

Regional rural planning is undertaken by the Jewish Agency's Settlement Department together with the government. Central to each
planned region is a county town where doctors, teachers and special-
ists live; from there they serve the surrounding villages.

The moshav concept and Israel's experiment in regional planning
have aroused interest in Africa, Asia and Latin America. Israeli instruc-
tors have set up moshavim in developing countries across the globe,
and thousands of students and leaders from the Third World have

undergone training in Israel. Israel has also sent many teams abroad to Third World countries to impart skills in agriculture and in water conservation.

The land of Israel or the Lord?

> Thus says the LORD of hosts: "Return to Me," says the LORD of hosts, "and I will return to you," says the LORD of hosts.
>
> (Zechariah 1:3 NKJV)

While Jewish people will enjoy and share in the delights of a restored land of Israel, Orthodox rabbi David Hartman (formerly director of the Shalom Hartman Institute for Advanced Jewish Studies and professor of philosophy at the Hebrew University) warned some years ago of what he called "a new idolatry." His warning is still relevant today.

He took issue with Jewish Bible students who demonstrated against the Israeli withdrawal from the Sinai in 1979. He spoke in admonition against unholy alliances between extreme nationalist groups and those committed to the covenantal spirit of Judaism:

> No one who is sober can deny that there are serious risks in the withdrawal from Sinai. But how should these be approached by one who values statehood as an instrument to serve the spiritual life of our people ... one who believes that God, *not the land*, Torah [Scripture] and peoplehood are primary in Judaism?
>
> It is not the withdrawal from Sinai that threatens the future wellbeing of this country, but the apathy and indifference of many Israelis to the spiritual significance of Jewish statehood.
>
> The loss of belief in the moral significance of our political re-birth is the dangerous cancer that is eating at the soul of our people.
>
> I appreciate the call to modern religious youth to return to Sinai, but it is folly for this to be a return to the physical Sinai separating Israel from Egypt, instead of a return to the spiritual symbol of Sinai which signifies the centrality of the covenant and the prophetic spirit of Judaism. The fact that the Torah was given to Moses at Sinai [that is, outside the historic boundaries of *Eretz Yisrael*] teaches us that

the challenge to become a holy people precedes the holiness of the land.

The land was given as an instrument for achieving the holiness of the people. To reverse the priorities is to distort the true significance of our love for Sinai. Absolute loyalty to a land irrespective of the quality of life of its people is idolatrous and undermines the covenantal destiny of Israel.[1]

What searing words these are! Wisdom that challenges our Western materialism – which has replaced whatever sense we had at one time of real spiritual destiny. Yet, for Israel, these words telescope national needs into one single issue: "The land *or* the Lord?" In Britain and elsewhere it might be hoped that it could be "the land *and* the Lord" – that as we return to Him, He will heal our land.

Ye shall be holy, for I am holy

For Israel, however, there is the double challenge, for God *appointed* them to be a holy *nation* (Exodus 19:6) – a complete nation knowing its God. So many of us believers would be content for a good percentage to be God-fearing, God-following. But for Israel, God's plan and requirement is that *the whole nation be holy*. Legalistic obedience to the laws of Sinai is not the prerequisite, but is to be the *result*. The prerequisite is the personal knowledge of the indwelling of the Holy One of Israel in the individual heart. The apostle Peter, writing to scattered Jewish believers in the first century, reminded them that:

> His divine power has granted to [you] everything pertaining to life and godliness, through the true knowledge of Him who called [you] by His own glory ...
>
> (2 Peter 1:3 NASB)

Holiness of the people must indeed precede holiness of the land. It involves the Lord revealing *how* this can be achieved, and what he means by saying: "Ye shall ... be holy, for I am holy" (Leviticus 11:45 KJV).

No one can make themselves holy by what they do. We are fallen, and only God Himself, the Holy One, can effect the transformation ... and that by His changing and indwelling our repentant, contrite hearts.

Not by accident does the first mention of "holy" in the Bible (Exodus 3:5) precede Moses' encounter with God. At that point, he was not bidden to *do* something, but rather to *take off something – his shoes!* His natural aptitude to go wherever and to do whatever he wanted was to be laid aside. So it is for us: the subjugation of our wills and our self-life, to the inbreathing of His holiness.

The holiness of God, referred to some 141 times in the books of Exodus and Leviticus, was the first characteristic revealed to Moses. Is it a coincidence that 141 times in the Bible, God also promises the restoration of His firstborn son – Israel (Exodus 4:22)?

May God give us an appreciation of His holiness to the extent that we can effectively pray for the people of the Holy Land in the way that David Hartman's beautiful article motivates us.

The cults

Many Jewish people seeking spiritual fulfillment in Israel resort to the deceptive cults of New Age, TM (Transcendental Meditation), Mind Science (the Church of Scientology), and other cults. Although the confirming source cannot be given here, one Israeli girl who joined the Divine Light Mission in the USA reportedly writes: "For years I completely believed that Guru Ji was the Messiah, and only through him could I find complete fulfillment in life, also that only through him was peace going to be brought into the world!" When she joined the cult, this girl was looking not for personal development but for a spirituality that she had not found hitherto. She has now been "de-programmed" to follow her Jewish roots. The cults present a real danger to the seven million Jews of America, to the almost six million in Israel, and to Jews everywhere.

However, at the huge New Age festivals that now occur regularly in Israel, with sometimes as many as 50,000 attending, the great spiritual

hunger is bringing increasing numbers to the Lord. The Messianic
Body, once so apprehensive in its outreach in the early 1970s, is today
much emboldened – even in the face of strong opposition by orthodox
factions.

Achievements in Israel since 1948

Some of the achievements of Israel are listed in the following pages.
They are but a tiny glimpse into the miracle of her restoration – for
which all glory goes to God. Through the prophet Ezekiel, Israel is
promised:

> You, O mountains of Israel, will produce branches and fruit for my
> people Israel, for they will soon come home ... I will increase the num-
> ber of men and animals upon you, and they will be fruitful and become
> numerous. I will ... make you prosper more than before. Then will
> you will *know* that I am the LORD.
>
> (Ezekiel 36:8, 11 NIV, emphasis added)

Two interesting features accompany these achievements:

1. They occurred during
   (a) the periods of seven wars (1948–49, 1956, 1959–60 War of Attrition,
       1967, 1973, 1982–86, 2006 Lebanon), plus the incessant threats of war;
   (b) constant intimidation, and terrorism within Israeli towns and
       cities;
   (c) the widespread Arab economic boycott against Israel – subtly kept
       hidden, but aided by most Western nations, even today.
2. The figures of the phenomenal rise in agricultural production and
export accompany a drop in the number of people actually employed
therein. For something like a quadrupled overall production (in some
cases, thirty- or forty-fold), we see an overall reduction in manpower
utilized, reported to be of about 14.6 percent. One seriously wonders
if such figures could be paralleled anywhere else in the world. It is
no wonder that Third World countries and other nations are coming

to Israel to learn from them – again a fulfillment of Scripture (Isaiah 45:14).

Israeli technology

In addition to a thriving agriculture, Israel has one of the most inventive research and development programs in the world. It has served well to counter the serious effects of the Arab boycott. In spite of its small size, its youth, and its location far from the commercial markets of the Western world, in its few years of existence, *Israel has established itself in several key areas of sophisticated exports.*

These include electronics, agrotechnology, computer graphics and software, and medical engineering. Israel has a total population about three quarters of that of London, yet maintains seven universities, an aerospace industry, its own army, navy and airforce and competes with world leaders in a variety of technologies! It has over 10,000 scientists and more than 20,000 engineers out of a Jewish population of almost six million. The figure of 3,000 qualified personnel working in research and development in 1980 represented an 80 percent increase in five years – an increase which has since accelerated. Israel's firsthand experience of many of the problems facing Third World countries places it in a position to be of real help to both the developed and the developing world.

In an arid climate, severely limited in raw materials and the amount of fertile land, limited in water supplies and conventional energy sources, Israel's scientists and technologists have shown real ingenuity. Energy, power, wealth and even healing for skin diseases proliferate from the Dead Sea (literally, the lowest spot on earth!) and its shores. Structural components made out of desert sand are about to be marketed.

Leading the world in producing solar energy, Israel owes much to its first Prime Minister, David Ben Gurion, who, recognizing the country's need for self-sufficiency in this area, encouraged this industry in his opening years of office. Later, in December 1979, a 150 kilowatt pilot solar-electric power station was unveiled at Ein Bokek on the shores of the Dead Sea. This dramatically demonstrated to the world the feasibility of generating electricity from solar energy, day and night, summer and winter. Most Israeli apartments carry a cylindrical tank that generates heating for household purposes from the sun, enabling a 2 percent saving on the country's oil imports.

Israeli surgeons and engineers have led the world in the development of the use of laser beams for surgical purposes. Now past its developmental stage, this process has many advantages over conventional methods: a reduced loss of blood, greater sterility, less pain and trauma for the patient, and great accuracy in focusing to a predetermined depth and predetermined spot where surgery is required.

One kibbutz has developed a method of water sterilization that has great advantages over chemical methods, avoiding resultant side-effects. An ultraviolet radiation method is used which can deal with anything from fifteen to 950 gallons of water per hour on an electric current usage of seventy watts. For one kilowatt of electricity, 13,000 gallons can be sterilized!

Shortage of water in agriculture has led to the development of computer-controlled irrigation systems which monitor the amount of water needed, and supply accordingly – often directly to the root of the plants concerned, rather than just the area. To save the high costs of air-freight, a method has been developed of packing and sending cut flowers and other sensitive produce in specially refrigerated shipping containers, where the temperatures are maintained slightly above freezing point. Atmospheric control halts deterioration of the produce. In the Red Sea area there is even a large-scale algae farming experiment where an algae organism, being grown for the first time for commercial purposes, promises excellent by-products in the fields of glycerol, cosmetics and pharmaceutics.

In the physical sense, during its sixty years of existence, we have seen a transformation of the face and productivity of the land of Israel which far outmatch anything from the time of Joshua. Conversely, we see an inflation rate of 130–150 percent, at least one third of its income spent on defense forces to preserve Israel from the escalating hatred from its foes, and the peace which Jews have sought throughout their lifetime seemingly further away than ever.

The lamentable truth of the centuries, "You have fed them with the bread of tears; you have made them drink tears by the bowlful" (Psalm 80:5 NIV), is as applicable now as to any time in the traumatic history of God's elect nation. We ask, "How long, O Lord? How long?" Is God mocking, is it just a pipe dream, when we read, "I will never stop doing good to them, and I will inspire them to fear me" (Jeremiah 32:40 NIV)? Very few households in Israel have been without loss and sorrow, bereavement and tears in the wars since 1948. "To what purpose?" the average Israeli parent asks. "Should I raise sons and daughters to send them to die on the battlefield?" At such a question, the hearts of us at ease in other lands must overflow in compassion.

But God is faithful to His name, to His covenant, and to His promises. Following the twenty-six "I will's" of Ezekiel 36, we find the promise of resurrection life within Ezekiel 37, not simply to Israel, but to the "whole house of Israel" (Ezekiel 37:11 NIV).

The "I will's" speak, in Ezekiel 36:25–27, of a new spirit, and the Holy Spirit, of a heart of flesh and not a heart of stone, of a divine cleansing and an inward impulse to obey God's laws. *Whatever the appearances*, the Word of God assures us that God is in this regathering, and that spiritual restoration is not far away.

The resurrected nation of Israel is pictured in Ezekiel 37:10, not as a vast people but as a vast army. The Lord of hosts will be using His restored nation in spiritual warfare in a way that the world has not hitherto seen or imagined. And then the "whole" house of Israel will not be whole simply in the sense of complete numbers, but whole in the sense of health of mind, body *and* spirit.

"Behold, I am for you"

If God is *for* Israel, who can be against them and prosper? Anew, as we stand for and with Israel, let us share not only in their tears, but also in their ultra-clear hope that the Prince of Peace holds out for them. God wants and waits to use His body of believers to be channels to Israel for God's promises.

Then we your people, the sheep of your pasture,
    will praise you for ever;
from generation to generation
    we will recount your praise.

(Psalm 79:13 NIV)

Notes

1. David Hartman, "A New Idolatry," *Jerusalem Post* (International Edition), 28 February 1982.

Table 1: Agricultural Data

	Livestock Inventory					Cultivated Area (Thousand Dunams)				Selected Inputs (Thousand Tons)			Exports of Main Products (Thousand Tons)						
	Laying Hens (Millions)	Beef Cattle (Thousands)	Dairy Cattle Purebreds (Thousands)	Tractors (Thousands)	Total Employed in Agriculture (Thousands)	Fruit Plantations (Excl. Citrus)	Citrus	Vegetables, Potatoes, Melons & Pumpkins	Field Crops	Potash Fertilizer	Nitrogen Fertilizer	Feed Grains	Flowers ($ Million)	Bananas	Citrus	Water Melons & Sugar Melons	Vegetables	Groundnuts	Cotton Lint
1948-49	2.7	0.3	37.4	1.3	102.2 (1954-55)	230	125	106	1,094	2.2	10.7 (1953-54)	123.5 (1951-52)	—		154.6	—			
1959-60	7.8	58.4	127.0	7.4	121.1	394	328	264	2,882	9.4	16.9	473.6	0.1	6.1	398.0	3.7	4.4	6.4	0.3
1969-70	7.0	61.5	144.2	16.3	89.8	420	420	346	2,685		29.6	721.4	5.2	16.6	815.7	28.0	43.5	9.8	14.0
1979-80 59.1	8.6	93.5	178.5	27.0	87.3	490	396	355	355	2,800	22.9	41.6	1129.0	90.0	18.4	854.7	43.3	78.7	10.1
Approx X Factor	3	310	5	20	-14.6%	2	3	$3^{1/3}$	$2^{1/2}$	12.73*	4	9	14.7*		$5^{1/2}$	231*	9.8*	12.3*	33*

* Figures based on 1959-60 figures, X = % increase

Table 2: Agricultural Data

Production of Main Products
(Thousand Tons, Unless Otherwise Stated)

	Eggs (Millions)	Cows' Milk (Million litres)	Other Livestock for meat	Cattle for meat	Poultry for meat	Bananas	Wine Grapes	Table Grapes	Stone Fruit	Pomme Fruit	Vegetables	Groundnuts	Cotton, Fibre	Wheat
1948–49	242.5	78.8	0.5	2.0	5.0	3.5	7.2	10.6	5.2		80.0	0.3	—	21.2
1959–60	1,114.0	277.3	10.6	25.1	45.7	34.3	21.6	31.1	10.6	26.9	296.2	17.0	10.7	41.3
1969–70	1,320.0	440.5	15.5	35.6	101.7	61.1	36.0	24.7	40.7	98.6	472.3	18.7	35.3	125.0
1979–80	1,614.9	670.3	21.2	40.2	200.0	75.0	37.2	39.3	50.8	113.0	607.0	19.5	79.1	253.2
Approx X Factor	7	$8^{1/2}$	42	20	40	22	5	4	33		$7^{1/2}$		7.4	11

CHAPTER 3

The Appointed Time to Favor Zion (A Twin Restoration)

But you, O LORD, sit enthroned for ever ...
You will arise and have compassion on Zion,
    for it is time to show favor to her;
    the appointed time has come.

(Psalm 102:12–13 NIV)

We are living in the actual period of this "appointed time." Out of the bones and flames of the Holocaust – synonymous with the greatest effort yet made to exterminate the scattered Jewish people – we have simultaneously witnessed the most remarkable regathering of all time.

Jewish people from almost 100 nations, whose forebears last dwelt together 1,900 years ago, have suddenly been put together again as a nation ... and they are situated, of all places, at the "center of the earth" – Israel (Ezekiel 38:12 NASB margin). It is *so* important to grasp the significance today of this term, by which the Bible describes the nation that had ceased to exist for almost two millennia – Israel.

Rees Howells, founder of the Bible College of Wales, described this restoration as "the greatest miracle since Pentecost!" And he himself had prayed through and seen many other miracles in his own ministry during World War Two. So he meant what he said – it was not just a passing phrase!

However, there are many who see all this as simply some political maneuver; many have violently opposed it, and continue to do so, while many others remain utterly indifferent. But there *are* some who are excited, and gladly involved.

The fact remains that *the most repeated promise within the Bible* concerns the restoration of Israel – the bringing back of God's people to His land. We are told that any single matter in the Bible is important. But if it is repeated twice it is even more important. However, if we find it (say) four times – as we do some important doctrines – God is obviously wanting us to take heed. He is underlining His Word, knowing how prone we are to ignorance, blindness or neglect. *How much store then, should we place upon a promise repeated something like 141 times in different ways within the Bible?*

> I will restore the fortunes of My people Israel and Judah [declares the LORD].
>
> (Jeremiah 30:3 NASB)

> I will restore their fortunes, declares the LORD.
>
> (Jeremiah 32:44 NIV)

> I will restore the fortunes of Judah and the fortunes of Israel ...
>
> (Jeremiah 33:7 NASB)

> I will restore the fortunes of the land as they were at first, says the LORD.
>
> (Jeremiah 33:11 NASB)

> I will restore their fortunes and will have mercy on them.
>
> (Jeremiah 33:26 NASB)

I will bring your children from the east, and gather you from the west.
I will say to the north, "Give them up!" and to the south, "Do not hold
them back."

(Isaiah 43:5–6 NIV)

I will take you from among the nations, gather you out of all countries, and bring you into your own land.

(Ezekiel 36:24 NKJV)

The Lord your God will bring you into the land which your fathers
possessed, and you shall possess it; and He will prosper you and multi-
ply you more than your fathers.

(Deuteronomy 30:5 NASB)

I will signal for them and gather them in. Surely I will redeem them ...

(Zechariah 10:8 NIV)

This change in fortunes is beautifully expressed in Isaiah:

No longer will they call you Deserted,
   or name your land Desolate.
But you will be called Hephzibah,
   and your land Beulah;
for the Lord will take delight in you,
   and your land will be married.

(Isaiah 62:4 NIV)

From desertion to delight – God's delight over His people Israel. From
desolation to marriage – the devotion of the Israelis to their land. Their
diligence, love and care for it have certainly led to a fruitful marriage
between land and people. But it is the Lord that gives the increase.
A "higher" marriage, between the Lord Himself and His people, is
spoken of for future days in Hosea 2:19–20.

The "No longer" of Isaiah 62 and the "appointed time" of Psalm
102 took a dramatic step forward on 29 November 1947 when, after
the management of thirty years (mostly *mis*management) by Britain,

a vote was taken at the United Nations on the "to be or not to be" of partition in what was then left of Palestine.

Two thirds of the territory, *originally mandated to Britain*, in which to establish a Jewish homeland, had *already* been given away to form Transjordan and to appease Arab demands. From this historic UN vote, by a big majority (two thirds), Israel came into being – after the first voting had to be repeated. It will surprise many to know that Russia was one of the countries which, under Stalin, voted *for* Israel's existence. Partition meant that Israel would have her own government, her own boundaries and land.

The fact that Israel came under military attack from the very outset (15 May 1948) proves *indisputedly* that the present unending dissension is not (in reality) over territorial boundaries, but rather over Israel's very existence. Politicians fail to grasp that Islam and the Koran cannot tolerate a Jewish State in their midst, nor can they tolerate any territory that they have once held (i.e. during the Turkish occupation) falling back into non-Muslim hands.

How much Israel still owes its rebirth to the prayers of Rees Howells and the Christians of his Bible College of Wales at that time, only eternity will reveal. They were amongst *the few who realized, the few who knew* that God's Word was at stake. So they prayed and prayed and prayed throughout the hours of the UN voting. Hearkening angels must have bent their ears to catch the voting results, and to report back to the Father! What a trumpet sound must have then echoed in Heaven! *Your word has not returned unto you void!* (See Isaiah 55:11.)

Times and seasons

Winter

To His disciples' last question, "Lord, will You at this time restore the kingdom to Israel?" Jesus did not reply with a straight "No!" Instead, He simply said, "It is not for you to know times or seasons which the Father has put in His own authority" (Acts 1:6–7 NKJV). In other words: "The restoration is going to come, but it is not for you to know when that will occur. There are times, there are seasons ahead which you are not to know of at present." However, each season has a character and a sequence. We can usually tell where we are by what we see and feel, by climate, by trees and by temperature, even if we have no calendar.

If we look again at Psalm 102 we find that Zion's "appointed time," when God will "show favor to her," is preceded by a long period of desolation and withering:

> My days vanish like smoke;
>   my bones burn like glowing embers.
> My heart is ... withered like grass ...
> my enemies taunt me ...
> I eat ashes as my food ...
>   I wither away like grass.
>
> (Psalm 102:3–4, 8–9, 11 NIV)

What an appalling summary of 1,900 years of desolation, ending with the Holocaust – everything withered away! Obviously it is "winter time."

There was little sign of a national life or land for Israel before the twentieth century. But the buds of spring made their first tiny sprout with Theodore Herzl calling the first Zionist Congress in Basle, Switzerland in 1897. It was there and then that the world first saw the founding of the World Zionist Organization. However, there had been stirrings amongst Jewish people earlier, in the nineteenth century, and some had begun to return to the land. In 1880, Jerusalem was the largest city and had a Jewish majority. "Zionism" – the Jewish National Liberation Movement – became the channel by which God was to favor Zion.

If the Lord is not in this movement we must question why He declares,

> For the LORD has chosen Zion,
>   he has desired it for his dwelling.
>
> (Psalm 132:13 NIV)

Those who today either unbelievingly, ignorantly, or even maliciously oppose Zionism (the restoration of the Jewish people) are set upon a collision course with God! While wonderful Church and Christian connotations evolve justifiably from the term "Zion" (Hebrews

12:22ff.), the Church (particularly in the West) has nonetheless been
guilty of totally spiritualizing the term, thereby robbing the Jews of
their irrevocable and priceless spiritual heritage (Deuteronomy 32:9;
Psalm 135:4; Romans 11:29).

One clear example of this occurred in New Zealand in the 1980s
when it was decided to expunge from the Anglican Book of Common
Prayer all references to Zion and Israel, and to substitute terms that
referred only to the Church. In effect, this was altering Scripture – against
which the Holy Spirit explicitly warns – both at the beginning and at the
end of the Bible (Deuteronomy 4:2; Revelation 22:18–19):

> If anyone takes away from the words of the book of this prophecy,
> God will take away his part from the tree of life ...
>
> (Revelation 22:19 NASB)

A fairly simple study of Scripture reveals that the term "Zion" repeatedly embraces the land and the people or nation, and also the holy
hill of Zion, *and* all the aspirations linked with the spiritual rebirth
of those whom God calls "My people" (Jeremiah 31:1; Ezekiel 36:28;
37:23) – the Jewish nation of Israel. In addition to this, *but not in place
of it*, the term "Zion" does, of course, have some application to the
Church (Hebrews 12:22).

A further great herald of the end of "winter" occurred when, in
1917, Jerusalem fell directly into the hands of the leading Christian
country of the day, Great Britain. After 400 years of Turkish rule, and
without a shot being fired, it came under British control – twenty
years after the first Zionist Congress! General Allenby, a fine Christian acquainted with God's Word and will, would not ride, but instead
walked bareheaded into this city – deeply aware of the Biblical and historic significance of the event. It was 11 December 1917, the occasion
of the Jewish Feast of *Hanukkah* (or Feast of Dedication, as in John
10:22). It was also winter, and General Allenby had spent much of
the previous night in prayer. While hidden within British history, this
was God's work. We could reflect that, 1,900 years earlier, on that
same festive and Biblical occasion, the unbelieving Jews had been

asking Jesus, "How long will you keep us in suspense? If you are the [Messiah], tell us plainly" (John 10:22–24 NIV).

So the Lord chose the annual celebration of the rededication of the Temple (dating from 168 BC) as the occasion on which to bring Jerusalem back into the hands of Great Britain, at that time a Bible-believing country. He had replied to the unbelieving Jews, "I did tell you, but you do not believe." What was not believed? That "I am the good shepherd. The good shepherd lays down his life for the sheep" (John 10:11 NIV). That Jesus *was and is* the Good Shepherd, and that His life laid down for His people was not in vain, we see clearly underlined today in the current restoration of Israel, and in what He began to do for Jerusalem in 1917.

While Purim (February / March) marks the rescue of the Jews from physical destruction by Haman (see the book of Esther), Hanukkah marks the rescue of Judaism, as a faith and a way of life, from obliteration. Such a faith awaits the inbreathing of the knowledge of the Good Shepherd. *But it is He who will breathe upon His people again.* The rabbis, who lay stress on the spiritual aspects of Hanukkah, habitually read at this time the Zechariah passage:

> "Not by might nor by power, but by My Spirit," says the LORD of hosts.
>
> (Zechariah 4:6 NKJV)

Spring

Matthew 24, the "spinal cord" of prophecy, tells us

> Now learn the parable from the fig tree: when its branch [or twigs] has already become tender and puts forth its leaves, you know that summer is near.
>
> (Matthew 24:32 NASB)

Not that summer is "here" … but *near.*

The fig tree is Israel. In Mark 11:12–14, 20–21 (and Matthew 21:19ff.) we find it withering under the word of the Lord, his prophetic utterance encapsulating the long winter and the withering of Israel in the picture of a single tree – the fig tree. It is at this very point in the Bible that we find the oft-quoted phrase "Have faith in God" (Mark 11:22 NIV). The setting of this verse in the context of a withered and unfruitful Israel is *primarily to instill faith in us* for God's beloved Jewish people; not merely that God is *able* to restore them, but that he *will* do so. Mountains of unbelief are to be cast into the sea!

And so, harmonizing with "the appointed time" to "favor [Zion]," Jesus tells His disciples of a time when the fig tree will become tender and will blossom. In other words, not only will life be flowing again through the living tree, but a season of fruitfulness is at hand! "Learn, profit from this; you *know* that summer is near."

Summer is the time of sun and warmth, and of fruit development. We are led to expect a time of spiritual fruitfulness ahead, with Israel leading the way (Isaiah 27:6; Romans 11:12, 15).

It was indeed spring for Israel when Jerusalem so unexpectedly and miraculously came back into Jewish hands during Pentecost (the Feast of Weeks or *Shavuot*) in 1967 – for the first time in 2,500 years! Thus fulfilled was the Lord's own prophetic word:

Jerusalem will be trampled on by the Gentiles *until* the times of the Gentiles are fulfilled.

(Luke 21:24 NIV, emphasis added)

Had Jordan not entered the Six-Day War in 1967 (against Israel's plea to remain neutral), she would never have lost the eastern half of Jerusalem which she had illegally seized and controlled for twenty years. However, this was God's intervention; it was *His appointed time*!

Although Jewish people had danced for three days (until exhausted!) in May 1948 (when Israel reappeared on the map of the world), on 7 June 1967 there were uncontrollable tears, even from the soldiers, as Jerusalem itself fell so suddenly into Jewish hands.

Spring's produce

> My beloved spoke, and said to me:
> "Rise up, my love, my fair one,
> And come away.
> For lo, the winter is past,
> the rain is over and gone.
> The flowers appear on the earth;
> The time of singing has come,
> And the voice of the turtledove
> Is heard in our land."
>
> (Song of Solomon 2:10–12 NKJV)

In these beautiful words we find two of the seasons, with the Lord calling His people out of the retreats and hidden places of winter: "Rise up, my love, my fair one, and come away" ("I will bring [you back] from the east ... west ... north ... and ... south"). Spring is here and there are flowers on the earth – winter has gone.

All who know a little about Israel will recall the incessant cooing of turtledoves, morn till night, from the onset of spring (late March) until their winter migration. They sing, as it were, in praise to God, *because* it is spring and "we are in our land." The singing, for the Jews, is indelibly related to the possession of the land that God has given to them. No other people on the face of this globe have had a portion of earth's territory so specifically allocated to them by the Creator Himself. *That it is written on their hearts is not a political matter, but a divine ordination.* History proves, in fact, that the land blossoms with the Jews in it, and withers in their absence. God has ordained the marriage of the two – land and people. Of what other place does the Bible say, "thy land shall be married," other than of Zion (Isaiah 62:4 KJV)?

Twin restoration

> The fig tree puts forth her green figs,
> And the vines with the tender grapes
> Give a good smell.

Rise up, my love, my fair one,
And come away!

(Song of Solomon 2:13 NKJV)

While the fig tree is Israel in Scripture, the vine is the Church, the body of born-again believers (Jew and Gentile) who love the Jewish Messiah. You will often find them together in Scripture, and the one (Israel) is often a picture of the other (the Church).

During the "winter years" of Israel – its desolation and dispersion for centuries – we find a parallel in the spiritual desolation of the Church: the medieval darkness and rigidity, the lack of vibrant, corporate spiritual life until the twentieth century, the Word of God stifled, traditional liturgy as the highest release, minimal record or use of spiritual gifts, and the Church sharply divided into doctrinal divisions with little or no inter-communication.

Many will admit that the dry bones of Ezekiel 37 have represented the Church as well as Israel! *If we could but see it, the timing of the outpouring of the Holy Spirit on the Church in the twentieth century was clearly linked with the restoration of Israel.* Where there were barren sands in the Negev desert in Israel we now find fruit – sometimes even tomatoes – completely surrounded by desert! Today, in many Christian denominations, we find folk joyfully filled with the Spirit, released into a praise and strength in the Lord that has not been seen since Pentecost.

A spiritual unity and intermingling of Christian believers has begun which typify the coming together of the dry bones of centuries. However, it is still only spring. The Lord has a great deal yet to do within us to make us really fruitful. Much pruning of the vine is needed to bring forth fruit – and some withered branches need to be burned. We can take confidence in the Lord's words: "I will build my church; and the gates of hell shall not prevail against it" (Matthew 16:18 KJV).

The time will come when the glory of the Lord *will* be revealed to all the earth through His Body – and we shall see the Lord's words fulfilled: "… that they may be made perfect in one; and that the world may know that thou hast sent me, and hast loved them, as thou hast loved me" (John 17:23 KJV).

The process of restorative work is bringing Israel into its *own* heritage. It is *we* who have "crossed over" into knowing and serving the God of the Jews (the God of Israel) who have already partaken of that heritage. They will not be coming into "our" heritage but into their own – the *commonwealth of Israel* (Ephesians 2:12)!

The winter of the fig tree and the vine are pictured together in Joel:

> The vine has dried up,
> And the fig tree has withered;
> The pomegranate tree,
> The palm tree also,
> And the apple tree –
> All the trees of the field are withered.

> (Joel 1:12 NKJV)

Meditation on the chapter will reveal how it mirrors Israel's and the Church's histories – with demonic forces described as "locusts" invading each. Joel 2 goes on to refer to what lies ahead – *restoration*. Here the fig tree and the vine give an abundant full yield – with the outpouring of the latter rain in full measure, following the early rain (which was Pentecost). This is a time of *twin* spiritual restoration that yet lies ahead for the Church and for Israel – the "summer" of Matthew 24:32.

So, in God's unique way, we can look at Israel today and gain some picture of the Church. Heard by the author, and part of a prophecy given at a Dennis Clark Prayer and Bible Week (at Ashburnham in January 1972), was:

> Do you not see, my people, that Israel is a picture of the Church – at ease, settled down in foreign lands and speaking different languages? And my cry is still, "Let my people go!"

Figs

In Mark 11, the Lord was looking for figs on the tree but was disappointed to find none. Hence the withering. The figs represent spiritual fruit – those who satisfy the Master's longing in yielding themselves to Him. (Did He not give Himself to us completely?)

"The fig tree puts forth her green figs" (Song of Solomon 2:13 NKJV). The physical restoration of Israel has its parallel in a far less obvious, but nonetheless _real_ spiritual restoration within. One has to "part the leaves" to find the figs.

The amazing change that has taken place in the Jewish attitude towards Jesus in the twentieth century may be judged from the fact that, until World War One, the bulk of the Jewish people would not even mention the name of Jesus, let alone write about Him! I know of this from my own youth.

The following statement is attributed to Dr Isidore Singer, managing editor of the Jewish Encyclopedia:

> The great change in Jewish thought concerning Jesus of Nazareth I cannot better illustrate than by this fact: When I was a boy, had my father, who was a very pious man, heard the name of Jesus uttered from the pulpit of our synagogue, he and every other man in the congregation would have left the building, and the Rabbi would have been dismissed at once. Now it is not strange, in many synagogues, to hear sermons preached eulogistic of this Jesus, and nobody thinks of protesting – in fact, we are all glad to claim Jesus as one of our people ...
>
> I regard Jesus of Nazareth as a Jew of Jews, one whom all Jewish people are learning to love. His teachings have been an immense service to the world in bringing Israel's God to the knowledge of hundreds of millions of mankind.[1]

The deepening Jewish interest in the mission and message of Jesus is reflected in the mounting number of books and articles Jews have written about Him. _Since Israel regained statehood, more books have been written about Jesus by Jews in the State of Israel than world Jewry had produced in all the preceding eighteen centuries!_

The visit to Jerusalem in the early 1980s of Pope John Paul II (of Polish origin) aroused considerable Jewish interest in the subject of Christianity. The New Testament became front-page news in Israel. Within one year of his visit, attendance at the Department of Christian Studies of the Hebrew University almost trebled, and three new books on Jesus made their appearance. Within thirty years of the establishment of the State of Israel in 1948, Israeli authors had published 187 books, essays, poems, and articles in Hebrew, and 223 other works – all about Jesus.[2]

However, the main and most dramatic change has occurred since 1967, since when we have seen a fulfillment of:

1. "I will sprinkle clean water on you" (Ezekiel 36:25 NIV)
2. "the washing with water through the word" (Ephesians 5:26 NIV)
3. "I will give you a new heart and put a new spirit in you" (Ezekiel 36:26 NIV).

The Bible is Israel's book and it fits her like a glove. It is *required* reading in schools and colleges – the opposite trend of the Western world today. The change in attitude to the Christian, and especially to Jesus, although gradual, has been quite remarkable.

More recently, it is very significant to find the "common people" ("the common people heard Him gladly" – Mark 12:37 NKJV), that is, Jewish people in general, defying an official rabbinic ban not to join in with Christians in the traditional Feast of Tabernacles celebratory march through the streets of Jerusalem. Instead, in October 2007, in a march of some 80,000 people, about 73,000 were Jews and the remainder were some 7,000 Christians coming specifically to celebrate this annual festival. This is but a forerunner to the prophecy of Zechariah 14:16 where we learn that, in the Millennium, representatives from around the globe will come annually to worship the Lord in Jerusalem at their *Succoth* Festival. What is happening amongst the people shows the new heart and the new spirit that the Lord is giving to them.

Grapes

In Israel the greatest impact in conveying some sense of real Christian love has been made through the coming together of such Christians who love Israel, pray for her, see her place in God's plans, etc. We must not make the error of thinking that such people are in any way anti-Arab: on the contrary, their relief program embraces Arab and Jewish needs. The point is that here also, in the Christian, there is the new heart. For the first time for centuries, a body of Christians is found willing to identify openly with the land and nation of Israel according to God's Word. This again is "restoration" because *it has restored an important element of the Christian faith*, lost since the persecution by the early Church fathers, and their removal of much of its original Jewish content.

Now we see groups of these Christians, representative of many other thousands worldwide, establishing, as it were, a foothold for the Messiah in Jerusalem. In their visits to the city from their homes abroad they tread the soil, walk the streets and declare faith in the Word of God that speaks so clearly of it becoming "a praise in the earth" (Isaiah 62:7 NKJV), and of it one day becoming the city of "the Throne of the LORD" (Jeremiah 3:17 NKJV).

This sharing in the annual Feast of Tabernacles (a "feast of the Lord" rather than a "Jewish feast" – see Leviticus 23:33–44) is particularly open to the non-Jewish believer. It has always formed the basis for the harvest festivals of the West. In the Lord's millennial reign, it will be obligatory for all nations to send representatives to Jerusalem "to worship the King" (Zechariah 14:16 NIV). Restoring this festival to the Christian calendar may seem strange to the Church at large, but it is Biblical and will only be putting back what was arbitrarily removed by the early Church fathers.

It is God's supreme plan that Jew and Gentile worship the one God, and thus form what is called the "one new man." This feast will then be the "autumn" completion of our seasons, when the Lord returns to Zion, and peace for the earth flows from its center – Jerusalem.

... the appointed time has come.

(Psalm 102:13 NIV)

While "parting the leaves" to uncover the hidden fruit of what God has been doing in the land (particularly since the miraculous Six-Day War), the West in general and the Church in particular are unaware of the remarkable growth of the numbers of Jewish people coming to saving faith in the Lord Jesus – the Messiah of Israel!

While, in the main, these believers have come from, and have settled from, abroad (i.e. they have made "Aliyah"), they have come sacrificially and purposefully. They represent the heart of God and the "remnant of Israel" in a way that no others can do. They represent the firstfruits of the end-time harvest that the Lord will soon be reaping from amongst His people. They represent the fruit of the prayers of those around the globe who have been praying for Israel. They represent the fruit of the prayers of other believers who, long centuries before Israel was even re-established, prayed with faith for their restoration. (See some of the matchless hymns written by Charles Wesley, Horatio Bonar, Isaac Watts, E.R. Vine.)

This remnant, while sadly hidden through ignorance, indifference or antipathy from most of the Church, is increasingly known of within Israel itself. Why? Because step by step since the Six-Day War, they have increased in size, boldness and influence. Known as Messianic believers or fellowships, less than a handful existed in 1969. But today, with constant increase, it is extremely difficult – impossible – to number them. Even though increasingly ostracized and persecuted by some ultra-orthodox Jews, it is an amazing transition from the 1980s to find the term "Messianic" so frequently used in media reference to them. While in some cases that same term "Messianic" is used by Orthodox Jews to refer to their particular interpretation of a coming "Messiah," *in the main it is used to speak of the activity of believing fellowships.*

So, whether favorably reported upon or not, the public are increasingly exposed to the gospel in one way or another. *There are more believing Jews in the land of Israel today than at any other time since the first century.* A large proportion of these are of Russian stock – having come amongst the one million or more Russians who flooded into the country after the fall of communism in 1991. Probably the Lord had these in mind in telling us, "Behold, I am bringing them from the *north* country ... For I am a father to Israel ..." (Jeremiah 31:8, 9 NASB, emphasis added). But just as encouraging has been the sight of Spanish-speaking Jews trickling back into their homeland from the south – notably Argentina, where, until fairly recently, the Jewish population reached 500,000.

Although there is so much else to pray for, *if the readers of this book prayed only for this aspect of the Lord's work in Israel, they would be doing well indeed.* Simultaneously, it is good to remember that there is increasing unity in the land between Jewish and Arab believers – particularly in Galilee. Bearing Islam in mind, *pressures and difficulties for the Arab believer can be very much greater than for the Jew.*

Israel's "winter" preservation

It is a most remarkable thing that the people who have suffered more than any other nation on earth are the ones who have consistently clung to and worshiped God. How many thousands of Jews went to their deaths in the Holocaust – singing to the Lord? Which of us has suffered such a test and how can we tell how many of these had a real saving faith? Eternity will disclose things that will amaze us all.

In the meantime, as we see God's appointed time to favor Zion – spring and summer – it is worth looking back over our shoulder for a moment to consider Jewish history, and to perceive that *it is the Lord who has preserved His people for His purposes and for this hour.*

> This people have I formed for myself;
> they shall shew forth my praise.
>
> (Isaiah 43:21 KJV)

It was the Jewish prophet Habakkuk who claimed that, *whatever* happened, he would rejoice in the God of his salvation:

> Although the fig tree shall not blossom, neither shall fruit be in the vines; the labour of the olive shall fail, and the fields shall yield no meat; the flock shall be cut off from the fold, and there shall be no herd in the stalls: Yet I will rejoice in the LORD, I will joy in the God of my salvation. The LORD God is my strength …
>
> (Habakkuk 3:17–19 KJV)

This pictures complete desolation – but also complete captivation, wholly trusting in God in the most barren circumstances! The Lord is bringing the Christian to this point of trust also. We have something to learn from the Jews who have thus clung to God. A living testimony to God throughout the centuries – and never more so than now – has been the existence of the Jew.

The appointed time to favor Zion *has* come. God *has* arisen in compassion. He awaits our partnership in His plans to bless Israel and the world through Israel. "He remembers [present tense] His covenant forever" (Psalm 105:8 NKJV):

> Forgotten! no; that cannot be,
> All other names may pass away;
> But thine My Israel shall remain
> In everlasting memory.
>
> Forgotten! no; that cannot be,
> Inscribed upon My palms thou art,
> The name I gave in days of old
> Is graven still upon My heart.
>
> Forgotten! no; that cannot be,
> He who upon thee named His name,
> Assures thee of eternal love,
> A love for evermore the same.

Forgotten! no; that cannot be,
The oath of Him who cannot lie
Is on thy city and thy land,
An oath to all eternity.

Forgotten! no; that cannot be,
Sun, moon, and stars may cease to shine,
But thou shalt be remembered still,
For thou art His, and He is thine.

Forgotten of the Lord thy God!
No, Israel, no, that cannot be,
He chose thee in the days of old
And still His favour rests on thee.

(Horatio Bonar 1808–89)

Notes

1. Reproduced from *The Messiahship of Jesus*, by Arthur W. Kac (Moody Press USA).
2. Reproduced from *The Messiahship of Jesus*, by Arthur W. Kac (Moody Press USA).

CHAPTER 4

Their Own Olive Tree

> For if you were cut off from what is by nature a wild olive tree, and were grafted contrary to nature into a cultivated olive tree, how much more [readily] will these who are the natural branches be grafted into their own olive tree?
>
> (Romans 11:24 NASB)

In the "you" of this text, the apostle Paul here specifically addresses Gentiles (see Romans 11:13). And, in contrast, and by "they" or by "the natural branches" he refers to the Jewish nation – Israel. He is writing to the Church in Rome (which later became the Church *of* Rome). A careful reading of the chapter shows that Paul is dealing with what appears to be the early stages of replacement theology.

The theological backbone of the Bible is generally acknowledged to be the book of Romans. While Bible colleges spend months and months on this book as a whole, it is normal and common to find little attention paid to chapters 9–11, which deal with Israel in an unambiguous way.

So important are those chapters that Paul immediately goes on to say in chapter 12:

> Therefore [i.e. as a result of the foregoing], I *urge* you, brothers, in view of God's mercy, to offer your bodies as living sacrifices, holy and pleasing to God – this is your spiritual act of worship.
>
> (Romans 12:1 NIV, emphasis added)

In his impassioned plea to the Gentiles in Romans 11, Paul likens the whole spiritual heritage of Israel to the olive tree (verse 24). It is into this "tree" that the born-again Jew and the born-again Gentile have each been brought. The olive tree is simply another metaphor or term for the "commonwealth of Israel" (Ephesians 2:12 KJV). But it is *theirs*, Israel's, by right – their *own* olive tree! Let it be understood here that the "you" and the "they" of this chapter consistently refer to Gentiles and Israelites. It is strategic to note this point – the emphasis being on the nation of Israel, the elect remnant of the nation, rather than on individual Jews. Paul is emphasizing: (a) what God is yet to do *for and through them as a nation* – again for world blessing (Romans 12, 15); and (b) the *responsibility* of the Gentiles – because of their indebtedness to the Jewish nation – to show compassion and mercy (Romans 11:30–31).

This indebtedness stems not merely from Israel having pioneered the gospel from Abraham's day, nor from God's entrustment to them of Scripture, nor merely from the Jewish prophets but, surprisingly, from God's judgments upon Israel after the crucifixion: "through their [Israel's] fall salvation is come unto the Gentiles" (Romans 11:11 KJV). What an indebtedness this really is!

Hypothetically, this is saying that had the Jewish nation not stumbled or fallen, there would have been no salvation for the Gentiles. However, it had of course been predestined (a) that Jesus was to die – "for this cause came I unto this hour" – John 12:27; see also 1:29); and (b) that there would therefore be an instrument of crucifixion.

This indebtedness is echoed in Romans 11:28, where the arresting statement is made: "From the standpoint of the gospel they [Israel] are enemies for your [i.e. the Gentiles'] sake" (NASB).

This scripture virtually tells us that while Israel became "God's scapegoat" for the crucifixion, and judgment has fallen (vicariously) upon them, in actuality, both Jew and Gentile were ultimately responsible (Matthew 20:18–19).

A national role

While we have seen elsewhere that Israel alone, in servanthood to the Lord, is allocated a specific *land* (and that at the center of the world), we see here also that she is given *a central role* to reach that world with the spiritual riches that are hers in the Messiah.

While the Gentile and the Jew before God are of equal standing (Galatians 3:28), God in His sovereignty has nonetheless chosen the *nation* of the Jews as His particular channel of revelation. Although Jewish people often prefer to call themselves a "choosing nation," indicating that *they* have chosen God, the real truth is that *God* has made the choice. God's call to them out of Egypt makes no mention whatever of "their" choice or of "our choice" – but only of *His*!

> ... the LORD your God has chosen you to be a people for His own possession out of all the peoples who are on the face of the earth.
>
> (Deuteronomy 7:6 NASB)

"You did not choose me, but I chose you ... to go and bear fruit" (John 15:16 NIV) shows the Messiah's words to the Jewish disciples, but they apply to the nation as a whole. Another illustration of this is found in Saul who later became Paul:

> But for that very reason I was shown mercy so that in me, the worst of sinners, [the Messiah] Jesus might display his unlimited patience as an example for those who would [hereafter] believe on him and receive eternal life.
>
> (1 Timothy 1:16 NIV)

A comparative study of the lives of Saul and Israel, past, present and future, will bring out many parallels, both in Saul's dealings with God, and God's dealings with him.

- Saul's/Paul's *zeal* for God, though not fully enlightened (Romans 10:2)
- The sovereign act of *mercy* that saved Saul/Paul by grace (1 Corinthians 15:9–10; Romans 11:5)
- The very *mode of his salvation* (Acts 9:4; 26:14; Isaiah 52:2 – Jerusalem to rise from the dust – a cameo of Paul's experience; 60:1)

- In *suffering* (cf. Acts 9:16; 2 Corinthians 6:4–5; Isaiah 43:2)
- Saul's/Paul's *fruitfulness* and Israel's yet-to-be (Romans 11:12, 15; Isaiah 27:6)

Of Zion it is said:

> Arise, shine; for your light has come,
>   And the glory of the Lord has risen upon you.
> For behold, darkness will cover the earth
>   And deep darkness the peoples;
>   *But* the Lord will rise upon you,
>   And His glory will appear upon you.
> Nations [Hebrew: *goyim*] will come to your light,
>   And kings to the brightness of your rising.
>
> (Isaiah 60:1–3 NASB, emphasis added)

While this also has application to the Church, by the text and context, it is *initially and primarily* addressed to Israel, prophesying of *the worldwide role yet to be fulfilled!* No wonder that in Romans 15:13 the Holy Spirit calls us to joyful faith – having just reminded us that Jesus, the Messiah, became "a servant of the Jews… to *confirm* [not to nullify] the promises made to the patriarchs" (Romans 15:8 NIV, emphasis added).

Professor Charles Feinberg says of the Isaiah 60 passage that it is in language *too glorious to apply to anything that has yet happened!* How truthful that is! And what an arising that is to be! The effect to be worldwide! A brightness that *all* shall see, with ships, wealth, kings and foreigners converging upon the world center.

Take note that Gentile nations come to this light and glory in Zion. Notice that it is not Israel's glory, but *the glory of the Lord!*

So, while we affirm that the original outpouring of the Spirit at Pentecost was but the early rain, there is to be (harmonizing with the climate in Israel) a latter rain to accomplish the above. What has been portrayed "in miniature" in Saul's life is to be reproduced on a grand national scale throughout Israel in the days ahead.

The latter rain (of springtime) is yet to come. That outpouring, for which we should now be praying, will see a far greater enactment of Acts 1:8. We are specifically bidden to pray for "the spring rain" (Zechariah 10:1 NRSV), and amongst the various terms used in Hebrew therein for rain, *geshem* (abundant rain) is chosen to tell us what the latter rain (*malqosh*) will be like! But there will also be "storm clouds": where God is at work, our adversary is not asleep!

God's answer to the present West Bank problem (Jerusalem, Judea, Samaria) will be found, not in political maneuvering or ingenuity, but in the coming abundant outpouring of the Holy Spirit ... *geshem*!

> You will receive power when the Holy Spirit has come upon you; and you shall be My witnesses both in Jerusalem, and in all Judea and Samaria, and even to the remotest part of the earth.
>
> (Acts 1:8 NASB)

Several other scriptures confirm this outpouring on Israel, and we do well to seek the Lord as to how we should be praying for the land and the people (Joel 2:23–24).

Homer Duncan writes in his *Helpful Hints on Romans*:

> Chapter 11 can be summarized in this way: (1) Israel's rejection is not total (v. 1–10), and (2) Israel's rejection is not final (v. 11–36). Most of the present day teaching is that God is through with Israel as a nation and now the Church as "spiritual Israel" has taken her place.
>
> This chapter as well as many other portions in the Word of God clearly teaches that this is not true. The Bible makes a clear cut distinction between Israel and the Church (v. 26). The nation of Israel is an earthly people whereas the Church is a heavenly people. A man would not be honourable if he were to make a promise to one person and then fulfil that promise to another person. In the same way, God cannot be holy and just if He makes promises to Israel and fails to keep them. It is folly to teach that the promises that God made to Israel are now being fulfilled in the Church. A study of God's covenants, promises and His Word will keep us straight on this.[1]

Israel and the Church

In the writer's opinion, Scripture teaches that God will pour out his Spirit on Israel while the Church is *still* here, that is, before the so-called rapture. There is only *one* olive tree and this will still be "on earth" in spiritual form for the time when the natural branches, the Jewish nation, are grafted back in. If it is "their *own* olive tree" it would seem most incongruous – as is taught in many circles – that the Church be lifted away to heaven beforehand, leaving Israel to face the music and the great tribulation.

The teaching of the pre-tribulation rapture of the Church has the scantiest scriptural basis, and serves simply to lull to sleep those who are not already slumbering! God is working through all of Israel's troubles to bring her to Himself. A close and prayerful study of this subject in the Bible will lead one to see the world-wide role He has for His elect nation, after the remnant is saved. (This is the subject of another study, not to be included within this book.)

Characteristics of the olive tree and God's dealings with Israel

The Holy Spirit closes the emotive book of Hosea as follows:

> I will heal their apostasy,
>   I will love them freely,
>   For My anger has turned away from them.
> *I will be like the dew to Israel* ...
> his beauty will be like the olive tree ...
>
> (Hosea 14:4–6 NASB)

The dew here speaks of the renewal of the Holy Spirit upon Israel. Dew is indispensable to plant life in the Middle East, and Israel's renewal will bestow upon her an olive tree likeness.

Seven characteristics of the olive tree

1. The olive tree has the habit of not dying, even when cut down. Its roots and stumps will still push forth, even after hundreds of years: *indestructibility and vitality*. The Garden of Gethsemane contains trees that predate the birth of the Messiah of Israel – the Lord Jesus!
2. There is a marked and lovely fragrance to the tree and its leaves (2 Corinthians 2:14).
3. The green of the leaf speaks of prosperity (Psalm 52:8). The silver underside of the leaf speaks of redemption. The trees make a beautiful picture as they shimmer in the sun and light breeze. "The Spirit Himself bears witness with our spirit that we are children of God" (Romans 8:16 NKJV). The olive groves, which proliferate across Israel, are a beautiful sight to all.
4. The timber is hard, durable and beautifully grained. It needs skilled handling to shape it into the desired figures for use. Its color, yellow, speaks of the Holy Spirit.
5. It is a *low* tree with wandering branches. It loves the sun. It is slow-growing.
6. The tree fruits with great regularity, but only in a pure Mediterranean atmosphere and climate will this fruit ripen. A full-grown tree can yield half a ton of olive oil a year.
7. Its trunk is well gnarled – typifying the tortuous history of Israel. And the marked grain reminds us of how the Word of God records "their own olive tree" – Israel.

The use of the olive

1. The tree has to be beaten or shaken to remove the olives. The beating is often done with a heavy stick.
2. There is a specific time for that beating. A week before the olives are ready, they will not respond.
3. After removal from the tree, the olives have to be pressed or crushed to release the oil. The stones of the olive presses of Bible days can still be seen in parts of Israel.

The Lord disciplines those he loves, and he punishes everyone he accepts as a son.

(Hebrews 12:6 NIV)

No discipline seems pleasant at the time, but painful. Later on, however, it produces a harvest of righteousness and peace for those who have been trained by it.

(Hebrews 12:11 NIV)

There is no such thing as a fruitful, godly life in the Lord that has not walked in the way of brokenness, trial and affliction. The forerunner of this was the Messiah Himself (see 1 Peter 2:21):

... smitten by him [God], and afflicted.
But he was pierced for our transgressions,
        he was crushed for our iniquities;
the punishment that brought us peace [*shalom*]
was upon him ...

(Isaiah 53:4–5 NIV)

Without the Messiah going before Israel and us, and without the Jewish nation firstly seeing Him as "The Lord our righteousness" neither they nor we would have had pardon and peace. That *shalom*, spoken of incessantly in Israel, but which (except for the Messianic believers) still eludes them, will one day be found in Him who says, "My peace I give unto you: not as the world giveth" (John 14:17 KJV).

"Abraham believed God, and it was credited to him as righteousness" (Romans 4:3 NIV).

From this oil (of crushing) there are seven uses:

Lighting: Psalm 18:28; Exodus 27:20

Food and cooking: Exodus 29:2; Leviticus 2:4

Anointing: Psalm 23:5; Exodus 30:31

Medicinal purposes: Isaiah 61:1; Proverbs 17:22

Cosmetic: Psalm 104:15; Isaiah 61:3

Cleansing: Psalm 51:10; Psalm 19:12

Lubrication: Psalm 133; Proverbs 27:9 NASB

What is God saying to Gentiles in Romans 11?

1. **God's faithfulness** (verses 1–2 NIV): "Did God reject his people? By no means! ... God did not reject his people, whom he foreknew."

   In less than a dozen words, in this leading epistle on New Testament doctrine, the Holy Spirit, through His servant Paul, specifically refutes the widespread teaching by the Church today that God has finished with Israel as His elect people.

   Note that this does not read, "God did not reject the Jews" but "God did not reject *his* people" (emphasis added). They may have been laid aside, *but they still belong to Him,* and they are just as much His own "treasured possession" (Exodus 19:5; Psalm 135:4 NIV) as at the time of coming out of Egypt!

   Paul's common phrase, "By no means," can be translated "Impossible!" That is, that rejection would be totally out of keeping with God's character and faithfulness. *It is unthinkable!* Moses' declaration to Pharaoh of God's choice 3,500 years ago: "Israel is my firstborn son ... Let my son go," has lost *none* of its meaning and support from the Father of Israel, God Himself (Exodus 4:22–23 NIV).

   If only we, the Church and the world could see it, to the Gentile, Israel in history is the ultimate example of God's faithfulness, in both kindness and severity (Romans 11:22).

2. **Indebtedness**: This is commented upon in part earlier in this same chapter, but Romans 11 actually *pivots* on this issue. "You do not support the root, but the root supports you" (verse 18 NIV). No plant can exist without its root, though a root may well live on its own (especially the root of an olive tree), without its eventual fruit.

   "... the root supports you" is in the continuous present tense. *Do you realize just how important this is?* It is like the lungs which breathe in to give life to the body. Gentile Christian anti-Semitism has caused endless harm to the Body of Christ over the centuries, and only the grace of God in His kindness has overruled to see His blessing continued – in spite of the obstinacy of the Church.

   But this kindness will not continue for ever. Romans 2:4 tells us that God's kindness and forbearance are meant to lead us to repentance...

The Jewish patriarchs, prophets, pilgrims and scribes were the instruments by which your salvation has come. Under God, their faith has laid the foundation for all that you today believe and follow. You are to nurture your roots – not ignore or destroy them!

3. **Avoid pride at all costs** (verses 20–21 NIV): "Do not be arrogant, but be afraid. For if God did not spare the natural branches, he will not spare you either." What a sobering verse! It says, in effect, "Take great care or else what happened to Israel will happen to you. If God in His anger destroyed Solomon's cedar, gilded Temple, what makes you think that your cathedrals are immunized from His judgments?'

   Romans 11:22 goes on to warn, "Behold then the kindness *and* severity of God; to those who fell, severity, but to you, God's kindness, *if* you continue in His kindness; otherwise you also will be cut off" (NASB, emphasis added). Which of the readers of this book have ever heard a sermon preached on this dire warning?

   Countless Bible teachers maintain that "We are the New Israel" or "the Israel of God" – in the one inventing an unscriptural term, and in the other misapplying what refers to born-again Jewish believers. This (a) feeds our pride; (b) deprives the Jewish nation of their inheritance; and (c) hinders the work of the Holy Spirit which, in contrast, we should be assisting by our prayers.

4. **Attracting the Jew** (verse 11): "… salvation has come to the Gentiles to make Israel jealous." While there are notable exceptions, we cannot say that the lives and witness of Gentile believers as a whole have caused Jewish people to desire to know the secret of our inward spiritual life. On the contrary, culminating with the Holocaust, the centuries have seen forced conversions, mass expulsions, deprivations, murders, pogroms, false accusations, shepherding into ghettoes – the entire opposite of what the Holy Spirit intended.

   However, while the above is true of the Church and of countries as a whole, *since the Six-Day War of June 1967, when – after 1,900 years – Jerusalem came back into Jewish hands, God has been working to raise a pro-Israel prayer-force, bands of praying people and prayer warriors throughout the world.* And while the Church in general has been largely asleep, God has not slumbered. *Coupled with this prayer, practical aid of many kinds has also been flowing into the land and towards the Jewish people. In most cases, it has been through the para-church organizations that God has raised and worked through – each with its own specific calling.*

He has remembered His covenant with Abraham, Isaac and Jacob:

Behold, I am against the shepherds [of Israel], and I will demand My sheep from them ... Behold, I Myself will search for My sheep and seek them out.

(Ezekiel 34:10–11 NASB)

Then I will give you shepherds after My own heart, who will feed you on knowledge and understanding.

(Jeremiah 3:15 NASB)

5. **Making Israel *jealous*:** Although mistrust still continues in many Jewish quarters, many of us are today seeing an amazing transformation in attitudes to Christians. Our motivation must be pure, and we must allow the Spirit to do *His* work, as opposed to using *our* ideas. But it can be said that He, the Holy Spirit, is searching and yearning for those who will bend the knee, and pour out their hearts for "the outcasts of Israel" – *as the whole world turns increasingly against "Zion."*

"... I will heal you of your wounds," declares the LORD, "Because they have called you an outcast, saying: '*It is Zion; no one cares for her.*'"

(Jeremiah 30:17 NASB, emphasis added)

6. **All Israel will be saved** (verses 25–26 NIV): "I do not want you to be ignorant of *this mystery*, brothers, so that you may not be conceited: Israel has experienced a hardening in part until the full number of the Gentiles has come in. And so [i.e. in this way] all Israel shall be saved ... " (emphasis added)

(a) Paul is warning Gentiles of ignorance of what God is doing and plans to do for the Jewish nation. It is precisely this ignorance (coupled with apathy) that blinds the Church at this hour. *It cannot be blithely excused. It is a very serious matter.*

(b) Insight into the truth about Israel does not come just with the intellect, nor via the news media. It is a "mystery" which only the Holy Spirit by the Word of God can uncover. The Bible speaks of a dozen "mysteries": the mystery of Christ, the mystery of iniquity, the mystery of the gospel, the mystery of faith, etc. *None* can be understood without the specific revelatory work of the Holy Spirit.

The author of this book, himself a zealous believer for eight years, had nonetheless, for many months on end, to pray through his own initial unwillingness to accept God's call: to understand His purposes for Israel. When light did eventually dawn, his own life was totally transformed. *Maybe the Lord wants to transform your thinking and life also? Are you willing for this?*

While the "mystery" is hidden from the world and even from most in the Church, "The secret of the LORD is for those who fear Him" (Psalm 25:14 NASB). Therefore remember that a major step for revelation in all of this is *an accompanying willingness to do His will, whatever it may be.* "If anyone is willing to do His will, he will *know* of the teaching, whether it is of God …" (John 7:17 NASB).

"Teach me thy way, O LORD; I will walk in thy truth" (Psalm 86:11 KJV).

7. **Life for the world** (verse 15 NASB): "If their rejection is the reconciliation of the world, what will their acceptance be but life from the dead?" In the original, this is meant to be a proclamation – more than a question! The Holy Spirit is saying: "If, in spite of Israel's initial rejection of their own Messiah Jesus, the blessings of the gospel nonetheless reached the world, *consider the transforming, worldwide effect that will follow when Israel finally receives (and obeys) Him!*"

There are two fullnesses in this chapter – that of the Gentiles in verse 25, and that of the Jews, which is yet to come, as in verse 12. The fullness is a kind of spiritual zenith or "ripeness" – which, for the Gentiles, seems to be in its closing stages and which, for Israel, yet lies ahead. Verse 12 re-echoes the truth of verse 15: If through their sin and failure, riches *still* flowed out to the Gentiles, how much greater spiritual richness will follow when Israel actually fulfills its calling.

We are reminded that both "God's gifts and his call [in this case to the Jewish nation] are *irrevocable*" (verse 29 NIV, emphasis added). In other words, God has not and will not withdraw them. This is important, because the general (mis)understanding today is that the Church, which is to "Christianize" the world, has replaced Israel.

8. **"... because of the mercy shown to you [Gentiles], they also [Israel] may now be shown mercy"**. (verse 31 NASB). Paul's argument here is that just as the Jewish people have been the vehicle of God's mercy to the Gentiles, so – *in reverse* – the Gentiles today (now!) are to be God's instruments to portray God's love, God's truth, God's wonderful faithfulness to the Jewish people.

How totally opposite to what the Church and the world says and does today! Can you begin to calculate the blessings we all might have known, had there been recognition and obedience to this call of God to the Gentiles? Yes! We can thank God for the exceptions, and for the faithful few – mainly parachurch organizations which do manifest God's mercy through faith, prayer and practical help. *But there was a specific call to Britain*, culminating in 1917, to foster this child, this prodigal son called Israel, and Britain and other nations have faltered, fumbled and failed.

Nonetheless, with this call for Gentile and Church response, Paul reaches the pinnacle of his epistle to the Romans, *and it is at this very point* that he bursts into that unquenchable, overflowing doxology, unmatched anywhere else in Scripture:

Oh, the depth of the riches both of the wisdom and knowledge of God! How unsearchable are His judgments and unfathomable His ways!

(Romans 11:33 NASB)

The infinitude of both the wisdom and the knowledge of God bring us to a fresh prostration in worship and praise. We are impressed even more deeply, that neither Jew nor Gentile has anything whatever of which to boast, save in the Lord Himself.

> Exalt the Lord our God
>> And worship at His footstool;
>> Holy is He.
>
> (Psalm 99:5 NASB)

Let us add our own "Amen!" to the above, and turn to consider what the Holy Spirit is saying and doing amongst the Jewish people today.

> I will give you a new heart and put a new spirit within you.
> (Ezekiel 36:26 NASB)

In Roman times, Judea was represented on coins by an olive tree, and a somewhat similar emblem is used to this day. Today the Embassy of Israel uses two olive branches and a *menorah* (a seven-branched candlestick) as its emblem. These Biblical symbols come from Zechariah 4 for the world to see. The two branches probably represent the natural *and* the wild branches (the Jew and the Gentile) brought together in one tree, as in Romans 11.

Let us add our own "Amen" and go on to consider the attitude of Jews towards Jesus changing over the last century. Here are some comments from a cross-section of Jewish leaders of this century:

1. Martin Buber (1878–1965), celebrated Jewish philosopher:

That Christianity has regarded and does regard him as God and Saviour has always appeared to me a fact of the highest importance which, for his sake and my own, I must endeavour to understand. I am more than ever certain that a great place belongs to him in Israel's history of faith and that this place cannot be described by any of the usual categories.[2]

2. Sholem Asch (1880–1957), Jewish author of international fame:

Jesus Christ, to me, is the outstanding personality of all time, of all history, both as Son of God and as Son of Man. Everything he ever said or did has value for us today, and that is something you can say of no other man, alive or dead. Every act and word of Jesus has value for all of us, wherever we are. He became the Light of the world. Why shouldn't I, a Jew, be proud of that? No other religious leader, either, has ever become so personal a part of people as the Nazarene. When you understand Jesus, you understand that he came to save you, to come into your personality. It isn't just a case of a misty, uncertain relationship between a worshipper and an unseen God; that is abstract: Jesus is personal.[3]

3. Rabbi Stephen S. Wise (1874–1949), founder of the American Jewish Congress and the Federation of American Zionists:

Even if Jesus had not been born unto Israel, even if he had borne no relation to the people of Israel, it becomes of importance for Israel to determine for itself what shall be its relation to the man who has touched the world for nearly two thousand years as has no other single figure in history . . . Jesus was not only a Jew but he was *the* Jew, the Jew of Jews. Whatever the death of Jesus may have been, we believe that his life was Jewish, and we devoutly affirm that Jewish was his teaching.[4]

4. Israel Zangwill (1864–1926), famous Jewish novelist:

To us, my brethren, in this our day, is given the privilege to reclaim the Christ we have lost for so many centuries. Has not the crucified Christ more than fulfilled the highest and noblest of our greatest prophets? Is not he the incarnation of what the Law, the Psalms and the prophets taught?[5]

5. Constantine Brunner (1862–1937), the great German philosopher:

His profound and holy words, and all that is true and heart-appealing in the New Testament, must from now on be heard in our synagogues and taught to our children.[6]

6. Solomon B. Freehof, reform rabbi, scholar and author:

Jesus of Nazareth is the most famous name in the world. The
Galilean teacher looms as large today as he did centuries ago. Millions praise him, but for widely differing reasons. To some he is
divine, the veritable Son of God, foretold by inspired prophecy, born
miraculously, who lived and died in order to fulfil his Father's plan
of salvation, and after death was resurrected from the tomb, and
enthroned in heaven as part of the three-fold Godhead ... Scores of
men have believed themselves to be the Messiah and have convinced
many of their contemporaries, but those who believed Jesus to be
the Messiah have built a great church upon the rock of their belief.
He is still the living comrade of countless lives. No Moslem ever
sings "Mohammed, lover of my soul" nor does any Jew say of Moses,
the teacher, "I need Thee every hour!"[7]

7. Ellis Rivkin, professor of Jewish history at Hebrew Union College:

Of these messianic claimants, only one – Jesus of Nazareth – so
impressed his disciples that he became their Messiah. And he did so
after the very crucifixion which should have refuted his claims deci-
sively. But it was not Jesus' life which proved beyond question that he
was the Messiah, the Christ. It was his Resurrection.[8]

8. Pinchas E. Lapide, former visiting professor of New Testament
   studies at West Germany's Gottingen University:

[The Church] was born of an act of the will of God, which all the
New Testament authors call the Resurrection of Jesus from the
dead. One thing is certain: Since all the witnesses of the resurrected Jesus were sons and daughters of Israel – since, moreover,
he appeared only in the land of Israel – his Resurrection was a
Jewish affair which must therefore be judged by Jewish standards
if we are to gauge its authenticity. If the disciples were totally disappointed and on the verge of desperate flight because of the very
real reason of the crucifixion, it took another very real reason in

order to transform them from a band of disheartened and dejected Jews into the most self-confident missionary society in world history.[9]

9. **David Flusser**, at one time, famous professor of religious history at Hebrew University in Jerusalem:

I do not think that many Jews would object if the Messiah – when he came – was the Jew Jesus.[10]

Israel and God

Extracts from an article on penitence and atonement by Rabbi David Hartman (professor of Jewish philosophy at the Hebrew University), who wrote (referring to the Old Testament doctrine):

The biblical description of the procedure to gain atonement is distinctly cultic and sacrificial. In fact, the only active person in the rites of the atonement is the high priest, who utters confession on behalf of the community. The cleansing of the people's sins was expressed in the ritual of banishing the scapegoat upon which the sins of the people were symbolically placed.

The Rabbinic emphasis upon "Teshuva" with regard to Rosh Hashana and Yom Kippur is an example of their efforts to develop a "Teshuva Culture". "Teshuva" which stems from the root verb "to return", indicates the man-initiated response in repentance; "Teshuva" presupposes human freedom to transcend habit and established patterns of conduct and to effect meaningful change in a person's relationship with God.

Nevertheless, as the biblical account of Rosh Hashana and Yom Kippur indicates, there is another aspect of forgiveness:

"Kappara" involves divine forgiveness and acceptance, which are beyond human initiative and action. While man may repent and become worthy of divine forgiveness, it is God who ultimately must grant "kappara". "Teshuva" is action-oriented, "Kappara" is grace-dependent.[11]

Russia

The spiritual hunger amongst Jews in Russia in the latter part of the twentieth century was clearly highlighted in a folder of 176 questions collected by two Moscow activists. Here are a few random samples, showing how the Holy Spirit was then moving amongst them. The activists write:

> This stream of questions came from our friends in only a few days. They show how big is the hunger to know.
>
> What does it mean to believe in God? Does it mean to fulfil Jewish ritual or something else?
>
> Is it true that people begin to believe in God after some misfortune?
>
> Is it the truth that Jesus was a Jew?
>
> Is it possible to be a Jew and a Christian at the same time? or a Jew and a Buddhist?
>
> What does the Tora mean that the Jews are "chosen people"? What is "sin" from the Jewish religious point of view?
>
> What is the difference between the sufferings of the believer and the non believer?
>
> Can a Jew be a good man and not religious?
>
> Is it possible to say when the Messiah will come? What does Judaism say about the Messiah?[12]

As shown in the opening text to this chapter, our summary must be: "... how much more readily will these, the natural branches, be grafted into their own olive tree!" (Romans 11:24 NIV)

Christians of earlier centuries did not have the added blessing and thrill of seeing, as we do with our own eyes today, Israel and its people being restored! How amazing that with both this visual proof *and* the Word of God, so much of the Church continues in ignorance and unbelief. In Romans 11, Paul repeatedly warns us, the Church, of the potential of God's great severity if we continue to ignore His call and the debt we owe to Israel.

The olive tree is still "their *own* olive tree," and there is not a "New Israel" but only the "old" Israel which God is grafting back into their own tree, and of which we became a part when we were saved! Hallelujah!

> God's gifts and his call are irrevocable.
>
> (Romans 11:29 NIV)

In the later and briefly referred-to purifying work of the Lord within the city of Jerusalem (Revelation 11:1–4), we should note the "*two* olive trees and the *two* lampstands that stand before the Lord of the earth" (Revelation 11:4 NIV, emphasis added).

Many may question here who or what the second olive tree (and the second witness) will represent in the days and tribulation time ahead. Let me draw deep attention to prayer and to the somewhat similar Scripture reference (three times) in Zechariah 4:3, 11, 14. This can have several meanings, including reference to both Jew and Gentile.

Although the foundation of the Church itself has come through the patriarchs of Israel (see Ephesians 2:12: the root of the olive tree; and Acts 7:38 KJV: the "church [congregation] in the wilderness"), Romans 11 tells us additionally of the *wild* olive tree. And the Gentile believers are to be co-witnesses with Israel and the Jewish believers in the days ahead. We may not by any means yet fully understand or have revelation on this, but clearly we can pray towards that end. Let us repeat:

> God's gifts and his call are irrevocable.
>
> (Romans 11:29 NIV)

Notes

1. Study Genesis 15:18–21; Deuteronomy 4:31ff. and 31–34; 2 Samuel 7:23–24; Romans 15:8; Hebrews 8:8–13.
2. Martin Buber, *Two Types of Faith* (Macmillan).
3. Frank S. Mead, "An Interview with Sholem Asch," *Christian Herald*, January 1944.

4. Stephen S. Wise, "The Life and Teaching of Jesus the Jew," *The Outlook*, 7 June 1913.

5. Jacob Jocz, *The Jewish People and Jesus Christ* (Baker Book House, USA).

6. Dr Arthur W. Kac, *The Rebirth of the State of Israel* (Baker Book House, USA).

7. Rabbi Solomon B. Freehof, *Stormers of Heaven* (Harper & Brothers, USA).

8. Ellis Rivkin, *The Meaning of Messiah in Jewish Thought: Evangelicals and Jews in Conversation* (Baker Book House, USA).

9. *Time*, May 1979.

10. *Newsweek*, 18 April 1977.

11. David Hartman, "Penitence and Atonement," *The Jerusalem Post* (International Edition), 4 October 1981.

12. Friends of Shamir, *176 Questions from Moscow*, PO Box 94, Tring, Hertfordshire, UK.

CHAPTER 5

Muddied Waters

Must my flock ... drink what you have muddied ...?
(Ezekiel 34:19 NIV)

How much we have to thank God for the rich spiritual life into which, as the Great Shepherd, He has led us! *How anxious He is that we leave a clear and inviting pathway for others to follow!*

With that in mind, we turn to the somber, sobering chapter 34 of Ezekiel, which speaks of the shepherds God has appointed, or allowed, over His people Israel. If read with honesty and contrition, it is impossible to deny the initial application to Christian responsibility for the Jewish people. After all, God does not appoint unsaved folk as shepherds over any part of his flock. While the chapter also has application in some measure to Christian oversight of the Church itself, its setting – just before chapters 35–37 which speak of the geographic, physical and spiritual restoration of Israel – points to a *specific and primary reference to care for the Jewish people.*

The Great Shepherd proclaimed, "I was sent only to the lost sheep of the house of Israel" (Matthew 15:24 NASB), later adding "as my Father hath sent me, even so send I you" (John 20:21 KJV). Ezekiel 34 summarizes, quite bluntly, the historical lack of practical and spiritual love and care for the house of Israel:

The weak you have not strengthened, nor have you healed those who were sick, nor bound up the broken, nor brought back what was driven away, nor sought what was lost ... My flock was scattered ... and no one was ... searching for them.

(Ezekiel 34:4, 6 NKJV, emphasis added)

We also read:

Woe to the shepherds of Israel who feed themselves! Should not the shepherds feed the flocks? You ... clothe yourselves with the wool ... but you do not feed the flock.

(Ezekiel 34:2–3 NKJV)

While we are to learn from past history, Ezekiel 34 speaks of something that is *happening now* in the very face of the work of restoration that God is currently doing: "Is it not enough for you to feed on the good pasture? Must you also trample the rest of your pasture with your feet?" (Ezekiel 34:18 NIV)

Alluding to the distortion of Scripture, one Bible commentary on this verse reads, "Not content with appropriating to their own use the goods of others, they spoiled from wantonness that which they did not use, so as to be of no use to others!" (cf. *Isaiah 62:8–9*, Jamieson, Fausset & Brown's one-volume Bible *Commentary*).

Many of God's specific promises to Israel have become "spoiled pastures," i.e. trodden down, "discolored," meaningless or irrelevant to the Jew and the Christian when they are taught that they no longer apply, or that today they are not meant for literal interpretation. Some examples are:

1. **"All Israel will be saved" refers to Israel** (its remnant) and it means mercy for Israel. It *does not and cannot* refer to the Church, as has been taught (Romans 11:26).
2. **Jewish identity** is actually enriched and confirmed, not eroded, by trusting and knowing the Messiah. Their true identity is found, not lost (Romans 2:29)! The apostle Paul said, "I am [not was] a

Jew" (Acts 22:3 NIV). To avoid the impression that he has lost
his Jewish identity, the born-again Jew today tends to think and
speak of himself as Messianic rather than Christian, although the
two terms virtually mean the same thing.

3. **The ownership of the land** of Israel by Abraham and his physical
   descendants was to be permanent and unconditional, even though
   its occupation by the Jewish nation was later interrupted and made
   conditional (Genesis 15:18; 17:8; Ezekiel 36:28; Leviticus 26:32–33,
   44–45).

4. **Election:** In spite of being temporarily set aside, Israel's ongoing
   election and calling are *confirmed* in many parts of the New
   Testament.

   (a) In Romans 9:4 Paul tells us: "To them *belong* [present continuous
   tense] the adoption, the glory, the covenants ... the promises ..."
   (NRSV, emphasis added).

   (b) In Romans 11:29 we are reminded that these very gifts (of
   Romans 9:4–5) and God's calling are irrevocable.

   (c) If God has finished with the Jewish race, why do we find James,
   long after the crucifixion, writing to "the twelve tribes who are
   dispersed abroad" (James 1:1 NASB)?

   (d) If God has finished with the Hebrew race, why is the new covenant
   mentioned four times in the epistle to the Hebrews, chapter 8:8–13
   giving great detail?

   (e) If God has finished with Israel, why does the Holy Spirit tell us
   that the Messiah became a servant to the Jewish people in order
   to *confirm* the promises given to the patriarchs (Romans 15:8)?

   In this single verse God virtually appends His signature in
   the New Testament to every Old Testament promise. Jesus did
   not come in order to annul or to modify, but to *confirm* the
   Old Testament promises given to such as Abraham, Isaac and
   Jacob.

   (f) Did not David, king of Israel, have full understanding when he wrote:
   "Your lovingkindness, O LORD, extends to the heavens, Your *faithfulness* reaches to the skies" (Psalm 36:5 NASB, emphasis added)?

5. **"Give Him no rest until He establishes And makes Jerusalem
   a praise in the earth"** (Isaiah 62:7 NASB). So often, the term
   "Jerusalem" is used for the Church, or in reference to the heavenly

Jerusalem of the book of Revelation. But here we are instructed to be ceaseless in prayer for the *earthly* city – the place to which the two angels promised the heaven-gazing disciples that Jesus would return "in like manner" (Acts 1:11 KJV)!

Note that the "muddied waters" of this chapter refer to the beclouded Christian testimony of centuries. While we remember the shining, sacrificial lives of some who have cared for Jewish people, on the whole there has been another picture.

Let us wash this history clean through repentance and prayer, and ask the Lord for good shepherds in particular localities, and a *move of his Spirit in Bible colleges and pulpits to bring Zion into focus*, to remind Him of His "time to be gracious to her" (Psalm 102:13 NASB).

Repentance versus God's grace

We are not told that at this time of favor Israel will have beforehand reached some suitable state of worthiness or even repentance. Rather, *God's prerogative* is highlighted: "I will have mercy on whom I have mercy … It does not, therefore, depend on man's desire or effort, but on God's mercy" (Romans 9:15–16 NIV).

Even repentance is a gift received through God's mercy and grace. Do you remember how King Saul sought for that earnestly with tears, yet did not find it? Do you remember how repentance came to you? Was it when you willed it, or when God Himself granted it (2 Timothy 2:25)? How sad it is that we Spirit-filled Christians feel unable to comfort the Jewish people because (in our eyes) "they have not yet repented."

Spoiled pastures! Muddied waters!

… they too may now receive mercy as a result of God's mercy to you.

(Romans 11:31 NIV)

What we have received by God's undeserved favor we are to share with Israel, as explicitly commanded in the well-known scripture:

> Comfort ye, comfort ye my people, saith your God.
>   Speak ye comfortably to Jerusalem, and cry unto her, that her [appointed time] is accomplished, that her iniquity is pardoned [or "paid for"]: for she hath received of the LORD's hand [the] double for all her sins.
>
> (Isaiah 40:1–2 KJV)

1. Three people are referred to herein: "ye" – meaning the Church or believers; "my people" – here clearly meaning the Jewish nation; and "your God."
2. The command to comfort is in the imperative. It is not a mere suggestion, but a strong command. Do we understand that? And that it is addressed to believers? Further, you will find on rereading it that the same command is twice-repeated. Why? Could it be that the Lord foresees reluctance and indifference from His Church?

    Why does he call the Jews "*my* people" if not to remind us of His special fatherhood to them, and of His being known in the Word as "the God of Israel"? Could He be jealous of and concerned for those He calls "my" people? Have these waters become so muddy over the years that *no one* cares for, and few even think about, Israel, and even less consider them as God's people?
3. Does "comfort ye" mean a little "There, there" and a pat on the back? Or does it mean (after the horrors of the Holocaust and the worldwide indifference of Christian nations), as the Hebrew root indicates, "encourage, strengthen, come alongside"? Isn't the exhortation and command verified a hundred times by other scriptures (see the first verses of Isaiah 43; 44; 52; 60; 61)?
4. The timing: the passage we are looking at begins what is known as "Second Isaiah." In general, it is from chapter 40 onwards that the whole tone of Isaiah changes from one of judgment and affliction to one of encouragement and restoration. Bearing in mind that it was the scroll of the prophet Isaiah that, after 1,900 years, was discovered in its entirety in the summer of 1947 (only a few months before the United Nations met to vote on

the recognition of the State of Israel), special attention needs to be given to this section.

It was a copy of this chapter 40 that was placed in front of every member of the very first Israeli Parliament (the Knesset) on 14 May 1948! God was speaking to them again after some 1,978 years of dispersion.

O Israel, you will not be forgotten by Me.

(Isaiah 44:21 NASB)

... [the] Double for all her sins.

(Isaiah 40:2 NASB)

Most translators omit "the" from "the double," not realizing that what is referred to here is the earlier Eastern custom of wealthy travelers occasionally stopping to pay the debts of a tent dweller. The latter would list on parchment his debts, and pin this hopefully to his tent pole for the gaze of any passing wealthy sheikh. If such mercy was shown, the sheikh would undertake to pay the debts, sign the list and double over the parchment so that the clean side showed. This was called "receiving the double."

Although repentance and faith must be involved as gifts from God, Jesus did not say from the cross, "Father, do not forgive them until they repent" but "Father, forgive them; for they know not what they do" (Luke 23: 34 KJV).

"The double" is available to them, to you and me, simply because the redemptive price for our sinful nature and deeds has been paid by the life blood of the wealthy Prince. But Jesus was not a casual passer-by – He came for the very purpose of paying that price: "... for this cause came I unto this hour" (John 12:27 KJV).

God's "double" following Israel's shame, hardship and privation is beautifully found in Isaiah 61:7 and Zechariah 9:12.

Instead of your shame you will have a double portion ...

(Isaiah 61:7 NASB)

... O prisoners who have the hope [title of Israel's national anthem],
This very day I am declaring that I will restore double to you.

(Zechariah 9:12 NASB)

That is why we can speak tenderly to Jerusalem! All humankind, Jew
and Gentile, bears a responsibility for the crucifixion, and if God the
Father and Jesus the Son say "Forgive," do you not think the Holy
Spirit prompts us also to forgive? Who are we to condemn? Our
unconditional Christian love is the channel along which God's Spirit
of revelation will flow – and something will be awakened in hunger
for God.

This is a general principle in all of our lives which, if followed, will
cause huge transformations.

Then, perhaps, is the fitting time to speak and share more directly
of our Lord. We use the term "witnessing" of giving out tracts and
telling people of the gospel. But in Greek the term means "martyr"
– laying one's life down! "The good shepherd lays down his life for the
sheep." This is not to say that there are not times when boldness *should*
be exercised. But let our words and attitude be tempered with God's
love and humility, having ourselves tasted of His comfort. May our
lives shine far more than our lips speak.

Jewish identity and the Messiah

In all, five epistles in the New Testament are addressed specifically to
Jewish people (James, Hebrews, 1 and 2 Peter and Jude). It is therefore
obvious that they retained their identity after coming to faith – leaving
us to wonder today why God's purposes for Israel and the Jews are
hardly known of, let alone understood by the Church. It is another
instance of muddied waters.

We misread Galatians 3:28: "There is neither Jew nor Greek [Gen-
tile] ... neither slave nor free ... neither male nor female; for you are all
one in Christ Jesus" (NASB).

Waters are muddied when we fail to realize that this scripture
merely tells us that born-again folk are all of equal standing before

God, *whatever* our gender or background. It is obvious that, just as we remain men or women after salvation, we likewise retain our Gentile or Jewish origins. This is not some spiritual trickery to persuade the house of Israel to desert their fold – some pill of inducement to dull their senses to the truth. Rather, it is the expressed truth and joy of countless Jews who today have become spiritually alive, thankfully proud of their Jewishness, of which, in the past, they may have been ashamed (Isaiah 61:7), ignorant or unconcerned. However, Jewish people face a very real double opposition to both finding and acclaiming this identity – apart from any family antagonism.

1. Many Christians, even of mature standing, cannot grasp the reality of the Jew not only *remaining* Jewish in his encounter with his Messiah, but of actually *finding* a fulfillment and purpose therein that is inspired by the Holy Spirit. So, instead of the Jew being encouraged in this, he is often blinded and side-tracked by the advice and comments of Christians who are ignorant on this topic.

2. More confusion is caused by Gentile Christian leaders who proudly state, "I am a Jew – I am a child of Abraham. We are all spiritual Jews." The same persons would not be so willing to take the yellow star of shame. "… a man is a Jew who is one inwardly" is intended for Jews who have been born again, not for Gentiles (see Romans 2:29).

3. The term "Israel of God" is often misinterpreted to mean the Church. But in fact it refers to those Jewish people who have come to faith, as opposed to Jews who have not: "those who will walk by this rule [faith], peace and mercy be upon them [Gentiles], *and* upon the Israel of God [Jews]" (Galatians 6:16 NASB, emphasis added).

Israel, the Church and the Bible

Centuries of anti-Semitism and distortion of the Scriptures have led to a spiritualizing of all the "nice" parts of the Bible for the Church, while relegating all the curses and warnings to Israel.

What is still taught verbally in many places is exemplified in the following study of page headings in Isaiah from an Oxford edition of the Authorized Version of the Bible.

Table 3: A short study of Isaiah Bible passages and interpretive Bible headings

Ref.	Leading or general verse(s) from page	Explanatory page heading
30:19	For the people shall dwell ... at Jerusalem	God's mercies ...
30:20	And though the Lord give you the bread of adversity ...	
30:29	Ye shall have a song ...	... to His Church
29:13	... this people [Jerusalem] draw near me with their mouth ... but have removed their heart far from me ...	Deep hypocrisy of the Jews
40:2	Speak ye comfortably to Jerusalem ...	The promulgation of the gospel
41:8	But thou, Israel, art my servant, Jacob whom I have chosen ...	God ... about His mercies to the Church
43:1	... thus saith the LORD that created thee, O Jacob ... O Israel, Fear not ...	God comforteth the Church ...
43:22	... thou hast not called upon me, O Jacob ...	Israel ...

(Continued)

Table 3: (Continued)

Ref.	Leading or general verse(s) from page	Explanatory page heading
43:24	… thou hast wearied me with thine iniquities	… reproved
44:1–3	… hear, O Jacob, my servant; and Israel, whom I have chosen… For I will pour water on him that is thirsty …	The Church comforted
49:14	But Zion said, The LORD hath forsaken me …	God's constant love …
49:15	… they may forget, yet will I not forget thee.	… to His Church
51:11	… the redeemed … shall return, and come with singing unto Zion …	The Church comforted
51:17–19	O Jerusalem … who shall be sorry for thee?	The woes of …
51:19	… by whom shall I comfort thee?	… Jerusalem
52:1	… put on thy beautiful garments, O Jerusalem …	Christ persuadeth the Church
57:3	… draw near hither, ye sons of the sorceress, the seed of the adulterer and the whore.	The Jews reproved for their idolatry

(Continued)

Table 3: (Continued)

Ref.	Leading or general verse(s) from page	Explanatory page heading
59:2	... your iniquities have separated between you and your God ...	The sins of the Jews
60:1	Arise, shine; for thy light is come ...	Gentiles convert
60:14–16	... they shall call thee ... The Zion of the Holy One of Israel ... Thou shalt also suck the milk of the Gentiles ...	The Church's blessings
65:2	I have spread out my hands ... unto a rebellious people ...	Jews rejected
65:18	... I create Jerusalem a rejoicing, and her people a joy.	The New Jerusalem
66:20	... they shall bring all your brethren ... out of all nations ... to ... Jerusalem ...	Gentiles shall have an holy Church

Nothing less than deep self-deception and spiritual gymnastics are needed
to hop from page to page and verse to verse in this way, alternately
allowing Jerusalem or Israel to be literal or "spiritual" (i.e. the Church)
according to our whim and our liking of the passage.

"We are the Israel of God" is the sentiment often on the lips of
ministers who fail to take account of the fact that what we call the
Church had a Jewish beginning, and will have a Jewish completion
when God chooses to pour out His Spirit on His elect nation. This
event is as certain as the coming of the dawn (Hosea 6:2–3) and
warrants our prayers of faith. The Church must discern that God has
a wonderful place for His temporarily set aside nation, as well as for
the parallel remnant within His Church. Otherwise the words of the
prophet Jeremiah, promising both perpetuity and pardon, would be
meaningless:

> This is what the LORD says,
> he who appoints the sun
>   to shine by day,
> who decrees the moon and stars
>   to shine by night,
> who stirs up the sea
>   so that its waves roar—
>   the LORD Almighty is his name:
> "Only if these decrees vanish from my
> sight," declares the LORD,
> "will the descendants of Israel ever cease
>   to be a nation before me."
>
> This is what the LORD says:
> "Only if the heavens above can be measured,
>   and the foundations of the earth
> below be searched out
> will I reject all the descendants of Israel
>   because of all they have done,"
> declares the LORD.

(Jeremiah 31:35–37 NIV)

These are God-breathed, Spirit-inspired words – exactly like the rest of Scripture. They bring incontrovertible assurance of Israel's permanence as a nation, and that God's forgiveness of them will not be withheld.

The centrality of Israel's coming salvation to world and Church blessing

The true teaching of the Word of God is hidden when we plan for world evangelism "to reach the world for Christ" with *no* reference whatever to the land or nation of the gospel's birth. Consider the exciting promise and proclamation of Paul's words:

> If their transgression means riches for the world, and their loss means riches for the Gentiles, how much greater riches will their fullness bring!
>
> (Romans 11:12 NIV)

Simeon declared some 2,000 years ago: "Behold, this Child is appointed for the fall *and* rise of many in Israel" (Luke 2:34 NASB, emphasis added). All expositors agree on the fall of many in Israel – but how many agree or teach upon the *rise* of many in Israel? Simeon prophesied not only of Israel's long apostasy, but equally of her coming restoration – harmonizing with much other Scripture. The basic root of his word "rise" is *anastasis* – resurrection, and this parallels Isaiah's prophecy

> Arise, shine; for your light has come
> And the glory of the LORD has risen upon you.
> For behold, darkness will cover the earth
> And deep darkness the peoples;
> But the LORD will rise upon you,
> And His glory will appear upon you.
> Nations [Gentiles] will come to your light,
> And kings to the brightness of your rising.
>
> (Isaiah 60:1–3 NASB)

Let no unbelieving heart fail to absorb the blessing of Isaiah's parallel prophecy

> In days to come Jacob will take root,
>   Israel will bud and blossom,
>   and *fill* all the world with fruit.
>
> (Isaiah 27:6 NIV, emphasis added)

In our own day and age, we have seen the unbelieving Jewish folk (Jacob) take root in the land. We have seen melons, citrus fruits, pineapple and all sorts going over the whole globe from Israel. What God has begun, He will finish – and soon the spiritual fulfillment of this will follow. First the natural, and then the spiritual (1 Corinthians 15:46). Then, as Habakkuk promises:

> The earth shall be *filled* with the knowledge of the glory of the LORD, as the waters cover the sea.
>
> (Habakkuk 2:14 KJV, emphasis added)

Remember, this worldwide knowledge of God's glory hinges upon the salvation of Israel. The Church *cannot* be complete and will not accomplish this task without the grafting back in of the natural branches – Israel. *Do you need any further reason to pray?*

The Jewish people and the cross

Waters are muddied when Jews see in the cross *not* God's great redemptive act of love for Israel and humankind, but a hateful, condemning, even vengeful spirit of accusation.

"You killed Christ" and "Christ killers" are insults hurled at the Jews not only by nominal Christians, but at times from born-again ones. At other times it is just thought and not said. How else have Jewish children come to flee from cross-bearing ministers? An adult Czechoslovakian once told the writer how, as a lad of twelve, he had fled in fear from all such characters. Let us remind ourselves again that "he was wounded for *our* transgressions" (Isaiah 53:5 KJV, emphasis added) and that both Jews *and* Gentiles were involved in that awful act of deicide, for which specific purpose Jesus, the Messiah, came.

The crucifixion separated the Western calendar into two parts (BC and AD), and humankind into two classes – those who mock the Savior, as did one criminal on the cross, and those who suddenly realize Who Jesus is and what we are, as did the other repenting criminal on the cross:

> We receive the due reward of our deeds ... Lord, remember me when thou comest into thy kingdom.
>
> (Luke 23:41–42 KJV)

Five people, or groups of people, are involved in the crucifixion:

1. *The Father* who so loved the world that he gave His only begotten Son.
2. *The Son* who said, "No-one takes [my life] from me, but I lay it down of my own accord" (John 10:18 NIV).
3. *The Jewish leaders* (rather than the common people who "heard him gladly" (Mark 12:37 KJV)) who made false accusations and handed Jesus over after a mock trial.
4. *The Gentiles* who carried out the physical crucifixion.
5. *Yourself – and myself.*

> He was wounded for our transgressions ... bruised for our iniquities ... and the LORD hath laid on him the iniquity of us all.
>
> (Isaiah 53:5–6 KJV)

Waters are muddied and Scripture beclouded when we fail to realize the world's indebtedness to Israel, *even in this matter of crucifixion!* She has been the scapegoat of God's judgment for the Gentile world, bearing the brunt of His hand these past centuries: "From the standpoint of the gospel they [Israel] are enemies for *your* sake" (Romans 11:28 NASB). This is the period of "hardship" – the "appointed time" referred to in Isaiah 40:2.

Has it ever occurred to you that had your nation (be it Britain, America, South Africa, Germany or any other nation) been the elect nation, then inevitably, following the path of sin, Jesus would still have been rejected and crucified, and upon you and your nation would have fallen God's hand of judgment?

Instead, that has fallen on Israel, scattered to the four corners of the globe for nineteen centuries. There is a substitutionary role here that impels Gentile indebtedness.

Jesus the Shepherd

Instead of presenting Jesus to Jewish people as their Shepherd and Friend, by living out His life in our bodies, we have given them such a false image over the centuries that many have come to regard Him as their enemy. Whereas the Eastern shepherd goes *before* the sheep and the good shepherd *lays his life down* for them, "official" Christianity has given up the house of Israel to the wild beasts, the Crusades, the Spanish Inquisition, the Russian pogroms, the Nazi Holocaust. Unsuccessful attempts to convert them in the past have almost always been followed by periods of anti-Semitism.

Stemming from this sad side of Church history, it is not surprising to find the Babylon of Jeremiah, whether symbolizing the world or the false Church, recorded as Israel's enemy and saying this:

> ... We are not guilty,
> for *they* [Israel] sinned against the LORD, their true pasture,
>   the LORD, the hope of their fathers.
>
> (Jeremiah 50:7 NIV)

But God says:

> Israel and Judah have not been forsaken
>   by their God, the LORD Almighty,
> though their land is full of guilt ...
>
> (Jeremiah 51:5 NIV)

Babylon must fall because of Israel's slain ...

(Jeremiah 51:49 NIV)

The same section speaks gloriously of the salvation of Israel at the same time as Babylon is dealt with by the northern army:

... the people of Israel and ... Judah together
will go in tears to seek the LORD their God.
They will ask the way to Zion
and turn their faces toward it ...
and bind themselves to the LORD
in an everlasting covenant
that will not be forgotten.

(Jeremiah 50:4–5 NIV)

God's pardon

... at that time ... search will be made for Israel's guilt,
but there will be none [!],
and for the sins of Judah,
but none will be found,
for I will forgive the remnant I spare.

(Jeremiah 50:20 NIV)

God's plea to us, His Church:

You who have escaped the sword,
Depart! Do not stay!
Remember the LORD from afar,
And let Jerusalem come upon your heart.

(Jeremiah 51:50 NASB margin, emphasis added)

So, let us who know these things, do no less than that! Jerusalem, the heart of Israel, is to be on our hearts – even as it is upon God's heart (Luke 19:41).

CHAPTER 6

Israel: God's Bridge into the World

While looking at more or less the exact center of almost any map of the world, you will see a tiny country (almost invisible unless you draw close) ... Israel. In Ezekiel 38:12 it is prophetically described as "the people who are gathered from the nations ... who live at the center of the world" (NASB). More accurately, in the margin of some Bibles (e.g. NASB) this is rendered as "the navel of the world."

Ezekiel had no map to guide him – only the Holy Spirit. Yet, in a few prophetic words, he could present what God would be doing 2,600 years later for His people – the miracle of Israel being re-gathered back to the same land given to their patriarchs of long ago (Abraham, Isaac and Jacob). This continues to this very day, amidst the escalating hatred of her neighbors and the rest of the world.

But the miracle is far more than a physical regathering *to* a central point. It is *from* that starting point in Bible history that Israel has been *God's umbilical cord* – God's lifeline to the rest of the world (Acts 1:8). The term "navel" (Ezekiel 38:12 margin) aptly describes how the life-giving flow of God's Word, and the knowledge of Him Who is the Fountain of Life, has reached and transformed whole nations.

A further look at any world map reveals that Israel is actually a *land bridge to three continents*: Africa, Asia and Europe. She is the bridge by which God Almighty, El Shaddai, has uniquely and initially entered and made Himself known to the world!

This was solely through God's election and grace, and not because Israel in themselves were superior. No land or people could possibly be worthy enough to bear the footprints of the Messiah. Jewish people are special *only because they are chosen*. They and we are *not* chosen because we are special.

Christian indebtedness to Israel and the Jew – Abram set apart

Realizing that our own spiritual heritage has come to us through Israel, and that far from finishing with them, God has *much more yet to reveal and achieve*, let us look at the earlier stages of God's choice. *Israel is not simply a promised land, but a land and a people of promise*, much of which has been received, *but much more of which is yet to come.*

Fatherhood of the nation

The land and its people had its fatherhood in Abram, who was the first Hebrew (Genesis 14:13). "Hebrew" is taken from *Eber* meaning "to cross over." Abram forsook the wealth of his father's city and country, and the idols of his father's household. He not only crossed over the River Euphrates into a promised land, but he passed from idol worship to the worship of the one true God, a physical *and* spiritual separation from the pollution and sin of the world. *In the world, yet not of the world* (John 17:15–16).

None of us ever lost anything in obeying God's call, even in giving up houses, land or reputation for the Lord, but especially in forsaking the idolatry of this present age.

> Get thee out of thy country, and from thy kindred, and from thy father's house, unto a land that I will shew thee.
>
> (Genesis 12:1 KJV)

A costly call! Abram is and was the human father of our faith. Where would we have been today, had he not responded? It has been said that the birth of the Jewish race began with "Get out" and that the same cry has constantly been hurled at them down through the centuries. *The Jew is essentially the testimony to God which the world does not want, and which even his Christian beneficiaries often fail to see or evaluate correctly.* This "Get out" has come not only from Muslim countries and Germany in the past, but from many other countries – including Britain.

Whereas God's "Get out" is an invitation with promised blessing, the world's "Get out" is a malevolent "Go – we don't want you!" The very fact that the latter is still a prevalent and a *growing* attitude (Matthew 24:9) underlines the fact that God has *not* finished with His people! He wants them, loves them and has a greater purpose for them than anything we have seen so far.

If the election of Abram, the first Hebrew, was not important, we could well question why:

(a) only two chapters are used in Genesis for the whole story of creation (Genesis 1–2);

(b) only a further nine chapters in Genesis are used to cover the first 2,000 years of Bible and world history (Genesis 3–11);

(c) whereas fourteen chapters follow *just* for the life of Abraham – 175 years (Genesis 12–25);

(d) twenty-five chapters then follow to tell us of Abraham's offspring – mostly devoted to Jacob (Genesis 26–50).

God's emphasis

God's emphasis is on one speck of humanity, not upon cosmic origins – *the speck by which He would bless the world, and ultimately all humankind.* Starting from Abraham's death, 929 chapters follow covering Israel's birth and history over the next 2,000 years, and revealing God's purposes and means of blessing the world.

This takes us right up to Malachi, the last book in the Old Testament, which opens with the Lord's words: "Was not Esau Jacob's brother? ... Yet I have loved Jacob; but I have hated Esau" (Malachi 1:1–3 NASB).

While this is a comparative love (so strong for Jacob that other loves seem like hatred alongside it), God nonetheless underlines, at the close of the Old Testament, *His prerogative in election*. Who are we to question God and His ways?

Genesis 12, then, becomes the great dividing line, where God chooses Abram, father of Ishmael and Isaac, and then grandfather of Jacob, from whom come the heads of the twelve tribes of Israel, and through whom, at God's appointed time, the Messiah Himself came. Note the promises in this chapter:

(a) "I will bless thee" – the *individual*
(b) "I will … make thy name great" – the *family*
(c) "I will make of thee a great nation" – the *nation*
(d) "In thee shall all families of the earth be blessed" – the *world* (Genesis 12:2–3 KJV)

Neither humanity's sin or failure, nor even Israel's breaking of God's laws could alter these purposes and promises of God. Abram's confidence in God (not in his own righteousness) was of the order that God was able to perform *all* that He promised. This confidence or faith was the ground of his acceptance before God – it was "counted … to him as righteousness" (Genesis 15:6). *Hallelujah!*

The Source of blessing

The Source of blessing would be *the Messiah and the Scriptures*.

Moses wrote of the Messiah being the seed of the woman (Genesis 3:15), although seed is normally masculine. This exception pointed to the day of the miraculous sign when "a virgin [would] conceive, and bear a son" and His name would be called "Immanuel" (Isaiah 7:14 KJV).

That the Messiah would be of a Jewish mother, brought up in a Jewish home to observe the Jewish way of life, that His family line would be traced back to King David and to Abraham through both

His mother Mary and His (foster) father Joseph, are facts we do well to remember as Bible-believing Christians.

Remembering the line of our spiritual heritage through the Jewish people, consider these facts about the Messiah of the world:

He was *promised* to Abraham (Genesis 22:1–8).

He was *figured* as the Passover lamb to Moses (Exodus 12).

The purpose was *announced* through Moses (Leviticus 17:11).

He was *revealed* to David (2 Samuel 7:12–13).

His coming was *confirmed* to Isaiah (Isaiah 9:7).

His coming was *fulfilled* through Mary (Luke 1:32–33).

Jacob *predicts the tribe* through which Messiah would come (Genesis 49:10).

David foretells the *family* (2 Samuel 7:12–13).

Daniel prophesies the *date* (Daniel 9:24–27).

Isaiah describes the *channel* – a virgin (Isaiah 7:14).

Micah describes the *place* of birth (Micah 5:2).

Zechariah speaks of His *coming* in lowliness *to Jerusalem* (Zechariah 9:9) and of His later *return* in Lordship and glory (Zechariah 14:4–12).

The last of these thirteen prophecies (showing the Lord returning to destroy the enemies of Israel), should itself give us a careful regard for Israel. A fourteenth prophecy follows:

> … the LORD will strike all the peoples who have gone to war against Jerusalem …
>
> (Zechariah 14:12 NASB)

The Christian who sides with world hatred and condemnation of Israel simply sides with the satanic effort to destroy the nation and to frustrate God's purposes through them for the world.

The prophets named above were Jewish, a few of the many by whom God has revealed Himself to humankind. Were it not for this ostracized race, the world would have had neither patriarch or prophet, apostle or Savior, and *no* Bible. The *entire* writings of the Bible – forty authors – were from Jewish hands and hearts, with the possible exception of Luke.

All that we know of God has come down to us through these Jewish authors who themselves write of the Jewish nation, Jewish lives, Jewish victories, Jewish failures, Jewish sin, Jewish joy and Jewish sorrow. Even in their sin and failure, as well as in their obedience and victory, Israel has indelibly engraved for us in Scripture God's do's and don'ts!

God's servant nation

> But you, Israel, My servant,
>> Jacob whom I have chosen,
>> Descendant of Abraham My friend,
> You whom I have taken from the ends of the earth,
>> And called from its remotest parts,
>> And said to you, "You are My servant,
>> I have chosen you and not rejected you.
> Do not fear, for I am with you;
>> Do not anxiously look about you, for I am your God!
>>>>> (Isaiah 41:8–10 NASB)

How relevant and living, contemporary and strengthening this is! God's prescription for Israel at her hour of trial! If we needed any proof of God's faithfulness, even when we ourselves are so unfaithful, here it is. Take note of the central part of this quote from Israel's own Scriptures: "You *are* [not were] My servant" (Isaiah 41:8 NASB, emphasis added).

Even in her present sin and unbelief, Israel has not lost her calling as servant. The New Testament simply confirms this: "God has *not* rejected His people whom He foreknew" (Romans 11:2 NASB, emphasis added). While Israel has been God's bridge and umbilical cord, that has been merely the beginning. *Much more* is to follow.

While not overlooking the fact that the most severe conflict still lays ahead, Israel is destined to become the major source in the world of an abundant spiritual river that is yet to flow out east and west (Romans 11:12).

> In that day living waters will flow out of Jerusalem, half of them
> toward the eastern sea and the other half toward the western sea; it
> will be in summer as well as in winter.
>
> (Zechariah 14:8 NASB)

Whatever physical interpretation we place upon this passage, the "living waters" are nothing less than the Spirit of the Lord (John 7:38–39), whose going forth from Jerusalem in yet greater power is much foretold elsewhere (Joel 2:23, 28–29; Ezekiel 47:1ff.; Revelation 22:1).

Even if the Jew himself is unaware of his role and calling as part of the servant nation of God, *the Christian is not to be ignorant – and (still less) ungrateful* for this calling. We need not be surprised at ignorance amongst non-Christians, or even amongst high-ranking government officials – *but the Christian is specifically counseled by the Word and Spirit*:

> I do not want you to be ignorant of this mystery, brothers, so that you
> may not be conceited ...
>
> (Romans 11:25 NIV)

This "mystery", of course, is the whole subject of Israel, culminating in her salvation.

> Breathe on me, Breath of God,
> Fill me with life anew,
> That I may love what *Thou* dost love
> And do what *Thou* wouldst do.
>
> (Edwin Hatch 1835–89, emphasis added)

To keep us from arrogance, we need to be aware of our present ignorance – particularly amongst those who handle the Word of God. At the same time let us admit and face indifference. The writer of this book was himself characterized by these traits for eight whole years. And only after lengthy, persevering prayer did revelation come.

The ancient hymn above, originally heartfelt but quite forgotten today, reminds us that "of ourselves we can do nothing." We need the Holy Spirit to breathe on us, to open up our minds to the Scriptures, and even more, to open up our hearts to God. Let us not merely give lip service in assent here, but *yield* to Him. He so desires that we earnestly seek Him, not merely on the topic of Israel, but rather *to come to know Him* on an increasingly personal level (Colossians 1:10; 2:2–3).

The widespread ignorance, and also arrogance, within the Church concerning Israel, is in direct contrast to the Word of God. We are not called to love Israel or the Jews, or even our enemies, because they are lovable, nor because they love us. We are called to love what God loves! It is as simple, and as profound, as that.

The fact is that we cannot do that, nor live and love in that way *without* God's help – given by Him *Himself* – the Holy Spirit. It is not to be merely "Breathe on me" but "Breathe *into* me, Breath of God"! The Lord wants to deal with our personal attitudes that have developed since our birth. Let Him show you what this means.

Israel is "a land for which the LORD your God cares; the eyes of the LORD your God are always on it, from the beginning even to the end of the year" (Deuteronomy 11:12 NASB).

As His under-shepherds, God calls us to be constantly vigilant for His land and people. It is very disturbing to see how hatred against Israel, with its annihilation as the goal, has actually *snowballed* since the Holocaust Memorial Day was instituted in the year 2000. The whole purpose of that Memorial Day had been to see that cruelty and anti-Semitism diminish – not to increase; not to ever happen again.

When the Lord commanded Moses to tell Pharaoh, "Israel is my firstborn son ... Let my son go, so that he may worship me" (Exodus 4:22–23 NIV), He was not merely conjuring up some apt phrase, but speaking of a relationship which, in Jeremiah's day some 900 years later (even after Israel's checkered spiritual history, the Lord still cherishes the nation):

I *am* a father to Israel,
And Ephraim is My firstborn ...

He who scattered Israel will gather him
And keep him as a shepherd keeps his flock.

>   (Jeremiah 31:9–10 NASB, emphasis added)

We, as Christians, often do not "see" this special love, nor the servant-role for which God has chosen Israel. Many think that God's purposes for Israel as a nation ended at Calvary. In this way, we are blinded to our tremendous indebtedness to Israel and the Jews for the past, the present *and the future*. The gospel began with Israel, and it was years before Peter went (for example) to Cornelius (Acts 10).

Salvation is of the Jews (1)

In that moving encounter with the Samaritan woman at Jacob's well (John 4), Messiah Jesus deftly crosses all boundaries (intellectual, cultural, racial and religious), to draw this thirsting woman to the well-spring of life eternal – Himself.

In the process, He says to her, "You Samaritans worship what you do not know; we worship what we do know, for salvation is from the Jews" (John 4:22 NIV). Jesus openly identifies with His own earthly race and condenses into a few words that salvation for all *had* come, *was* coming and *would* come through the Jews

So let us note the Lord's word that salvation *is* (not was) of the Jews. As far as His own humanity is concerned, the Savior of the world remains Jewish – born as He was with God and man mysteriously intertwined.

The Ten Commandments which have formed the basis for the world's ethical code came through Jewish lips and scribes. And they are *still* the guidelines to which we must return to rescue the world from its moral, idolatrous and godless plunge. The hearts that burned for the upholding of these, and the martyrs who died for them, initially came from Jewish stock. Apparently, Israel is called to play a leading part when God comes to judge the nations: "... with you (Israel) I shatter nations... destroy kingdoms" (Jeremiah 51:20 NIV).

Even in their failure, Israel has brought blessing to the Gentiles –
never more so than in their greatest failure, when the leadership, if not
the laity, failed to recognize the Messiah!

Through their fall, salvation has come to the Gentiles (Romans
11:11). In some way, unforeseen at the time, God took the stumbling
of Israel to bless the world. In theory at least, had there been no stumbling and no crucifixion, there would have been no Savior, and no
sending out of apostles to the Gentiles. *There is a huge substitutionary
role here played by Israel on behalf of the Gentile nations.* To repeat what
has been said earlier, we come back again to Paul in Romans 11:28:
"From the standpoint of the gospel they [Israel] are enemies for *your*
[the Gentiles'] sake" (NASB, emphasis added). It would not be inaccurate to interpret this as saying, *The judgment of God is upon the Jews for the
sake of the Gentiles.* Nonetheless, there were cross-bearing Christians in
England in 1290 leading a crazed mob which killed 1,500 Jews; and centuries later, Martin Luther was displeased when the Jews in his region
resisted conversion.

In the Bible, we find the priest (with the right doctrine) passing by
on the other side of the victim who had fallen amongst robbers and
had been left half dead. At this same spot, it was the Samaritan (said to
hold the "wrong doctrine") who had compassion. Nor was it just cold
comfort, or some religious truth or tract that he passed on. Personal
attention was paid to the victim's wounds. The Samaritan provided
all that was needed to remedy the victim's condition. Time was spent
with him, the journey was broken – the routine forgotten – in order
to attend to the crisis. Finally, the Samaritan made a return journey to
follow up the matter (Luke 10:30–35).

Table 4: Some parallels between the sufferings of the heavenly Servant, Jesus the Messiah, and the earthly servant, Israel
"He had to be made like His brethren in all things, so that He might become a merciful and faithful high priest ... to make propitiation for the sins of the people" (Hebrews 2:17 NASB).

The Messiah	Israel
He was pierced for our transgressions. (Isaiah 53:5 NIV)	As far as the gospel is concerned, they are enemies on your account. (Romans 11:28 NIV)
Everyone deserted him and fled. (Mark 14:50 NIV)	No longer will they call you Deserted or ... your land ... Desolate. (Isaiah 62:4 NIV)
I am innocent of this man's blood. (Matthew 27:24 NIV)	We are not guilty, for they sinned against the LORD. (Jeremiah 50:7 NIV)
Peter insisted ... "I will never disown you." And all the others said the same. (Mark 14:31 NIV)	[God] saw that there was no-one ... he was appalled that there was no-one to intervene. (Isaiah 59:16 NIV)

(Continued)

Table 4: (Continued)

The Messiah	Israel
Many of his disciples turned back and no longer followed [Jesus]. "You do not want to leave too, do you?" Jesus asked the Twelve. (John 6:66–67 NIV)	A thing of horror and an object of scorn and ridicule to all the nations. (Deuteronomy 28:37 NIV)
Whatever you did for one of the least of these brothers of mine, you did for me. (Matthew 25:40 NIV)	In those days ten men from all ... nations will take firm hold of one Jew by the hem of his robe and say, "Let us go with you, because we have heard that God is with you." (Zechariah 8:23 NIV)
A stone that causes men to stumble and a rock that makes them fall. (1 Peter 2:8 NIV)	Some ... hold to the teaching of Balaam, the one who taught Balak to put a stumbling block before the people of Israel. (Revelation 2:14 NASB)
He was led like a lamb to the slaughter. (Isaiah 53:7 NIV)	For your sake we face death ... we are considered as sheep to be slaughtered. (Psalm 44:22 NIV)

Salvation is of the Jews (2): early signs of election

1. Although no fruit is actually named on the Tree of Knowledge, rabbis have speculated that it was a fig tree. Whether or not this was so, keys to the eventual Jewish *channel* of humankind's salvation are given:

    (a) In Adam and Eve sewing *fig leaves* together to cover their nakedness, after their sin had brought conviction (Genesis 3:7); and

    (b) In the fig tree later coming to represent Israel, withering in Mark 11:14, 20–22 and restored in Matthew 24:32. The fig leaf is the first foliage mentioned in the Bible.

    While this fig leaf covering itself proved unacceptable, and God Himself later provided skins as a covering for them (Genesis 3:21), it is a pointer to Israel as God's channel-of-salvation-to-be to the world, His "bridge." The blossoming fig tree in Solomon's Song (2:13) is again a reference to Israel.

2. The skins which God provided for Adam and Eve point us to the time when Jesus was first introduced to His own. He was firstly introduced not as "the Messiah" nor as the King of kings, but "Behold! *The Lamb of God* who takes away the sin of the world!" (John 1:29 NIV, emphasis added). Israel was the only nation which, up to that time, had been prepared to know and to understand the purpose of the sacrificial lamb.

3. The olive leaf which the dove brought to Noah (the second foliage mentioned in the Bible), reminds us of the olive tree in Romans, which is called "their *own* olive tree" (11:24).

4. The commandments which came to us through Moses, even though they are observed by fewer and fewer people today, have nonetheless given the world a basis for its ethical code. They remain the guidelines to which we need to return from our godless plunge. But the hearts that initially burned for these came from Jewish stock, and many Gentile martyrs have followed on.

5. A millenial prophecy and promise for Israel and the world:

    Many peoples will come and say,
    "Come, let us go up to the mountain of the LORD,
        to the house of the God of Jacob.

He will teach us his ways,
    so that we may walk in his paths."
The law will go out from Zion,
    the word of the LORD from Jerusalem.

(Isaiah 2:3 NIV)

This passage looks ahead to the time when the spiritual capital of this globe will be Jerusalem – affirmed many times in the Word of God. The shame, humiliation and degradation heaped upon Israel by the nations (and often by the Church) over the centuries will be wiped away!

Instead of your shame you will have a double portion,
    And instead of humiliation they will shout for joy ...

(Isaiah 61:7 NASB)

(Also, in the course of time, this will have its application to the consecrated Church, which becomes the overcomer of Revelation 2 and 3). Included in this shall be the saved remnant of Israel.)

Amongst those pilgrimaging annually to Jerusalem will be representatives from countries worldwide, celebrating that culminating Feast of the Lord (or the Feast of the Ingathering, of Tabernacles, of Booths, or of *Succoth*). In real measure this has already begun, and thousands of Christians have a victorious time in attending Succoth in Jerusalem.

Jesus certainly would have had all of this in mind when He confided in His Samaritan friend that He Himself was the long-waited Messiah. No wonder she abandoned her waterpot to broadcast the news!

6.

He declares His words to Jacob,
    His statutes and His ordinances to Israel.
He has not dealt thus with any [other] nation ...

(Psalm 147:19–20 NASB, emphasis added)

The answer as to why God chose Jacob (or Peter, Paul or even you or me) was not because of any inherent goodness. This is what causes many a Christian to stumble. We almost expect Israel to be the most "Christian" nation on earth. Well, one day she will indeed be that. But, in the meantime, let us take our measurements from the Word of God where, of Israel we read:

You are a holy people to the LORD your God ... [who] has chosen you to be a people for His own possession ... because the LORD loved you ...

(Deuteronomy 7:6, 8 NASB)

For by grace you have been saved through faith; and that not of yourselves, it is the gift of God; not as a result of works, so that no one may boast.

(Ephesians 2:8–9 NASB)

7. Humanity's bridge to God: Just as elsewhere we have seen that the Jewish nation has become God's bridge to humankind, so – in reverse – the Jewish Messiah has become and is humanity's bridge to God: "... no man cometh unto the Father, but by me" (John 14:6 KJV).

It is hoped that this short summary will spark within you an immeasurable sense of indebtedness to those who pioneered the Christian faith, and by whom you and countless millions have tasted God's mercy.

The first and the finest way of repaying that debt is through prayer. The following organizations provide resources to help support Israel through prayer. In the case of PFI the major goal in their calling is to pray for the believers in the land – Arab and Jewish, but mainly the Jewish ones:

PFI[1]
PO Box 328
Bromley
Kent BR1 2ZS
UK

CFI[2]
PO Box 2687

Eastbourne
East Sussex BN22 7LZ
UK

CMJ
PO Box 9510
Newark
Nottinghamshire NG24 9FW
UK

Gentiles: "aliens from the commonwealth of Israel" (Ephesians 2:12 NKJV)

Paul's letter to the Ephesians is deep in spiritual richness and truth. In chapter 2, Paul (himself of rabbinic Jewish stock), after speaking of salvation by grace alone, reminds Gentiles in detail of their formerly hopeless and pagan ancestry; the term "Gentiles" always refers to the nations, and is often used elsewhere as "heathen."

He refers to the time when "you were without [the Messiah], being aliens from the commonwealth of Israel" (Ephesians 2:12 NKJV). This spiritual wealth (originally the sole inheritance of Israelites), was opened up to the Gentiles as Jews went forth to tell and to share. While Paul himself led in this, many of us will recall the blessing and miracle of Peter's meeting with Cornelius and his household (Acts 10).

What does Paul mean by "commonwealth"? What does it consist of? Well – it must be that which belongs to the people of Israel, as listed in Romans 9:4–5:

- The sonship (of God)
- The glory (of the knowledge of God)
- The covenants (by God with His people)
- The giving of the law (by God to His people)
- The worship of God (in Spirit and truth)
- The promises (beyond enumerating)

- The patriarchs (headed by Abraham, Isaac and, above all, Jacob)
- The Messiah Himself

At that time you were without Christ, being aliens from the common-wealth of Israel and strangers from the covenants of promise, having *no* hope and without God in the world.

(Ephesians 2:12 NKJV, emphasis added)

- *No* vestige of hope
- *No* relationship with God
- *No* way out of the grip of the world

But now [how things change when God intervenes!] in [Messiah] Jesus you who once were far off have been brought near by the blood of [Messiah]. For He Himself is our peace, who has made both one, and has broken down the middle wall of separation.

(Ephesians 2:13–14 NKJV)

The Jews were "near" to God through His everlasting covenant. Gentiles had no such covenant and were far off.

Now, therefore, are no longer strangers ... but fellow citizens with the ... household of God, having been built on the foundation of the apostles and prophets, [Messiah] Jesus ... Himself being the chief cornerstone

(Ephesians 2:19–20 NKJV)

Paul doesn't say, "Once you had no hope; now you are in the (Gentile) Church." He says, "Once you had no hope, you were without God, lost in the world – *now you have been brought into Israel's commonwealth. Remember!"*

This amazing transformation for the Gentiles is wonderfully referred by a lovely hymn-writer, Jessie F. Webb:

O people of the grace of God
You people of the grace of God,

Standing enriched by Israel's fall;
Aliens you were and slaves to sin,
Till sweet and clear came mercy's call.

Were you by nature worthier found?
What merit yours, such place to win?
Wild olive, by a Hand Divine,
In Israel's stock now grafted in.

Think not, O Gentiles now brought nigh,
That here God's age-long purpose ends
With promises, yet unfulfilled,
While David's throne no King ascends.

Nay, from the furnace of His wrath
Subdued and purged, from dross made free,
The Lord shall lead His remnant forth
And every pledge fulfilled shall be.

O people of the grace of God,
Will you not pay the tribute due,
And Israel's blessing ever seek
For love of Him Who died a Jew?

(Jessie F. Webb 1866–1964)

This hymn, although totally unknown by the Church in general, brings
out through the revelation and understanding given to its writer, Jessie
F. Webb, *that God, so far from rejecting Israel, is calling the believing Gentile
remnant thus*:

O people of the grace of God,
Will you not pay the tribute due,
And Israel's blessing ever seek
For love of Him Who died a Jew?

This hymn, today lost and unknown but based upon the Word and will of God, has said what this very book is today calling you to. That is: *to remember, in prayer to God, the people with whom He worked in the first century to reveal Himself to the world – the nation of Israel,* the nation which God calls His firstborn son, and so told Pharaoh: "Israel is my firstborn son ... Let my son go, so that he may worship me" (Exodus 4:22–23 NIV).

How strange that Christians who praise God for His promises and faithfulness doubt that these will be fulfilled to those to whom they were first given! Why should God be faithful to all *except* those whom He chose as a nation, His instrument of revelation? Only in Israel was the marred image of God sufficiently repaired for revelation to be given.

We can say all we wish about Israel – but we cannot deny that they were the bridge by which God came to humankind! God prepared humanity nowhere else for this. By them came the only Bridge by which humankind comes to God – the Messiah Himself.

It was only with the later persecution by the early Church fathers and secular rulers that the original Jewishness of worship to God was expunged. We have a Gentilized form of Christianity today, but for many years after the crucifixion the followers of Jesus were Jews. The center of these for worship was the Temple in Jerusalem.

In fact, Peter had been admonished on his return there for preaching to a Gentile family. He was reproved: "You went into the house of uncircumcised men and ate with them" (Acts 11:3 NIV) – a doubly forbidden act in the teaching and revelation that Israel had received up to that date. Initially, when the believers were scattered, they preached *only* to Jews, and synagogues became the venue of Jewish believers. In fact, opposition arose amongst these through Paul's acceptance of the Gentiles into the Jewish promises, although Paul's teaching had been misquoted by his opposers.

Our Church assemblies today have evolved out of the Jewish synagogue, and the latter evolved when the Jews were in Babylon, the Jewish Temple having been destroyed by Nebuchadnezzar. The word *synagogu* means "assembly" and is so translated in one place in the New Testament (James 2:2 KJV).

Another contribution to Christendom was the organ. The Jewish Book of Knowledge tells of a "pneumatic-type organ operated by twin bellows, a prototype of the kind in use today." With the destruction of the Temple in AD 70, rabbis themselves banned (to this day) the use of all musical instruments in synagogues as a sign of mourning. Because of its original link with the Jewish Temple, the early Church first resisted the use of the organ in Church services. Some even thought its use could seduce some Christians to Judaism!

However, it is God who is finally in control. That which we see being restored in joyful worship to the Church is nothing less than Jewish in origin. The expressive dance, the joyful songs of Scripture, the instrumental accompaniments – all of these had largely vanished since Temple days. These are now flooding into worship times again – worldwide. While unrealized, the restoration of all this, even with its imperfection in places, is linked with the restoration of Israel to its land. The Holy Spirit is at work, and this began in the latter part of the nineteenth century and the beginning of the twentieth century, when the Jews had begun to return to their Land.

The work of the Spirit is involved, although the link may seem to be hidden. The coming back of the tambourine is a part of the work of the Spirit which lays behind what is today going on to restore Israel. Joyful worship to the God of the Jews began 3,500 years ago with their immense victory in coming through the drying up of the Red Sea – with Moses leading them. You will all remember that it was Miriam, the prophetess, who, complete with tambourine, led the women in song and dance after the exodus. It was an amazing revelation of the power of God. He is waiting to bless them today through your own overcoming and powerful faith and prayer! Joyful worship to the God of the Jews began exactly there – about 3,500 years ago – with the newly formed Jewish nation. And it is exactly there that we find the very first song in the Bible!

> The LORD is my strength and song,
> and he is become my salvation:

he is my God, and I will prepare him an habitation;
my father's God, and I will exalt him.

(Exodus 15:2 KJV)

At numerous Messianic fellowships right across the land of Israel these last thirty years, the writer of this book has increasingly seen, and been part of, wonderful Messianic worship – flooding back in as the believers of the land worship their Messiah. The height and depth and challenge of this response from the believers to their King are very precious and represent a big advance and growth, since the Body of Messiah only really began to grow after the Six-Day War of June 1967 – when Jerusalem fell back into Jewish hands in an incredible way:

Behold, I will do something new ...
    I will even make a roadway in the wilderness ...
    To give drink to My chosen people.
The people whom I formed for Myself
    Will declare My praise.

(Isaiah 43:19–21 NASB)

Notes

1. Prayer For Israel.
2. Christian Friends of Israel.

CHAPTER 7

Britain's Vision for Israel

The Church in England from 1600

It will surprise most readers to know that the title of this chapter is adapted from a little-known, out-of-print book published in 1956 by the World Jewish Congress, and written by a non-Christian, Jewish author: Franz Kobler. The book was entitled *The Vision Was There*. (What follows here is a prelude to Chapter 8.)

In an astonishing way, Franz Kobler traces the history of Britain from before the reign of Queen Elizabeth I up to the twentieth century, producing hundreds of names of statesmen, churchmen and spokesmen in Britain, each of whom had a vision for the restoration of the land and people of Israel. So harmonizing are his quotations from over three centuries of British history that it is reasonable to conclude that, *although Kobler may not have realized it, his research and labors were actually blessed and inspired by God.*

His book highlights God's choice of Britain as His servant nation, appointed early in the twentieth century to "shepherd" a restored Israel. While this may sound controversial, it is actually an important statement and observation. It is also important for the Church in Britain to take full note of it, so that we are aroused and shaken from the slumber, error and ignorance into which we have sunk.

The doctrine of the restoration of Israel did not emerge into the public arena in 1917. There had been centuries of Christian teaching on this matter in the Anglican and evangelical churches, particularly during the Puritan age. All of this merely culminated in the Balfour Declaration.

This fact is of cardinal importance to the Church in Britain today, where we are so bound and blinded by the gross lie and error of replacement theology, telling us: "We, the Church, are the 'New Israel,' the spiritual Israel, the Israel of God." We are close to the point where the Lord may have to set us aside because, in our ignorance and arrogance (Romans 11:18–22, 25), we shun the Word of light and truth, to serve our own will instead of His.

It was to proud Nebuchadnezzar that Daniel was bidden to disclose:

> The Most High rules in the kingdom of men,
> [and He] gives it to whomever He will.
>
> (Daniel 4:17 NKJV)

With this in mind, let us note how Franz Kobler uncovers British history to show that, for many centuries, what God has done in His faithfulness to restore His people Israel in the last 100 years *was foreseen and prayed for within these shores over 400 years ago!*

This should shake us and our church leaders out of slumber, and cause us to repent of error and false doctrine, and return to God. *This is Britain's primary sin and is undoubtedly the key to what we call "revival" in Britain.* We cannot diverge from the call of God and still expect His blessing, any more than did Israel in the first century. God waits for us to return:

> His compassions fail not.
>
> (Lamentations 3:22 NKJV)

Although his book is now sadly out of print, in his preface Kobler states (emphasis added):

Nowhere more than in Britain has the idea of the "Restoration of Israel" been developed into a doctrine and become the object of a movement extending over more than three centuries.

Only in Britain, the leading spokesmen of many generations have been inspired by the vision of a revived Israel. *Only there,* the creation of a Jewish National Home has been a serious and almost continuous political issue which was finally translated into reality ...

Only a comprehensive study tracing the movement from its origins, through all of its historical stages and cultural ramifications, can reveal how deeply the idea of Israel's Restoration is rooted in the fundamentals of the Commonwealth, how inseparable it is from the character and history of the British nation, in spite of a temporary abandonment.[1]

What weighty words these are for anyone who yearns to see Britain restored to that kind of relationship with God through which the gospel went out to so much of this world in the nineteenth and twentieth centuries!

Kobler continues:

The British Movement for the Restoration of Israel is in fact one of the rare instances of the continuous interest shown by one nation in the destiny of another people. Its specific historical significance lies in the recognition of Israel's Restoration as an organic part of British political ideals.[2]

To the [Puritans], as to the early Christians, there appeared the vision of a Zion, which was to take the place of Rome and bear out the biblical prophecies by becoming the heart of a kingdom of peace and justice ...

The profound faith of the Puritans in the Word of God enjoined moreover the acceptance of all the promises explicitly and unmistakably relating to the Jews, as contained in the [Bible]. This ... took place in a country [Britain] where almost no professing Jews had been seen for centuries, in consequence of their expulsion in 1290, [and] may be regarded as one of history's strangest paradoxes![3]

Kobler quotes from a hymn by William Cowper (1731–1800):

Oh Israel! Of all nations most undone,
Thy diadem displaced, thy sceptre gone,
Cry aloud, thou that sittest in the dust,
Cry to the proud, the cruel, the unjust!
Knock at the gates of the nations, rouse their fears,
Say "Wrath is coming, and the storm appears,"
But raise the shrillest cry in British ears![4]

[In 1621] a book appeared by another outstanding Elizabethan Christian [Sir Henry Finch] which gave a powerful impetus to the Restoration doctrine. [It was entitled] "The World's Great Restoration or The Calling of the Jews and of all the Nations ... to the Faith of Christ" ...

This reflection of the Restoration idea in one of the greatest literary documents of the epoch is an indication that it had taken root in the spiritual life of England ...

The anticipation of a Restoration of the Jews became an increasingly general notion in the forties of the 17th century. Oliver Cromwell himself spoke of the prophecies "that He will bring His people again from the depths of the sea, as once He led Israel through the Red Sea".[5]

The famous Rabbi of Amsterdam, Menasseh ben Israel, published a book in 1650 [*The Hope of Israel*] expounding the divinely-ordained conditions that must precede the Restoration of the Jews, the coming of the Messiah, and the realisation of the Kingdom of Heaven. These would only be fulfilled with the readmission of the Jews to England! The English version was dedicated to the High Court of the Parliament of England [printed in Spanish, Latin and English].

Menasseh ben Israel's work laid a foundation which did later open the gate to that return of the Jews to England ...

Thomas Milton and Isaac (William) Newton were associated with the vision. The Methodists strengthened the movement enormously through the inspired hymns of Charles Wesley, one of which reads:

1. Almighty God of love,
Set up the attracting sign,
And summon whom Thou dost approve
For messengers divine:
From favour'd Abraham's seed
The new apostles choose,
In Isles and Continents to spread
The dead-reviving news.

2. Them, snatched out of the flame,
Through every nation send,
The true Messiah to proclaim,
The universal Friend;
That all the God unknown
May learn of Jews to adore,
And see Thy glory in Thy Son,
Till time shall be no more.

3. O that the chosen band
Might now their brethren bring,
And, gather'd out of every land,
Present to Zion's King!
Of all the ancient race,
Not one be left behind;
But each impell'd by secret grace,
His way to Canaan find.

4. We know it must be done,
For God hath spoke the word:
All Israel shall her Saviour own,
To their first state restored:
Rebuilt by His command,
Jerusalem shall rise;
Her temple on Moriah stand
Again, and touch the skies.

5. Send then Thy servants forth,
To call the Hebrews home;
From East, and West, and South and North,
Let all the wanderers come:
Where'er in lands unknown
The fugitives remain,
Bid every creature help them on,
The Holy Mount to gain.

6. An offering to their Lord,
There let them all be seen.
Sprinkled with water and with blood,
In soul and body clean:
With Israel's myriads seal'd
Let all the nations meet,
And show the mystery fulfill'd,
The family complete!

[Written ca.1759][6]

In 1797, Thomas Witherby, commenting upon a book, "The Restoration of the Jews – the Crisis of all Nations," said that he felt confident that "England, under a new Cyrus, would be chosen to perform God's purposes of mercy towards Israel." Even Jonathan Edwards, America's great reformer and Christian, spoke of "the future glorious times, when Judah and Ephraim shall be united as one people."[7]

In the 1830's, amongst those who favoured the Restoration of Israel and who were active to that end, were: Lord Shaftesbury, Lord Palmerston and Edward Bickersteth. Shaftesbury wrote: "The ancient city of the people of God is about to resume a place among the nations, and England is the first of all the Gentile kingdoms that ceases to tread her down."

In 1840, the Ambassador to Turkey strongly recommended the Turkish government to use every encouragement to urge the Jews to return to Palestine. Shaftesbury drew up a kind of State letter urging Turkey to hand over Palestine to the Jews for their "indestructible Messianic hope."[8]

In the 1840's Charles Henry Churchill [ancestor of Sir Winston Churchill] notably spoke and wrote of "a pledge of England's friendship, and bonding union with the Jewish nation. May the Jewish nation regain its rank and position among the nations of the world ..."

As others had done, Churchill made a direct approach, together with Lord Shaftesbury, to western Jewry to co-operate with the British Government in planning for their return to Palestine.[9]

These extracts from Franz Kobler's book, giving his Jewish viewpoint, are all the more remarkable when, for example, we see how they parallel the teaching of one of Christendom's greatest preachers and theologians, Charles Haddon Spurgeon, given in London in 1855: "I think we do not attach sufficient importance to the Restoration of the Jews. We do not think enough of it. But certainly, if there is anything promised in the Bible it is this." He did not place the conversion of the Jews at the consummation of history but rather at the beginning of a period of general revival:

The day shall yet come when the Jews, who were the first apostles to the Gentiles, the first missionaries to us who were afar off, shall be gathered in again. Until that shall be, the fullness of the Church's glory can never come. Matchless benefits to the world are bound up with the Restoration of Israel. Their gathering in shall be as life from the dead.

With all that we have seen above, and much more available in confirmation of these things, it is obvious and incontestable that when Palestine and Jerusalem fell into British hands in 1917, *this was nothing less than the hand of God*. It was His express will to grant us in Britain both the responsibility and the privilege of establishing a homeland for the Jewish people.

In spite of Britain having, since those days, yielded continuously to intimidatory and relentless Islamic pressure, and in spite of the bulk of the Church in Britain having almost totally departed from Biblical prophetic truth (often calling herself the "New Israel"), Israel *still stands because of God's protection* (Psalms 121:4; 124). But, without doubt, God *also chose Britain* to be His "Cyrus" nation – the channel and shepherd nation by which He planned to see Israel rebuilt.

Now, because of our scarred history since 1917, having done far more to obstruct than to assist in Israel's restoration, *the Lord is very angry with Britain* (Zechariah 1:15). Referring to Daniel's repentance, we come to:

> We have not listened to your servants the prophets, who spoke in your name to our kings, our princes and our fathers, and to all the people of the land ...
>
> O LORD, we and our kings, our princes and our fathers are covered with shame because we have sinned against you.
>
> (Daniel 9:6, 8 NIV)

To repeat what has been said earlier in this chapter: The *root* sin and *root* cause of Britain's ongoing spiritual decline is our *failure to heed God and His Word* in connection with His specific calling for us to shepherd His sheep, Israel (Ezekiel 34:10; John 21:15–17).

There are countless examples – too many to begin quoting from – but they are exemplified by the excellent DVD series *The Forsaken Promise*.[10] Most of us in Britain have forgotten, or have not even discerned, that our worldwide empire disappeared "overnight" – shortly after our refusal even to vote for Israel's restoration at the United Nations in November 1947. *This abstention should cause Bible-believing Christians almost to vomit, at such outrageous opposition to God's revealed will.*

The loss of our empire, together with our ongoing moral, social and spiritual decline, are an indication of God's displeasure with us. Yet, even given those criteria, "The LORD longs to be gracious to [us] ... He waits on high to have compassion" (Isaiah 30:18 NASB). Do you catch the throb of God's heartbeat here? He, the God of the universe, longs and waits to be gracious to us – this undeserving, pleasure-loving nation!

He is looking for that appropriate and godly remnant who will "humble themselves and pray and seek [His] face and turn from their wicked ways," so that He may "hear from heaven and ... heal [our] land" (2 Chronicles 7:14 NIV). This is a huge step for us to take, a huge truth for us to grasp, particularly with our inbuilt, innate pride and our total ignorance about Israel. However, Elijah discovered that there were 7,000 others besides him, and God looks for "a man" to "stand in the gap" (Ezekiel 22:30 NASB), not an army!

Perhaps there are some pastors and teachers who will foster prayer amongst their flock. Perhaps there are those whose tears will touch the Throne of Grace. Perhaps a tiny remnant – even such as prayed Britain through, during World War Two – will be found behind closed doors, and the God of Abraham will bend His ear and listen to them. Perhaps... Will you yourself make this a goal in prayer: to pray for pastors, teachers and leaders, and the "whosoever"?

Is there an "Esther" who will risk her life – "If I perish, I perish" (Esther 4:16 NIV) – and stand before the King in her royal apparel (Esther 5:1–2; Isaiah 61:10), touching the extended scepter and seeing the Jewish people, God's people, delivered? As a nation, are we desiring that the God of Heaven will turn us back to Himself, breaking and motivating our hearts concerning His elect people?

> I searched for a man among them who would build up the wall [of prayer] and stand in the gap before Me for the land, that I should not destroy it; but I found no one.
>
> (Ezekiel 22:30 NASB)

The paradox is that while God in His justice should destroy us, in His mercy – which exceeds His judgmental assessment of us all (James 2:13b) – He yearns to be gracious, and looks for an intercessor. Will you be such a one?

The distorted theology

"Replacement theology," known also as "supercessionism," centers around the belief that when some of the Jewish people rejected Jesus as the Messiah, God rejected the Jews as a nation. It takes the view that the Church is the "New Israel" and has replaced the "original Israel." The blessings that God promised to Israel now pertain to the Church; however, His curses still apply to Israel (see Chapter 5: "Muddied Waters").

The spiritual gymnastics needed to fit this evil theology into Scripture are enormous, leading to Britain's increased departure from the truth of the Word of God. Derek Prince has taught that if someone gets the first button on his waistcoat in the wrong position, every other button will also be out of place. He thus illustrates that if we are wrong on God's purposes for and attitude to Israel, we shall be wrong on the rest of our doctrine. There are almost eighty references to Israel in the New Testament, every single one of which applies in the very first place to Israel. *There is no such term in the Bible as "the New Israel."*

The whole doctrine of replacement theology is therefore in direct contravention of the endlessly repeated declaration: "God is faithful." It is a huge blot on British history to have ever fostered such a lie, and it is appalling to realize that the lie and error permeate and mislead every section of the Church here in Britain today. In recent years, what appears to have been the last remaining major Bible college which had been teaching Bible prophecy *accurately* – including the place of Israel in the end times – was taken over and its former theology "ransacked" in order to substitute modern-day error. (There are still three lesser-known Bible colleges in Britain which accurately teach the Biblical place of Israel.)

It was at that same Bible college, during World War Two, that overcoming, all-night prayer had been made which

1. saw the planned German invasion-by-sea of Britain turned back in 1940;
2. *prayed through the UN vote on Israel in November 1947;*
3. saw the two-thirds majority vote then needed to secure Israel's rebirth and recognition as a State on the world map.

One of the inevitable results of such strategic error is the failure to prepare the Church for the difficult times ahead.

The prophetic word [is] as ... a lamp shining in a dark place.

(2 Peter 1:19 NASB)

This tells us that when things get tough and spiritual darkness covers the whole earth, it is the Word of God which alone guides us into God's truth and into the way ahead. There was never a time when this principle needed to be so much known and so much followed. The relevant scriptures are so important: 2 Peter 1:19; Isaiah 60:2. Ensure that you yourself refer to and study them.

Church responsibility

Few of us understand that the responsibility to shepherd Israel in restoration to their homeland was specifically laid by the Lord at the feet of Britain. It was in fact a privilege, and it should and could have been our joy, to welcome back the returning "prodigal son" at this first stage.

Instead, the life-giving breath of prayer that we have been called to release over Israel has been stifled and silenced. God, who is bound to His Word, will hold His shepherds responsible (Ezekiel 34:1–19). That is the whole essence of the judgment of nations about which we read in some detail in Matthew 25:31–46. In case there is some dissension in understanding that passage, remember that, whatever the application also to the Church, Christ's words, "one of the least of these my brethren" (Matthew 25:40 KJV), cannot be interpreted without inclusion of the poor, neglected, world-rejected Jews.

Remember that Jesus cannot and *will not* return until Israel's remnant is saved. He has overlooked our ignorance and indifference up till now, but He now demands that "all people everywhere should repent" (Acts 17:30 NASB). There are those of us who really believe that Israel will be saved during a short period before Jesus returns, and we should be working, praying and believing to that end today!

To those who do not believe that God would bring judgment on the Church because of her hostility, arrogance or indifference to Israel, the Holy Spirit would direct attention to the Word of God:

> Do not be arrogant towards the branches [Israel] ... it is not you who supports the root, but the root [patriarchal ancestry and teaching] supports you ... If God did not spare the natural branches [Israel], He will not spare you [Gentiles] either. Behold then the kindness *and severity* of God.
>
> (Romans 11:18–22 NASB, emphasis added)

In passing, let us note that it is nothing to do with whether or not Israel deserves God's mercy, any more than either you or I did. Israel will be saved by grace, as we were, not by works. Please get on your knees and plead for the Lord to open the eyes and hearts of Christian leaders and teachers – to grant not merely revelation to them, but true humility and repentance for them and for all of us.

Time is short – very, very short!

> It is high time to awake out of sleep.
>
> (Romans 13:11a KJV)

The sword of Islam is poised, hanging over Britain, pointing directly at the Houses of Parliament – the long-planned takeover bid being amply evident to the few church leaders who are awake. For correction (and judgment), Israel was sold so often into the hands of her enemies. Whatever mouths or media may say, if Islam is a friend of Christendom, why is the "Church" an underground affair in Saudi Arabia? Why are Christians forbidden to pray on the Temple site or near the Mosque of Omar in Jerusalem? Why have so many Christians left Bethlehem? Why are Christians fleeing today from Iran and Iraq? [11]

Thank God that, in three places in the Bible, we are assured that the time *will* come when "the earth shall be filled with the knowledge of the glory of the LORD, as the waters cover the sea" (Habakkuk 2:14 KJV; see also Numbers 14:21; Isaiah 11:9).

Notes

1. Franz Kobler, *The Vision Was There* (World Jewish Congress, 1956), p. 7.
2. *ibid.* p. 9.
3. *ibid.* pp. 13–14.
4. *ibid.* p. 18.
5. *ibid.* p. 21.
6. *ibid.* pp. 26–27.
7. *ibid.* p. 47.
8. *ibid.* pp. 58–59.
9. *ibid.* pp. 63–64, 66.
10. *The Forsaken Promise* is available from PFI, PO Box 328, Bromley, Kent BR1 2ZS, UK.
11. A booklet entitled *A Nation Called by God* is available from CFI UK, PO Box 2687, Eastbourne, East Sussex BN22 7LZ, UK.

CHAPTER 8

Did God Choose Britain?

For the nation or kingdom that will not serve you [Israel] will perish;
it will be utterly ruined.

(Isaiah 60:12 NIV)

At this time of mounting anarchy, lawlessness and terrorism – our prisons overflowing, young children becoming murderers, teachers fearful of pupils in the classroom, two out of three marriages ending in divorce, crime rising at an unprecedented rate, pornography rife, schoolchildren taught (and even encouraged) in the use of contraceptives – is it not imperative for the Christian, and the nation, earnestly to seek God and ask *where* we have gone wrong? Has there not been a removal of God's former blessings?

If my people, who are called by my name, will humble themselves and pray and seek my face and turn from their wicked ways, then will I hear from heaven and will forgive their sin and will heal their land.

(2 Chronicles 7:14 NIV)

The three promises given here depend on the four preceding conditions: humility, prayer, seeking God, and turning back from sin. There is the "If" of those conditions.

While we appropriate many of the spiritual promises to Israel, one of the characteristics of believers in Britain, and elsewhere for that matter, is that we seldom, if ever, follow the teaching of Moses and Joshua to go in and possess the land, and *to drive out our (spiritual) enemies before us* (Deuteronomy 2:24; Joshua 1:7, 15). Our opening text from Isaiah is a typical warning.

We may "possess" our parishes and church buildings, but a divine jealousy for the once-great land of Britain is lacking. In the historic Jewish / Israeli concept, both the secular and spiritual aspects of serving God used to blend together. Such a zest and view is needed today by Christians in Britain. We need to cry out to God over the pollution of our land, just as much as we, who may be of the house of Israel, cry out to Jehovah for mercy and pardon for Israel. While we are now accustomed to the volume of sin around us, it was the sin of just one man, Achan, that brought judgment on the whole nation of Israel (Joshua 7). Today, it is the Holy Spirit and the Word of God that seek to draw us to repentance. They assure us:

> The LORD longs to be gracious to you;
>> And therefore He waits on high to have compassion on you.
>> For the LORD is a God of justice;
>> How blessed are all those who long for Him.

> He will surely be gracious to you at the sound of your cry; when He hears it, He will answer you ... Your ears will hear a word behind you, "This is the way, walk in it."
>> (Isaiah 30:18, 19, 21 NASB)

Note that the Lord "waits" for us and "longs to be gracious;" his voice is heard "behind" us, showing that we have left the path of the Master. This is so with Britain at this hour, diverging more and more from the purposes of God, and – as far as Israel is concerned – even opposing them since the early part of the twentieth century.

Outside of Israel, God has entrusted to Britain the Word of God and the preaching of the gospel more than to any other nation. Although small in size, Britain has produced many men and women to bless the world with the knowledge of the Lord and his Word; consider David Livingstone, William Carey, Hudson Taylor, C.T. Studd, "Praying Hyde," John and Charles Wesley, George Whitefield, Rees Howells, Smith Wigglesworth, Mary Slessor, Gladys Aylward, Elizabeth Fry, Helen Roseveare, Lady Jane Grey.

In addition to these, the United States of America has received its foundations of great faith from the shores of Britain. And the USA has been a great blessing to the world from its earlier Christian roots. Spiritually and politically, we need people today of similar caliber. We have lost our way, and we are groping for a way out. From one decade and government to another, we continue in moral, spiritual, economic and political decline.

We can choose: we can blindly pursue our existing course to the destruction of all our known spiritual and moral values, "doing our own thing" in turning to the right or to the left, or we can turn back and return to the point from which we left God and his appointed purposes for us early in the twentieth century. A notable freelance Bible teacher and evangelist recently stated: "We stand in greater danger today of the loss of our national heritage, of our freedom, of the foundations of our Christian civilization that have taken centuries to build up ... we stand in greater danger today than for centuries."

You do not need to be a great, learned person or even to have a spirit of discernment. It is plain for the ordinary person in the street to see and know that *something* is basically wrong with Britain. You can talk to ordinary people who know nothing of the gospel and you can sense that there is unease running through this nation today. The common people *know* that we are in danger. Something has gone wrong with the whole life of the nation, because nothing is going right. Everywhere you turn, you see the evidence of human inability to control the life of this nation.

The spirits of materialism and secularism that have taken a grip on the life of this nation have moved us through successive stages of corruption that have undermined the moral and spiritual foundations of life in an unprecedented way. The change has been rapid, leaving the sociologists with their mouths open, unable to understand what is happening! Sociologists usually pride themselves on being able to predict anything – nothing takes them by surprise. But there has been a basic change in the last twenty years: they realize that the forces of change at work in this nation are moving us in directions that we have never seen before.

Politicians, theologians and sociologists have an endless variety of reasons for Britain's decline, with an equal variety of cures. But what we see in Britain is not so much the *reason* for our condition as the *symptom*! The root cause lies deeper. It is embedded in the early years of the twentieth century and interwoven into our chapter heading: "Did God *choose* Britain?" Did he choose us to be not only the main custodian of the gospel for centuries, but also His channel of healing and care, His "under-shepherd" for the restoration of Israel, His first-born son, in 1917?

There can be no question that God began to set Britain apart in the 1600s and that the Puritans were early instruments (amongst many others) in preparing Britain to be His "Cyrus" nation in the 1900s to restore Israel.

Speaking of Abraham's offspring, Scripture declares:

> I will bless them that bless thee, and curse him that curseth thee.
>
> (Genesis 12:3 KJV)

To what extent has Britain been affected by this decree of Genesis 12?

It was God's divine prerogative that brought His land of Israel again under the control of a professedly Bible-believing people (the British) for the first time in 2,000 years. It was not some strange political quirk of no significance whatever in God's eyes.

If it is of the literal Zion, the land and the people, of which God says, "He who touches you touches the apple of [my] eye" (Zechariah 2:8 NKJV), how then have we in Britain "touched" and dealt with that which is Biblically recorded to be the most tender part of God's body – the "apple of His eye," His window onto the world? This is the same land that God describes in His Word as "a land for which

the LORD your God cares; the eyes of the LORD your God are always
on it, from the beginning of the year to the very end of the year"
(Deuteronomy 11:12 NKJV).

Did God choose Britain to be His eyes and heartbeat to bless Israel,
and, if so, have we been that blessing to the Jewish nation, or have
we closed our eyes and heart to them and instead been a curse and a
hindrance? There can be no question that God did choose Britain to be
His eyes and ears in putting the land of Israel (then called "Palestine")
under our oversight in 1917. Seven of the nine politicians involved in
the meaningful Balfour Declaration were believing Christians! *God was
answering their own prayers!*

When Jerusalem, after many centuries, fell into British hands in
1917 without a shot being fired from the hands of a Muslim nation
(Turkey), Britain's representative, General Allenby, marched bareheaded into the city as a token both of his respect for "Messiah King"
and for His Word. He knew that history was being made that day and
realized the importance of Jerusalem prophetically. The night before
it fell, he had prayed on his knees that the city of Jerusalem would be
spared the disaster of a bombardment, and in a remarkable way this
prayer was answered.

Within a month of the Balfour Declaration, Christians saw
this as a fulfillment of prophecy. The world saw it as a solution
to the terrible sufferings that the Jews were undergoing. Lord Balfour, Lloyd George, General Smuts and others who believed in the
Bible had a personal conviction that the return to Palestine was
a fulfillment of prophecy. With the close of World War One, the
Jews looked forward to the rapid implementation of Britain's Balfour Declaration, but *here is exactly where the problem began, for it
was only partially implemented and later repudiated.* Set now against
scriptures such as Psalm 105:14–15, we can see clearly how we have
thus grieved the Lord.

While mystery surrounds the sudden change of attitude and
policy, this must be linked with the non-co-operation of the British
military leaders of that day, as well as British governmental hindrance
ever since.

Events leading to British rule over Palestine

1. **Birth of Zionism.** After the infamous Dreyfus trial in 1894 in which the Jewish French military officer, Captain Alfred Dreyfus, was falsely accused, convicted and imprisoned as a scapegoat, Theodore Herzl realized that there was no hope anywhere in the world for sustained justice towards the Jews, other than *within a country they could call their own*. Thus the First Zionist Congress of 1897 was called, leading to the founding of the World Zionist Congress in Basle, Switzerland.

2. **Britain's support.** The only Great Power showing a flicker of practical interest was Britain which gave serious consideration in 1902 to Herzl's plea that the Sinai Peninsula be used for Jewish development.

3. **World War One.** As many will know, during the 1914–18 war, Britain fell into the most serious need. Having no stocks of gunpowder with which to continue the war against Germany, its situation was dramatically transformed by the Jewish scientist Chaim Weizmann. At the critical moment, he was able to produce a formula by which to manufacture synthetic TNT, using – of all things – horse chestnuts! Not only did this save the day, but it saved the British nation also.

4. **Balfour Declaration.** Declining all other offers of reward, Weizmann pleaded for Britain's help in establishing a homeland for the Jews, and to this, the British government acceded. Thus reads the official confirmation of the Foreign Office of this historic agreement:

November 2nd. 1917

Dear Lord Rothschild,
I have much pleasure in conveying to you, on behalf of His Majesty's Government, the following declaration of sympathy with Jewish Zionist aspirations which has been submitted to, and approved by, the Cabinet.

"His Majesty's Government view with favour the establishment in Palestine of a national home for the Jewish people, and will use their best endeavours to facilitate the achievement of this object, it being clearly understood that nothing shall be done which may prejudice the civic and religious rights of existing non-Jewish communities in Palestine, or the rights and political status enjoyed by Jews in any other country."

I should be grateful if you would bring this declaration to the knowledge of the Zionist Federation.

Yours
Arthur James Balfour

5. **1919.** The British military administration in Jerusalem showed little sympathy with the Balfour Declaration and withheld its publication! A Jewish delegation led by Weizmann met marked hostility, but Weizmann came to an understanding with the Emir Feisal, eldest son of Hussein and chief Arab delegate at the Paris Peace Conference. In their agreement of 3 January 1919, the Balfour Declaration was accepted. Palestine was recognized as a separate Jewish entity with which the about-to-be-created Arab state of Transjordan would maintain diplomatic relations, provided that Britain and France met Arab demands in other areas.

6. **1920: yielding to opposition to the Jewish return.** Sir Herbert Samuel, first British High Commissioner, arrived in Palestine on 1 July 1920 and worked to open the way for Jewish immigration and the continued development of the land. However, he simultaneously adopted a policy of appeasement towards an extremist Palestinian Arab minority which violently opposed the realization of Jewish national rights in Palestine. Sir Herbert believed that such a policy would eventually lead to renewed harmony between Arabs and Jews in Palestine. What happened was precisely the opposite:

   (a) The British released the leader of the Arab extremist movement, Haj Amin Al-Husseini, from prison, where he had been sent for instigating an Arab attack on Jews praying at the Western Wall in Jerusalem.

   (b) Al-Husseini was then helped to attain the two most powerful positions in the Palestinian Arab community: head of the supreme Muslim Council *and* Mufti of Jerusalem.

(c) In the ensuing years, this leader methodically set about strengthening his position, advancing his political aims through mounting terror and intimidation. These were directed not merely against the Jewish community, but also, during certain periods primarily, against the Palestinian Arabs who opposed his rule and policies.

(d) The rise of the Mufti to dominance on the Palestinian Arab scene in the early 1920s was a turning point in the course of Jewish–Arab relations in Palestine. It marked the end of any hope of implementing the Feisal-Weizmann Agreement of 1919 and it set the Arab world on a course of uncompromising hostility to the very idea of Jewish statehood, to which, regrettably, much of it adheres to this day. Britain's policy of appeasement and compromise, diverting from the spirit and terms of the Balfour Declaration, was a leading factor in this.

7. **First White Paper (1922).** In 1921, Feisal's brother, the Emir Abdullah, invaded eastern Palestine (Transjordan) and was recognized as its ruler by the British Colonial Secretary. This area east of the River Jordan was taken out of the territory designated in the Balfour Declaration, i.e. Palestine, and closed to Jewish settlement (!) although it was not excluded from the area of the later British Mandate. *Thus, approximately three quarters (77 percent) of the territory originally intended for a Jewish homeland was lost!* It was first called "Transjordan," and later, as it is still called today, simply "Jordan."

"Aliyah" (Jewish immigration) was temporarily halted because of large-scale anti-Jewish rioting. Lord Samuel's talks with Arab nationalists produced a Colonial Office White Paper in 1922, watering down the promises of the Balfour Declaration. Negotiations failed to establish a legislative council on which Arabs would agree to serve. The end-product was a British colonial regime.[1]

The British Mandate (1922–48)

In July 1922 the League of Nations (forerunner of the United Nations):

1. formally entrusted Britain with a Mandate to establish a homeland for the Jewish people, which incorporated the Balfour Declaration;

2. recognized the historical connection between the Jewish people and the land;

3. called upon Britain to smooth the way for the creation of the national home. This Mandate extended over the banks of the Jordan, east and west. Within a few months, Britain partitioned the area of the Mandate, establishing an autonomous Arab emirate in eastern Palestine, Transjordan, thus giving away 77 percent of the land entrusted to her!

Jewish immigration and its opposers (1919–29)

Between 1919 and 1929 the Jewish population almost tripled to a total of 160,000. However, the rioting of 1920–21 was minor compared to the violent outbreak in August 1929. Triggered by a challenge to Jewish worship at the Western Wall, Arabs murdered sixty-seven Jewish men, women and children in Hebron and destroyed the synagogues. This brought an end to a community which had dwelt in the city of the patriarchs for 2,000 years.

Thereafter, a British Parliamentary Commission of Enquiry recommended that Aliyah (Jewish immigration) and the purchase of land by Jews should be limited. In October 1929 a second White Paper foreshadowed new restrictions, although under the pressure of public and parliamentary indignation. Prime Minister Ramsey MacDonald rejected the extremism of the White Paper. *Jewish confidence, however, was by that time very badly shaken.*

First partition plan (1930–38)

1. A general strike, proclaimed in April 1937 by the Mufti of Jerusalem, led to heightened attacks on the Jews in Palestine.
2. Hosts of Arabs sympathetic to the Jewish cause were wiped out in 1938.
3. The Royal (Peel) Commission report of 1937 recommended partition of the area west of the Jordan into an Arab and Jewish state.
4. The opposing Arab Higher Committee was finally disbanded by the Mandatory Commission, and its leaders arrested and exiled to the Seychelles islands. However, the leader, the Mufti of

Jerusalem, Haj Amin Al-Husseini, fled to Syria and later joined the Nazis in Berlin in open collaboration to wipe out the Jews of Europe.

Closing the door to Jews in Europe

1. In November 1938, fearful that the Arabs might join the German–Italian axis in the event of war, Neville Chamberlain's government in Britain discarded the Peel Partition Plan, instead inviting Jewish and Arab leaders to roundtable talks. But the Arabs would not negotiate or come to these talks.
2. In the third White Paper published on 17 May 1939, the Colonial Secretarial laid down that annual Aliyah was not to exceed 10,000 Jews for the next five years. Thereafter its volume, if any, would depend upon Arab consent. *This virtually repudiated the Balfour Declaration of 1917.*

World War Two (1939–45)

It is significant that at the time when Nazi plans were crystallizing to wipe out the Jews of Europe, at the hands of the British the door to Palestine (the Jews' only escape route) virtually closed! It is also significant that although Prime Minister Neville Chamberlain returned to Britain in October 1938 triumphantly waving a piece of paper bearing his signature and those of Adolf Hitler and other European leaders, his "peace in our time" proved a very short-lived illusion. Around ten months later (fifteen weeks after the third White Paper of May 1939), Britain was at war with Germany. The face of the globe was to be darkened for almost six years. In spite of the foregoing, that world war saw Jewish volunteers from Palestine fighting side by side with British forces against Nazi Germany.

The Holocaust and its aftermath

Although the world has today lost its conscience about the Holocaust, the horrific truths concerning the systematic massacre of six million Jews by the Nazis during World War Two are well known. Nonetheless, a young generation is amongst us which hardly credits this greatest blot yet on human history. We are currently being lulled into a sleep and sense of complacency wherein circumstances could again permit and even approve similar unbelievable bestiality.

In 2007 there was news of a proposed scaling down of teaching on the Holocaust in schools, so as "not to cause offense" to Muslim pupils. This came only six years after Britain took a leading role (with Prime Minister Tony Blair present) in the international decision to establish an annual Holocaust Day (27 January) to commemorate the six million dead.

Did you realize that in the years immediately following the 1939–45 war, British efforts *against* Jewish immigration into Palestine redoubled? One would at least have thought that Jewish survivors of the Holocaust, who had suffered the most indescribable horrors, often losing their complete families, would have been unhesitatingly ushered and admitted into Palestine. But no! Almost 100,000 Jewish people, with no home in the world, denied entry to other countries, were also denied entry into Palestine by the British colonial rulers. (See the DVD *The Forsaken Promise.*[2])

But somehow, some of these desperate, homeless, bereaved and fleeing survivors were able to acquire old, unseaworthy ships in which to run the dangerous gauntlet of the British navy and air force in the Mediterranean Sea in their efforts to reach Palestine. However, few of these made it. Some ships were sunk, with the loss of many lives – *saved from the Holocaust, yet denied a place and a home in the world!*

Although God calls Zion the "apple of His eye" (Zechariah 2:8 NKJV), in the world's eyes Zion is called "an outcast – Zion for whom no one cares" (Jeremiah 30:17 NIV). In Britain, we cannot simply pull the curtain down on that period of history, nor can we, in our policies of expediency since then, purchase wealth at the expense of justice and righteousness. As a Church and as a nation, we need to confess and seriously to repent of all that we did.

An extract from the booklet *The Miracle of Israel* turns the clock back:

Herman Grabe, a German construction engineer, who worked in the
Ukraine at the time of the Jewish massacres, testified to what he saw
with his own eyes. He told how he and his foreman heard of 1,500
Jews at Dubno being killed daily. They drove out to the site and saw
large mounds of earth from pits that had been dug. There they witnessed Jews with regulation yellow patches on the front and back of
their clothes being driven off in trucks towards the pits. An SS man
with a whip ordered the men, women and children to disrobe.

Unprecedented horror

"Without screaming or weeping these people undressed [said Mr
Grabe], stood around in family groups, kissed each other, said fare-
wells, and waited for a sign from another SS man, who stood near
the pit, also with a whip in his hand. During the fifteen minutes that
I stood near I heard no complaint or plea for mercy. I watched a family of about eight persons, a man and a woman with their children of
about one, eight and ten and two grown-up daughters.

"An old woman with snow white hair was holding the one-year-old
child in her arms and singing to it and tickling it. The child was cooing
with delight. The couple were looking on with tears in their eyes. The
father was holding the hand of the boy about ten years old and speaking to him softly, the boy was fighting tears. The father pointed to the
sky, stroked his head, and seemed to explain something to him. At that
moment the SS man at the pit shouted something to his comrade. The
latter counted off about twenty persons and instructed them to get
behind the earth mound. Among them was the family which I have
mentioned. I well remember a girl, slim and with black hair, who as
she passed close to me pointed to herself and said, 'twenty-three.'

"I walked round the mound and found myself confronted by a
tremendous grave. People were closely wedged together and lying
on top of each other so that only their heads were visible. Nearly
all had blood running over their shoulders from their heads. Some
of the people shot were still moving. Some were lifting their arms
and turning their heads to show that they were still alive. The pit was
already two-thirds full. I estimated that it already contained about
1,000 people.

"I looked for the man who did the shooting. He was an SS man, who sat at the edge of the narrow pit, his feet dangling into the pit. He had a tommy-gun on his knees and was smoking a cigarette. The people, completely naked, went down some steps which were cut in the clay wall of the pit and clambered over the heads of the people lying there, to the place to which the SS man directed them. They lay down in front of the dead and injured people; some caressed those who were still alive and spoke to them in a low voice.

Down into the pit

"Then I heard a series of shots. I looked into the pit and saw that the bodies were twitching or the heads lying motionless on top of the bodies which lay before them. Blood was running away from their necks. I was surprised that I was not ordered away but I saw that there were two or three men in uniform nearby. The next batch was approaching already. They went down into the pit, lined themselves up against the previous victims and were shot. When I walked back around the mound I noticed another truckload of people who had just arrived. This time it included sick and infirm persons. An old, very thin woman, with terribly thin legs was undressed by others who were already naked, while two people held her up. The woman appeared to be paralyzed. The naked people carried the woman around the mound. I left with my foreman and drove back in my car to Dubno.

"On the morning of the next day, when I again visited the site, I saw about thirty naked people lying near the pit – about 30–50 metres away from it. Some of them were still alive; they looked straight in front of them with fixed stares and seemed to notice neither the chilliness of the morning nor the workers of my firm who stood around. A girl of about twenty spoke to me and asked me to give her clothes and help her escape. At that moment we heard a fast car approach, and I noticed that it was an SS Detail. I moved away to my site. Ten minutes later we heard shots from the vicinity of the pit. The Jews still alive had been ordered to throw the corpses into the pit; then they themselves had to lie down in it to be shot in the neck."

This first-hand report reveals only partly the hideousness of Hitler's hatred. As the United States armies penetrated the dark heart of Germany, they discovered and revealed to the world some examples of the most highly organised terror of all time. Reports began to flow in, and the world read in absolute horror the details of the death camps.

"There were two ovens here, each with six openings. The ovens are cold now, but before the Americans came their clean bright flame consumed between 150 and 200 people daily. And there are down in a cellar on a clean, white-washed wall many hooks jutting out near the low ceiling. Before we came, men were strung up on the hooks, pulled up till they choked. It took them a long time before they gave up the instinctive fight for breath, and there are scratches on the walls where they clawed vainly for support.

"We came up from the cellar and passed into another yard fenced in by a high wooden wall. There was a pile of bodies there, stacked more or less the way I stack my firewood back home, not too carefully. There were men and some of them were naked. They looked strange. Their mouths were open as though in pain and little streaks of blood flowed from their noses. A GI stared and stared and couldn't get one thought out of his mind, repeating it over and over. 'Those guys just starved to death. They just starved.'"

To counter this terrible threat to their people, Jewish underground leaders met together to inaugurate a full-scale programme of illegal immigration. So began a contest between the obstinate insistence of the British that Jews be kept out of Palestine and the Jews who knew their only chance to avoid the gas chambers of Hitler lay in escape to that land. It was a dreadful test between people who were on the same side in the war.

One of the first of the refugee ships to reach Tel-Aviv was the Tiger Hill. The ship ran aground on the beach on a Sabbath eve. The British trained machine guns on the people to keep them from disembarking. Two refugees were killed. Nevertheless, thousands of Tel Avivians waded in to help them. A large number of soldiers came on the scene to separate the refugees from the local inhabitants. They demanded identity cards, but the local inhabitants outwitted the British by lending their cards to the newcomers.

The flight of the immigrants was sometimes marked by heartbreaking tragedy. One ship arrived with 1,771 refugees who had lived for two months under terrible privations. The passengers were placed under arrest and transferred to the British ship Patria to be removed to a prison in the island of Mauritius in the Indian Ocean. Police guarded the docks so that none might leap ashore. Then came a terrific explosion. The ship sank rapidly. Before the eyes of a horrified population at Haifa, they saw the sea thick with the bodies of drowning refugees. Over 200 were drowned. It was rumoured at the time that the refugees blew up the ship rather than submit to the horrors of another prison camp.

There were ships crowded with refugees that never made it to Palestine. Some old vessels were leaking tubs that went down at sea. Others were torpedoed by the Germans. One vessel, the Struma, a river boat with 769 people aboard, waited two months for permits to proceed to Palestine. There was no response to their futile appeals. Finally the Turks ordered the ship out of the harbour. The vessel was without food or water, but it was tugged away into the open water. From its sides hung a banner, "Help!" A few hours later the leaky vessel sank. Out of 769 refugees only one survived. No wonder the hearts of the Hagana hardened. It was war on the White Paper. But as the Nazis tightened their grip on all of Europe, few Jews found it possible to escape.

The year 1945 came, and Allied armies were racing deep into Germany. The ghastly concentration camps of Buchenwald, Dachau, Bergen, and Belsen were liberated. The survivors, reduced to hollow-eyed skeletons, begged to be taken to Palestine. They had seen their loved ones taken to the gas chambers. They themselves had laboured as slaves under the lash to the point of starvation. Surely these pitiful creatures could be given their wish. But alas, it was not to be.[3]

The Jews battle for the right to exist

As we have seen, in view of these terrible experiences, during which six million Jews perished, it was hoped that with the ending of the war, the White Paper would be forgotten, and the surviving Jews would be given permission to emigrate to Palestine. *But fear of the Arabs still overruled all considerations.* To the shame of Britain, those refugees who entered Palestine without visas were herded into internment camps while their fate was debated by the government.

Churchill was favorable to the idea of Palestine being made a Jewish national homeland, but unfortunately, near the war's end, he was voted out of office. Nevertheless, the Labour Party had been friendly to the Zionist policy, and the Jews were hopeful. But help was not to come. Lord Ernest Bevin, who became Foreign Secretary, repudiated all the pledges made by Labour leaders during the previous ten years. President Truman sent an urgent request that 100,000 Jews be resettled in Palestine immediately. He was turned down.

In desperation, the Jews organized in self-defense. Underground vigilante groups were formed to protect Jewish communities from Arab attacks and to assist in the smuggling of refugees into the country. The Irgun was one of these parties. Its members sought to operate on an ethical level. Another group was called the "Stern Gang," after their leader Abraham Stern. Before the outbreak of World War Two, Stern was shot by the police.

From then on, his followers showed no restraint. The methods employed by members of the Stern Gang were greatly to be deplored, but under the circumstances one cannot be surprised at their conduct. They had seen Jewish immigrants at the doors of Palestine, in pitiful condition, not permitted to land, but instead turned back to meet the horrors of Hitler's Germany. When such things happen, one cannot expect people to think logically.

The British handover

After thirty years of oversight, the British government could find no solution whatever to the complete impasse of the Jewish–Arab Palestine question and took it to the United Nations. The fateful voting on 29 November 1947 and the outcome – the final formation of the Jewish State of Israel – are discussed in Chapter 6. Even in this voting, in spite of the Balfour Declaration and in spite of what the Bible should have taught us, the best Britain could do was to *abstain*! The table shows how the nations voted.

Table 5: Final voting on partitioning of Palestine

For:	Against:	Abstention:
Australia	Afghanistan	Argentina
Belgium	Cuba	Chile
Bolivia	Egypt	China
Brazil	Greece	Ethiopia
White Russia	India	Honduras
Canada	Iran	Mexico
Costa Rica	Iraq	United Kingdom
Czechoslovakia	Lebanon	Yugoslavia
Denmark	Pakistan	
Dominican Republic	Saudi Arabia	
Ecuador	Syria	
France	Turkey	
Guatemala	Yemen	
Haiti		
Iceland		
Liberia		
Luxembourg		
Netherlands		
New Zealand		
Nicaragua		
Norway		
Panama		
Paraguay		
Peru		
Philippines		
Poland		
Sweden		

(Continued)

Table 5: (Continued)

For:	Against:	Abstention:
Ukraine		
Union of South Africa		
Union of Soviet Socialist Republics (USSR)		
United States of America		
Uruguay		
Venezuela		

United Nations, Flushing Meadow, New York, 29 November 1947

As we well know, even this has not led to peace for the Israelis – far from it. But here we are concerned about Britain.

Although it is true that Britain has been a blessing and a safe harbor for many thousands of European Jews who gratefully acknowledge their indebtedness, it is also true that the lot fell upon Britain, God's appointed agent, to establish a homeland for His people. In this, and in compromising with the foes of Israel, we have most seriously obstructed God's purposes, and His coming judgments are hovering over us this very day.

Since 1947, we can no longer say that the sun never sets on the British Empire, nor that "Britannia rules the waves." For we do not now have an empire – it vanished almost overnight – and we certainly do not "rule the waves!" Once a world power to be feared and favored, Britain is now but one of the many members of the European Union, thereby increasingly losing our sovereignty, and often now elbowing for our minimal rights. There is no question that *this decline results from our neglect of and opposition to Israel*, past and present, particularly from within the Church.

What a disgrace that we are ashamed to be seen even as sympathetic to Israel and are reluctant to have any high Israeli official visit our country! The Lord's promise to Abraham has never been revoked:

> I will bless them that bless thee, and curse him that curseth thee.
>
> (Genesis 12:3 KJV)

Inasmuch as ye have done it [or not done it] unto one of the least of these my brethren, ye have done it [or not done it] unto me.

(Matthew 25:40 KJV; see also verse 45)

One notable speaker, Dr Clifford Hill, has declared:

> The nation is in disarray at its foundation with the break-up of family life. It is a pagan nation – multi-cultural, multi-religious. Whoever thought we would see a Hindu leader throwing rose petals over the capital, riding on an elephant, setting up temples in our nation? I have seen one church after another becoming a Hindu temple or a mosque in the inner city of London. The same thing has been happening in city after city of this land. We Christians share a large part of the responsibility for the paganizing of this nation.
>
> I tell you this: the Muslims, until they opened their great mosque in the heart of the capital city of this nation [i.e. in Regent's Park], for a number of years were renting Westminster Central Hall every Friday night to pray for the conversion of England to Islam! The headquarters of Methodism being used to pray for the conversion of England to Islam! Who ever heard of such a thing? When money becomes more important than faithfulness to the Word of God, the judgment of God hangs heavy over the Christian people of this land.[4]

A meeting of Christian television producers shared something of their anxiety over what was happening in the preparation stages for the opening of an additional television channel over fifty years ago. Bids were being made, with influences coming from the Arab world. The Muslims were really bidding to get in on the further channel. They had in mind the tremendously powerful effect on the life of this nation, were their hands on the religious teaching to be heard on that channel.

It appears that Muslims in Britain have been far more successful in acquiring control of the BBC which today ceaselessly promotes Islam on both radio and television. The BBC is an undisguised mouthpiece and platform for the spirit of Islam. *And Muslims are also adept with their impressive statistics showing their numbers in this country.*

The voice of the Church

We may hang our heads in shame at the political incompetence and cowardice shown in pursuing the course promised in 1917, but let us remember that Britain then and now owed its existence, and its ability to win World War One, to the work of Chaim Weizmann, a Jewish scientist. We must also realize that, in it all, the established Church has been silent to this very hour.

The onus of being a "shepherd" of Israel, as described in Ezekiel 34, falls on the Christian who has the Word of God, who seeks God's voice and God's will. If we, as the Church, say, in direct contravention of God's Word, that "we are the New Israel, the Israel of God," how can we simultaneously expect either that our government will act in accordance with God's Word for the true Israel of God, or that the Lord will hear our prayers on other matters?

While God is patient and long-suffering, He is speaking to Britain now on this matter. The Lord chose not only the British government to act for Him, but in the first place He also sought, and continues to seek, for the Church (His "militia," His "army" in Britain) to get involved.

> We wrestle not against flesh and blood, but against principalities, against powers, against the rulers of the darkness of this world, against spiritual wickedness in high places. Wherefore take unto you the whole armour of God.
>
> (Ephesians 6:10–13 KJV)

As has been aptly said before of this scripture, the truth so often is (concerning the Church) that "We wrestle not!" Although a spiritual battle of the highest significance rages before our very eyes, the Church (apart from some fine para-church organizations) on this matter is entirely asleep, ignorant, indifferent or (worse still) hostile! Yet *our destiny in Britain revolves around this issue*, as the opening text to this chapter clearly states:

> The nation or kingdom that will not serve you [Israel] will perish ...
>
> (Isaiah 60:12 NIV)

This warning is curt, concise and unambiguous. Do you believe it? And which church leader, which government leader, believes it? Therefore, even a "selfish" answer to the question "Why pray for Israel?" would be that it is in our own interests, in the interests of Britain and our spiritual standing with God, so to do!

Former British hindrances to Israel

1. Britain's sad record did not end in 1948 but continues to this day. In 1956, after Egypt had unilaterally nationalized the Suez Canal, Israel, France and Britain were involved in counter measures. Withdrawal was forced (this time under American pressure), leaving the Suez Canal in Egyptian hands and the sea artery closed to anything going to or from Israel.

2. In 1973, after the murderous, surprise all-out attack on Israel during Yom Kippur, where she was outnumbered 12:1 in personnel, and even more in tanks and armory (an attack, by the way, which nearly cost Israel her life), Britain, under the leadership of Prime Minister Ted Heath, specifically withheld Israel's much-needed, ship-loaded military spare parts that had been both ordered and paid for by Israel. One might have understood this, had Israel been the aggressor or were the same policy meted out to Israel's aggressors. It was not long afterward that the British government fell, and Ted Heath was out of office.

3. Neville Chamberlain's government had fallen in the same way in 1940 – one year after the third White Paper.

4. Anthony Eden lost his premiership just after the Suez crisis and withdrawal in 1956.

5. In 1982, a two-day visit to Israel (31 March–2 April) of the British Foreign Secretary, Lord Carrington, ended on a very sour note. It was his first visit, and the highest official British government visit

for many years. His insistence – and Israel's reluctance – that the PLO be included in any peace talks left relationships worse than when he had arrived. (The PLO does not give official recognition to Israel's right to exist.)

Within less than twelve hours, at six o'clock the next morning, Britain was facing a similar territorial crisis of her own, with the invasion of the Falkland Islands by Argentinian forces. The Argentinian claim was that the British annexation of the islands in 1833 had been by force and was illegal. This saw the urgent recall of the British Parliament to deal with perhaps the biggest crisis since World War Two, and the looming possibility of Britain's involvement in a war with Argentina over some territory of little consequence, 8,000 miles distant from the homeland. The war, of course, materialized. Was there some poetic justice here?

Within a matter of days, Lord Carrington had resigned – but what connection was there with attitudes to Israel in all of this?

6. President Anwar Sadat's demise occurred on the very day that he was celebrating his attack on Israel, precisely eight years earlier – in the Yom Kippur War which broke out on 6 October 1973. Sadat died by assassination on 6 October 1981. His celebration of that attack, only six months before the commencement of the Camp David Peace Agreement with Israel, arouses many serious questions on the value of that agreement.

One might at this point recall that in both the 1967 and 1973 wars there were many accounts of some mysterious, divine hand preserving Israel. In the former, Arab prisoners related how their arms had been paralyzed, preventing them from using their weapons against the Israelis! Secondly, no one can explain to this day why, in the 1973 war, the invading Syrian tanks did not just continue to sweep through the Golan Heights and Israel without stopping until they had reached the Mediterranean coast – thus severing Israel in two. What, or Who, allowed those twenty-four hours to Israel in order for her to regroup her own depleted and weary forces?

Is there a divine hand of love and jealousy preserving Israel? Is it the very heartbeat of God that we catch in Hosea's cry:

> How can I give you up, O Ephraim?
> How can I hand you over, O Israel?

(Hosea 11:8 RSV)

The story of Joseph

We all know the story of Joseph, sold into the hands of the Ishmaelites by his own brothers. His brothers were not happy about Joseph's dream, in which they were pictured as eventually bowing down and serving him. Their hatred led almost to his murder, and certainly to his being sold into Egypt.

It was in God's divine ordinance that those same brothers later had to go to their ostracized brother, Joseph, in order to survive. He held the key to their continued existence.

The situation has a parallel today. Many within the Church are, in selfish ways, "selling" Israel, Joseph's offspring, into Ishmaelite hands. With a gun in one hand, and an olive branch in the other, the arch-enemy of Israel says within the portals of the United Nations, "Of course, we want peace."

We in Britain, small nation though we may be, have sufficient light through God's Word, and power by God's strength, to speak up and to pray up. God will honor those denominational and church leaders who begin to teach and to pray openly, but with wisdom, on what God's Word says about Israel. There will unquestionably be opposition, but this is no license to remain silent.

If "the weapons of our warfare are not carnal, but mighty through God to the pulling down of strongholds" (2 Corinthians 10:4 KJV), then the time is here to use them!

The time of looking over our shoulders because the subject is so controversial or unpopular must end. Our *existence* as a nation depends upon God's blessing, which we cannot continue to expect without repenting and acting over our past follies in regard to Israel. A powerful little booklet, *A Nation Called by God*, is available, summarizing God's call to Britain, over five centuries, to be His "Cyrus" nation – His channel and shepherd nation to see Israel rebuilt![5]

Author's testimony

Since my founding of the ministry of Prayer For Israel under the hand of God in February 1969, thirty-four years of my directorship followed. It was the Six-Day War of 1967 that led to the formation of this first Christian "Zionist" work of its kind in Britain. It resulted in so many responding to the call to pray for the establishment, growth and maturity of the indigenous Body of Christ in Israel. In other words: Jewish people coming together in faith and forming Messianic fellowships.

It has to be at least a partly redeeming feature for Britain that, thirty years later, there were (apart from groups in other countries) over 400 prayer groups scattered across Britain, all interceding for God's ancient people. This is apart from many societies and people that have been raised to support and pray for Israel. These are a kind of seal on God's initial call to Britain – to be His "Cyrus" nation for the blessing and restoration of Israel.

At the very outset, through the precious Word of God, the Lord gave his blueprint to establish the home base; we were not to be traversing the globe in search of those to pray, but rather (at that stage) to let Him do the work.

> Set yourselves, stand ye still, and see the salvation of the Lord.
>
> (2 Chronicles 20:17 KJV)

It is amazing to see how God continually chooses "the foolish things of this world to confound the wise" (1 Corinthians 1:27 KJV). In my earlier years, nothing had been further from my Jewish mind than to get involved with Israel! That is why I can so confidently say today that the establishment of the work of Prayer For Israel was entirely of Him.

The calling was not merely one of setting up prayer groups, but also of teaching the Church in general. Just as I was initially with my *own* fixed ideas, *unaware* of my blindness to the Word of God, so today this seems to pervade many of us within the Church. I eventually confessed my unwillingness to be changed or to get involved, but at the same time telling God that *I wanted to do His will* (John 7:17). Subsequently, through His Word and Spirit, He taught and changed me. However, while there is a small but goodly remnant within Britain that do follow His prophetic Word and Spirit, the Lord is looking for a much wider and deeper response from the Church. To repeat: it was not by accident that Palestine fell into British hands in 1917.

I believe that the genuine heart and prophetic voice of God are contained in a vital prophetic word that was given back in February 1988, twenty years after I had personally come into the vision.

With a heart that feels deeply for Britain, that yearns for the Church in Britain through which one has received so much in the past, I reproduce this now (but keep it anonymous), trusting that it will reach leaders and laity alike, but particularly leaders. In my estimation, this is the utterance of the Spirit for then (1988) and for now – 2009.

Vision in the valley: a prophetic word that needs to be heard

Canterbury – 13 February 1988

This experience was in a time of prayer when I seemed to lapse into a kind of reverie, and I found myself experiencing a very vivid picture as an onlooker but it was extremely real. The picture of the Lord climbing up a mountain leading His followers. I was totally aware of this being the Lord, but as in other experiences of this kind, no actual identity was given to His person, so that I could not describe His appearance; it was totally irrelevant at the time. Nevertheless, I was aware of Him stopping and turning around to look back on His followers, only there were none.

Instead, right down at the bottom, there in the valley they all were, scurrying about in every conceivable direction in their thousands like great armies of tiny ants. Some groups of them were forming and heading off in different directions. It also appears that some groups were fighting with each other, but there was one major drift in particular – a great mass of people forming into a strong thick column surging up another mountain altogether on the opposite side of the valley, and heading in exactly the opposite direction from the Lord. It seemed as though the vast majority of people were more or less being pulled in that direction. The Lord was now wringing His hands in anguish.

There did, however, seem to be just a few people who were hesitant, and looking back discovering their mistake, and I saw people leaping off the road they were on but finding themselves in swamps and every kind of difficulty, not having set out in their right direction to begin with. The way back was going to be very perilous for those few.

When I had seen this picture I realized instantly that this was not just the populace at large but only referred to the Church, the actual followers of Christ. There was then also a great flow of words which came and these filled me with a deep sense of awe and heaviness, for it came to me that the words would be totally unacceptable by almost everyone who heard them. I will try to recall the words, as near as possible to the way I heard them. They came with a great rush and with a powerful sense of authority, so that at the end – still lying on the floor – I can remember saying over and over to myself, *"This is real. This is real."*

The words:

"I have the stench in My nostrils of Church history; yes, I say the stench in my nostrils. Can you not understand if I turn My head aside? The Church which calls itself by My name is drunken with the blood of the saints but particularly that of My ancient people, the people of the Covenant which I still honor. You do not discern the times and seasons, but My people are running around in circles... looking for minor self-indulgences... like dogs chasing their own tails instead of being where I am.

"Have I not given enough indication of what I am doing? Have I not miraculously preserved My ancient people and brought them back to the land on which I once walked and on which I will walk again in order to redeem them? To which land did I promise I would return? Yet many of you are joining with the hordes of hell in order to pervert My purposes. It is for the blood of the Jewish people that I grieve especially. The whole earth is again screaming with blood lust for them, and My followers are amongst them.

"Until there is repentance I can fulfill none of My promises of Spirit revival. There may instead come upon you times of great hardship, of a testing and a shaking until you cry out *"Where is God?"* Your enemies will laugh in your face and taunt you with the same words and you will feel deserted.

"There will be a great falling away but you must hang on to the end until My people truly repent and begin to share the global view that I have. I must have My people *where I am*, not deciding for Me *where they want Me to be*.

"Don't trust the opinions of the masses or of the media. Get back to My Word and hold tenaciously on to it and thus discern the times and My purposes, then I will be able to fulfill My promises."

If my people, who are called by my name, will humble themselves and pray and seek my face and turn from their wicked ways, *then* I will hear from heaven and will forgive their sin *and will heal their land*.

(2 Chronicles 7:14 NIV, emphasis added)

While God's judgments on Britain cannot be entirely averted, with true God-granted repentance, they can certainly be ameliorated.

Seek me and live ...

(Amos 5:4 NIV; see also verses 6, 14)

Notes

1. With grateful acknowledgment to the Israel Information Office, London, for permission to quote extracts from their book, *Facts about Israel*.
2. DVD *The Forsaken Promise* is available from CFI UK, PO Box 2687, Eastbourne, East Sussex BN22 7LZ, UK.
3. Gordon Lindsay, *The Miracle of Israel* (Christ for the Nations, Inc.), PO Box 769000, Dallas, Texas 75376/9000, USA, p. 34.
4. Dr Clifford Hill at the Family Bible Week, Elim Bible College, Capel, Surrey.
5. Booklet available from CFI, PO Box 2687, Eastbourne, East Sussex BN22 7LZ, UK.

CHAPTER 9

Whose Land?

This is what the Sovereign LORD says: In my burning zeal I have spoken against the rest of the nations, and against Edom, for with glee and with malice in their hearts they made my land their own possession so that they might plunder its pasture-land.

(Ezekiel 36:5 NIV)

No other single piece of territory, no other single subject, has so consistently filled the media over the last sixty years than this tiny sliver of land (less than 8,000 square miles, no bigger than Wales) – Israel! Even if standing close to a large map of the world, it is difficult to discern the tiny "thumbprint" that Israel represents at the very center. God's Word says of it, "How can Jacob survive? He is so small!" (Amos 7:2, 5 NIV), while elsewhere calling it the "navel of the world" (Ezekiel 38:12 - NASB margin).

One of the many "mysteries" of the Bible is Israel.

I do not want you, brethren, to be uninformed of this mystery – so that you will not be wise in your own estimation.

(Romans 11:25 NASB)

In this passage, the apostle Paul is implying that these mysteries (e.g. the mystery of Christ, the mystery of the gospel, the mystery of God, and the mystery of Israel) can *only* be understood through divine revelation.

Without that revelation, it is humanly impossible today to find one's way reliably through the flood of claims, and counter claims, about the land of Israel. To understand the "mystery of Israel" on which Paul writes three chapters in his epistle to the Romans (chapters 9, 10 and 11), the Word of God and the Holy Spirit (plus a teachable attitude) are indispensable.

While often interpreted in other ways, it seems clear that the "woman" of Revelation 12 is, in effect, Israel; she is "clothed with the sun" (Revelation 12:1 NIV), prophetically reflecting the coming glory of God. This presents the crown of twelve stars as being the twelve tribes of Israel – which incidentally are also specifically mentioned in Revelation 7. We find Revelation 12 drawing to a close with the words:

> And the serpent poured water like a river out of his mouth after the woman, so that he might cause her to be swept away with the flood [i.e. be destroyed].
>
> (Revelation 12:15 NASB)

I believe that, here, the flood of water represents the incessant negative, biased, distorted and lying media reports about Israel – the serpent's "mouth" being the plethora of media channels today under his control. Satan is also known as "the prince of the power of the air," (Ephesians 2:2 KJV) a fitting title for the one who controls the television and radio of this day and age.

The writer of this book was himself disinterested, and even confused, on the subject of Israel until, in 1967, he determined to set aside all other approaches and seek God through His Word. We are reminded, therefore, that in the final analysis, this is a struggle "not against flesh and blood, but against principalities, against powers, against the rulers of the darkness of this world, against spiritual wickedness in high places" (Ephesians 6:12 KJV). Ultimately, the struggle is not even between Arab and Jew, nor over a piece of territory, but over "*Allahu akbar!* God is most great!" Who is God? Who is sovereign and supreme: Jesus or Muhammad?

The goal on the one hand is:

1. the annihilation of the people of Israel;
2. the taking over of her land, frustrating the fulfillment of the prophecy that one day "His [Jesus'] feet will stand on the Mount of Olives" (Zechariah 14:4 NIV);
3. the elimination of Christians and the Church.

On the other hand, the goal, starting with the Temple site and the Mosque of Omar, is to spread the banner and sword of Islam throughout the earth.

These are some of the issues ensuing from the fearsome question, "Whose land?" Unlimited volumes have been written, and more will follow. Rhetoric will continue to swamp the audio-visual media. Voices, even Christian voices, will grow louder, to add to the flood that Satan will produce to obstruct God's purposes for Israel (and the Church) in these end-time days.

Paul tells us that he would not have us "ignorant of this mystery" (Romans 11:25 KJV). So, if you happen to be one of those who fall into that category, be honest and humble, go to God and His Word, and He will open your eyes and heart. He may also give you a loving heart for the Arabs, for the Muslims – as you realize that if you have any light on the matter, it comes to you *only* by the grace of God, not because of your stature or prowess!

God's imperishable Word: the "lamp in a dark place"

Before hearing even a little of what the media have been saying about the land of Israel, *be armed with God's Word*. Some 500 years before He shaped Abraham's descendants into a nation, God set aside the land of Canaan for them. He gave it *unconditionally*:

1. to Abraham (Genesis 12:1, 7; 13:14–17; 15:7 18–19);
2. to Abraham's son, Isaac (Genesis 26:2–5);
3. to Isaac's son, Jacob (Genesis 13–15). Affirmations followed to and from Joseph (Genesis 48:21; 50:24).

So, from the above we see that *ownership* of the land by Abraham (and his descendants through Isaac and Jacob) was unconditional. However, occupation of the land which they owned was later made conditional, with the warning that they would be widely scattered in the event of, for example, their turning to idolatry (Deuteronomy 4:25–27; 28:15ff. – see verse 64).

In the aftermath of that scattering, God speaks of His people turning to seek Him, and finding Him, having searched with all their hearts. Such prayers and such seeking were burned into Jewish hearts during the Holocaust, and that disaster (the world's greatest disaster thus far) actually led into *the world's greatest blessing since the death and resurrection of Christ in the first century – the rebirth of the nation of Israel!* As stated previously in this book, Rees Howells, formerly of the Bible College of Wales, called this "the greatest miracle since Pentecost."

That miraculous rebirth is foreshadowed in the same chapter which predicts the scattering of the Jewish people: Deuteronomy 4:29–31. Notice that it is "in distress" (i.e. during "Jacob's Tribulation," including perhaps the Holocaust) *in the latter days* that the people call on the Lord, and that He then remembers "the covenant with [their] fathers that He swore to them" (Deuteronomy 4:31 NASB), that is, the covenant with Abraham, Isaac and Jacob.

This is why we read that the Lord is a compassionate God, and we are repeatedly reminded in His Word that "His lovingkindness [Hebrew: *chesed*; mercy, steadfast love] is everlasting" and "endures forever" (Psalm 136:1 NASB, NKJV).

To the frequently asked question, "Where was God during the Holocaust?" we thus answer:

> In all their affliction *He* was afflicted.
> (Isaiah 63:9 NASB, emphasis added)

The title deed to the land (Psalm 105)

With Israel now back into place and at the center (together with the Church) of God's end-time purposes for this age, what assurance does the Word of God give us concerning all this fuss about the land of Israel? After all, most of the nations of the world are somewhere involved in resolving the conflict over this postage-stamp piece of territory. If Satan is behind the conflict, what does God say? We can do no better than to turn to Psalm 105, which is addressed to the "sons of Jacob" (Psalm 105:6 NASB). Verses 8 to 11 virtually read like the title deed to a property.

Putting verses 8 and 9 into the vernacular, and into the tense in which the original is written, we can read:

> He is remembering His covenant forever [continuous present], that which He commanded for 40,000 years ahead ["to a thousand generations"] from the days of Abraham, Isaac and Jacob. The covenant that he "cut" with Abraham was backed by His subsequent oath to Isaac, and later confirmed by His statute to Jacob, and then additionally sealed to Jacob after his name was changed to "Israel," and this covenant was to be everlasting [i.e. circumstances, and the passage of time, would not wipe it out nor change it].
>
> (Psalm 105:8–10, paraphrased)

And the essence of the covenant – its core – was:

> To you [Abraham, Isaac and Jacob] I will give the land of Canaan
> As the portion [the measuring line] of your inheritance.
> (Psalm 105:11 NASB)

In the original Hebrew, there is a seven-fold building up of God's commitment to give the land – and the whole of this is found, repeated for a second time, in 1 Chronicles 16:15–18. The Holy Spirit does not want us to miss this, so, in spite of Israel's sin, rebellion and unworthiness, He *twice* inscribes this record of His faithfulness into Holy Writ – to be noted by His Church and by the people of Israel! Even so, we *still* misread it!

It is most important to discern that, when the Lord Jesus, after His death and resurrection, said three times to Peter, "Do you love

Me? ... Feed My sheep" (John 21:15–17 NASB), He stipulated each time, "My sheep [or lambs]," not "the Church," not "the world," but "My sheep."

In Ezekiel 34, the chapter with correction and direction for the shepherds of Israel, "My sheep" or "My flock" are mentioned fourteen times! This is followed by the rebuke of Edom (i.e. Islam) in Ezekiel 35, and the regathering of Israel to her land in chapter 36. Do you see the continuity with which the Lord is speaking to His Church?

In our opening text (Ezekiel 36:5), Edom is mentioned. While initially "Edom" was another name for Esau, in following its usage in the Word and noting the heavy judgments pronounced thereon (embracing also "Mount Seir"), we need to ask ourselves about its present application. While I am personally thrilled that so many Muslims are coming to the Lord today, we must see the many prophecies concerning Edom and Mount Seir as being directed at Islam and its proponents (Numbers 24:18; Joel 3:19).

In that connection, the book of Obadiah is directly relevant. While being the Bible's shortest book and prophecy, it is awesome and uncompromisingly direct concerning the vengeance of the Lord and Israel. As the Church here in Britain, we need to truly fast and pray, and hear what the Spirit is saying. A triumphalist attitude will cause us not to hear. The Lord is today saying:

> I dwell on a high and holy place,
> And also with the contrite and lowly of spirit.
>
> (Isaiah 57:15 NASB)

As Bible believers, *we cannot spiritualize our opening text wherein God is calling Israel "my land."* He is angry with nations appropriating it for their own ends. In the very same chapter, speaking to re-gathered Jews, He further refers to Israel as "your *own* land" and "the land that I gave to *your fathers* [i.e. Abraham, Isaac and Jacob]" (Ezekiel 36:24, 28 KJV, emphasis added).

As mentioned elsewhere, that such an insignificantly small piece of territory – no bigger than Wales – should continue to arouse such bitter contention amongst its well-endowed neighbors is quite astonishing, to put it mildly. What are some of the myths or false claims that are being made?

"Palestine"

While this name was deliberately applied by the Romans in the first century to hide and obliterate Jewish ownership of the land of Israel, *nowhere in the Bible does the land bear that name*, which itself is derived from that of Israel's traditional enemies – the Philistines.

"Palestine" was never an Arab country. One of the myths of our time is that Israel, before it was settled by the "alien" Jews and "stolen" from the Arabs, was an independent state called "Palestine," whose majority residents were Muslim "Palestinians." However, the truth can be easily and historically seen.

Until the defeat by Britain of the Ottoman (Turkish) Empire in World War One, there was *no* geopolitical entity called "Palestine," *no* Arab nation ever set historical roots on this soil, and *no* national claim was ever made to the territory by any national group, other than the Jews!

Between the expulsion of the Jews by the Romans in AD 70 to 132, and the defeat of the Ottomans in 1918, Israel ("Palestine") was occupied by fourteen conquerors over thirteen centuries until, in 1948, the Jews once again declared their independence.

Thus, *during the entire period of recorded history, "Palestine" was never ruled by so-called "Palestinians,"* the name adopted today by the Muslim residents of the Holy Land. The rule of the various Muslim caliphates, which was a foreign rule, extended for a period of 432 years. Jewish rule of "Palestine" extended for over a period of 2,000 years.

The inhabitants of the land consisted of the conquering soldiers and their slaves, and only during the Muslim conquest of the area were these diverse ethnic inhabitants compelled to accept Islam and the Arabic tongue, or otherwise be put to the sword. The Jews, on the other hand, are in fact the sole survivors of the ancient inhabitants of "Palestine" to have maintained an uninterrupted link with the land since the dawn of recorded history.

It is one of the failures of our media today that, while almost complete acceptance is granted to an absurd, fabricated lie, no attention at all is paid to the fascinating story of the Jewish families and communities who have resided in the Holy Land without interruption since Biblical times. These people have, throughout hundreds and thousands of years, kept their national claim to God's given ownership of their homeland.

Arabs recognize Jewish sovereignty

The above facts were well known and publicly recognized by the international community in 1919, during the Allied Peace Conference in Paris, to which residents of the Middle East – Muslims as well as the Jewish people – were invited. At this conference, Emir (Crown Prince) Feisal, son of King Hussein (great-grandfather of the late King Hussein of Jordan), who headed the Muslim delegation, agreed that "Palestine" should be earmarked as the specific area in which Jewish sovereignty was to mature.

He announced his acceptance of the Balfour Declaration of 2 November 1917 and concluded an agreement with the World Zionist Organization, confirming that "all such measures shall be adopted as will afford the fullest guarantee of carrying into effect the British government's Balfour Declaration."

These same sentiments were later expressed by Emir Feisal in a letter (dated 3 March 1919) to Professor Felix Frankfurter, Justice of the United States Supreme Court (emphasis added):

> Our deputation here in Paris is fully acquainted with the proposals submitted by the Zionist organisation to the Peace Conference, and we regard them as modest and proper. We will do our best, insofar as we are concerned, to help them through. *We will wish the Jews a most hearty welcome.*

Jewish areas reduced

The two sets of promises officially made by Britain – one to the Muslims and the other to the Jews – were originally fully reconcilable.

The interesting historical fact is that between World War One and the UN partition of "Palestine" in 1947, British promises to the Muslims were over-fulfilled, while their promises to the Jews were constantly violated and whittled down. Far from being the victims of imperialism, the Muslims were handsomely rewarded when twenty sovereign states were artificially established by the British after carving up the former Turkish Empire. These new countries had no previous national history or independent culture.

The development of the part of "Palestine" allocated by the major powers for Jewish sovereignty took a different course. The area originally designated and agreed to by Hussein and Feisal was first reduced by four-fifths. Four-fifths of the Jewish homeland were given in a "land for peace" agreement, and on this land the present kingdom of Jordan was established. *On one fifth of the remaining land, the democratic country of Israel exists today.* In 1948, in the face of seven invading armies, Israel declared independence. The State of Israel consists of less than 8,300 square miles. Against this, only five Muslim states – Syria, Lebanon, Saudi Arabia, Jordan and Iraq – cover an area of 1,200,000 square miles!

It should be pointed out here that, at that time, over 70 percent of today's Israel consisted of Crown lands transferred from the outgoing Ottoman power to the incoming British Mandatory Authority. The remaining 30 percent of the land was largely swamp and barren hillside. It was in these areas that Jewish settlement began through land purchased from absent Muslim owners. *At no time did the Jews seek to displace the indigenous Muslim population.*

Under the Mandate granted to Britain by the League of Nations (forerunner to the UN), the Jewish population continued to grow, but while the immigration of Jews was progressively restricted, that of Muslims from the surrounding countries (e.g. Syria and Jordan) was completely free. As a result, attracted by the Jewish development of the country, the Muslim population increased rapidly and had attained majority by 1947.

(Conversely, Jewish immigration into the newly formed state of Transjordan/Jordan was totally barred – and remains so to this day.)

Palestinian Arabs never a nation

"Palestinian" Arab nationalism today is a product of comparatively recent political and religious currents. Until the 1920s, no such national community had even existed in "Palestine." This is why the Balfour Declaration and the League of Nations Mandate charged the Jews of the "national home" with guaranteeing the civil and religious rights of other inhabitants. *No mention was made of any national rights of other inhabitants, as it was recognized that the only national claim to the area was made by Jews.*

But the fiction of Palestinian nationality is still being exploited. If the "Palestinians" were in fact a separate nationality, then their anger over the past sixty years would have been directed as much against Jordan and Egypt as against Israel. It was the invading forces of these armies which captured (for example, in the 1948 war) a substantial portion of the territory allotted under the UN plan to the "Palestinian" Muslims. This included the West Bank, which was occupied by the Jordanian army and added to their kingdom, and the Gaza Strip, which was seized by the Egyptians.

The only people who have, in fact, maintained an historic connection with the area called "Palestine," over a period of 2,000 years, are the Jews. The Bible *never* uses the term "Palestine," but invariably calls this land "Judah" or "Israel."

The Jewish right to the land of Israel is based not only on history and the Bible, but on the physical process of the work, carried out by Jews, which transformed it into an area capable of supporting life. So much of the present fruitful land of Israel was rescued in the late 1800s and early 1900s from its centuries-old, deadly swamp.

Pray for the Arab people

Our calling to intercede for Israel and the Jewish people does not carry with it any suggestion that we rule the Arab people out of the realm of our love, prayer and compassion. First, we all know that it is God's sure desire for all people to be saved and to come to a knowledge of the truth.

Secondly, applicable to ourselves and to others, there is always the exhortation of the Lord himself:

> Love your enemies and pray for those who persecute you, that you may be the sons of your Father in heaven ... If you love those who love you, what reward will you get?
>
> (Matthew 5:44–46 NIV)

Muslims, no less than the rest of humankind, need the divine revelation of the gospel. The god of this world is the one who blinds all to this; it is against him that we wrestle. And wrestling matches are "all-out" unclean affairs! *The spirit of Islam is perhaps the most serious opponent with which we have to deal in the days ahead.*

There are many fine Arab Christians in the Middle East. It is not an easy road for them to take, faced with much opposition from their Arab brethren. Any scriptural thought of Israel as "God's land," or the "land of the Jews," is hard for them to accept in the present situation. At the same time, with escalating opposition from Islamic quarters, the Arab Christian population of the Middle East is being rapidly reduced as many flee to save their lives.

The media in the West

Whatever Israel may have achieved in the world of technology, at the moment she is by no means Master of Arts in diplomacy. She does not have the funds to counter the massive billion-dollar propaganda machine that the Arabs are using to permeate our Western culture, education, economy and politics; our radio, television, newspapers; and even our Christian faith.

Additionally, on top of limited finance, there is a great lack of force and finesse in Israeli diplomacy. The honest bluntness of the average Jew may be commendable, but in the world of politics it is the well-chosen words that so often win the day. Other than Benjamin Netanyahu, there are no notable Israeli spokesmen in that realm today.

However, if Israel has lost its faith in UN proclamations, we can hardly blame her. From the establishment of the State in 1947–48, right through the many successive wars, not *one* of the armistices called has seen any real peace.

Because the change has been gradual, many perhaps do not feel that the Western press today has a pro-Arab, pro-Islamic leaning, but this is actually the case. It is interesting to note that one of the mouthpieces of Islam, *New Horizon*, reported on 3 December 1979 that the Islamic Press Union had decided to monitor the Western press and to identify and name the papers which persistently indulge in malicious and mischievous propaganda against Islam and the Muslim world. To quote:

> The IPU shall communicate every month the names of such papers to the Information Ministries of the 42 Muslim countries besides the airlines, banks, insurance corporations, shipping lines and other major institutions of the Muslim World, and recommend them to withhold patronage from such papers.[1]

Given the present inaccuracies and imbalance of much Western reporting on the Middle East, it is apparent that this veiled threat is not without considerable effect. One of the characteristics of Islam is that it cannot bear reproach or criticism, hence the bid to muzzle the editor. We need to see through this veil in considering "Whose land?"

Israel the "aggressor"

One clear example of misreporting lies in the Western presentation of the March–April 1982 disturbances on the West Bank. One leading British newspaper boldly proclaimed on its front page: "Israeli soldiers kill Arab," while radio reports carried a similar story. What was not mentioned was the intrigue behind the disturbances, and the deliberate fostering of unrest on the West Bank by elements outside of Israel. For example: "The Jordanian Government warned the [West Bank] population to withdraw from the Israeli-sponsored civic organisations and threatened them with treason proceedings and the death penalty if they did not comply."[2]

These organizations were "village leagues" – self-help groups set up among the Arabs to provide a variety of facilities for rural Arab communities. The simultaneous dismissal by Israeli authorities of several Arab mayors was, according to the Israelis, on account of their collaboration with the PLO and certain influences from abroad, leading to the disturbances.

An articulate and politically experienced Arab, Mustafa Dudein, founder of the Hebron League, at his own personal request met with Menachem Begin, Israeli Prime Minister, only days earlier. In a later radio interview, Dudein alleged that,

> Saudi Arabia was behind the Jordanian move against the leagues … the Saudis had threatened to cut off support to the Hashemite throne unless Amman helped the PLO to counter the Leagues, which are acknowledged to be a serious threat to the PLO role in the area.[3]

The media and Israeli diplomacy

Although Israel has expertise in aerial and field warfare, her victories in the war of words have been absent. In spite of incessant demands for Arab autonomy and self-determination in Judea and Samaria (the West Bank), no one has dared to declare that the Arabs do not enjoy this option in their own countries. We have not seen it in Syria, Saudi Arabia, Egypt, Iraq or Libya – Israel's bitterest foes in earlier years. No one has said (and the West has not realized) that:

1. the only democracy in the Middle East is Israel;
2. the only country in the Middle East where Arabs do enjoy political, civic and private rights is Israel.

The media and Arab well-being

Were the media and the Arab nations to be truly enlightened, they would at once discern that a secure Israel is the one thing keeping Russia out of the Middle East. With Israel removed from the scene, the Russian takeover of the Arab states would be but a matter of time.

Her respect for the Muslim people has been seen in her earlier cruel endeavor to occupy Afghanistan. Instead of plotting endlessly for the destruction of Israel, the Arab nations should foster, feed and sustain it ... even if only for their own well-being!

Whose land?

This question is not raised in order to establish some political point, but rather to direct us in prayer. We need the heart of God for this. It is of Himself that He says:

> I am very jealous for Jerusalem and for Zion, but I am very angry with the nations that feel secure.
>
> (Zechariah 1:14–15 NIV)

Let us look at what seems to lie behind God's anger:

1. **1922:** In a policy of appeasement, from the territory given in Mandate to Britain by the League of Nations to form a Jewish homeland, Britain handed over 35,222 of the total of 45,760 square miles of Palestine (75 percent) to the Hashemite Emir Abdullah. He thus formed what is now called Jordan.
2. **1947:** Thus the Palestine partitioned by the UN in 1947 was of fractional size compared to the mandated territory entrusted to Britain in 1922. Nonetheless, both an Arab and Jewish state were declared for the area.
3. **1948:** On 14 May, when Israel (a nation composed of world refugees and death-camp survivors) finally came into being, one would have expected the world's conscience to have been so stirred that no effort would have been spared to rehouse, relocate and re-equip the Jewish outcasts. But when the Arab aerial and tank bombardments came on the virtually unarmed, fledgling nation (one day after its official birth!), the United Nations were voiceless and powerless to help.
4. **May 1948:** Under Arab direction, people using loudhailers were driven into all Arab sectors of western Palestine calling on all Arabs

to leave their homes at once, due to the impending Arab attack aimed at the destruction of Israel. *The Jewish authorities pleaded with the Arab residents not to leave.* While many complied, 500,000–600,000 still fled.

The Arab plan to destroy Israel did not succeed, so the plans for the fleeing Arabs to return also went astray. Those Arab "refugees" could and should, in any case, have been easily resettled in Jordan, Syria, Lebanon or elsewhere. But they were kept in shocking, appalling conditions as a political pawn. The amazing thing is that the West, via the UN, still pays the lion's share in their upkeep, while the wealthier Arab parent-nations contribute a minor fraction.

5. **May 1948–July 1949:** From the time of the attack by seven Arab states until July 1949, there were several ceasefire agreements and truces, all of which were broken. Egypt took over Gaza in 1948, but this was under legal entitlement and it became "occupied territory." Similarly, in February 1949, Jordan seized the West Bank areas of Judea and Samaria. Their later (1950) annexation of this land almost caused their expulsion from the Arab League, the anger of other Arab states being so intense.

6. **1950–56:** A Western tripartite agreement to control the arms flow to the Middle East proved impotent when in September 1955, Czechoslovakia and Egypt concluded a massive arms deal. This was a major cause of the 1956 Sinai War wherein President Nasser gathered his forces to attack Israel, and France and Britain lost control of the Suez Canal. Czechoslovakia later came under the heel of the Soviet invaders. Israel was saved from this Egyptian attack.

7. **1967:** For the second time, the "peacekeeping" forces of the UN withdrew from the Sinai at President Nasser's request, allowing Egypt to gather again far more strongly – this time aided by Syria – in order to "annihilate Israel" and "drive them into the sea." A lightning six-day war followed, which Israel miraculously won, and this led to their conquest of territories that had been used as springboards for terrorist activities into Israel over the preceding nineteen years.

Not a word of censure came from the UN against the loudly proclaimed Arab intentions. Censure came *only when Israel gained the upper hand*, and world powers bade her to cease her "attack." However, UN Resolution 242, which followed, has never been implemented or accepted by Israel's Arab neighbors! It was during this undesired and unprovoked war of self-defense that Israel gained control of the Sinai, Judea and Samaria. Furthermore, upon Jordan entering the war (despite Israel's plea that it should remain neutral), East Jerusalem fell into Jewish hands, bringing the city under Jewish control for the first time in almost 2,500 years.

8. **1973:** The unprovoked, surprise all-out attack on Israel by Egypt and Syria on 6 October 1973 nearly cost Israel her life. She knew, as her Prime Minister Golda Meir said at the time, that Israel has to lose only one war, and its survival will be no more. This became known as the Yom Kippur War. The day of attack was *Yom Kippur* – the Day of Atonement.

There was no word of censure from the UN until, at great cost in terms of lives lost, Israel somehow gained the upper hand in throwing back the invaders in the Golan Heights. In doing so, she advanced to within forty kilometers of Damascus in the north, and encircled the Egyptian third army in the south.

Not until this latter point did the UN vote for a ceasefire! Not until Israel was in a position to exert her own terms was the UN voice heard, telling Israel to withdraw. The preceding weeks – when the knife was at Israel's throat – had seen no flicker of concern from the UN. The UN today is still the platform of "international justice and law."

Relevant to that, it is no wonder that we read (in relation to Zion):

Justice is turned back,
And righteousness stands afar off ...
So truth fails,
And he who departs from evil makes himself a prey ...
Then the LORD saw it, and it displeased Him
That there was no justice.
He ... wondered [He was astonished] that there was no intercessor.
(Isaiah 59:14–16 NKJV; see also verse 20)

This is why God is angry. He says:

> I am very jealous for Jerusalem and for Zion, but I am very angry with
> the nations that feel secure ... they have added to the calamity.
>
> (Zechariah 1:14–15 NIV)

What is the calamity? Israel's sixty years of total insecurity, while others pass by as mere onlookers.

9. **28 October 1977:** The UN voted 131:1 to censure Israel. The single vote was Israel voting for herself! What was the voting for? An Egyptian resolution had been adopted declaring that "the Jewish settlements have no legal validity" in the territories occupied by Israel during and since the Six-Day War of June 1967.

Retribution and the nations

In 1974, within a few months of the Yom Kippur War and using the weapon of the oil barrel, the Islamic world forced the West into an economic recession of traumatic proportions. The price of motor fuel has skyrocketed since then.

Henry Kissinger writes:

> Never before in history has such a group of relatively weak nations
> been able to impose, with so little protest, such a dramatic change in
> the way of life of the overwhelming majority of mankind. The poetic
> justice, if such it is, is that this "achievement" threatens their own [the
> Arabs'] stability. A perception that may gradually be dawning. Few
> political structures can sustain the accelerated rate of growth made
> possible by such an enormous transfer of wealth. Dislocations are
> bound to occur.[4]

The Western world and Christendom will be making a serious mistake if we think we can be dispassionate and uninvolved spectators in the present Middle East impasse on the question of "Whose land?"

Whether or not Israel is a righteous nation is not the subject in hand. What matters is that she happens to be God's touchstone – whether we like it or not. She is God's yardstick for testing the genuineness of our love for God.

> After he has honored me and sent me against the nations that have plundered you – for whoever touches you touches the apple of his eye – I will surely raise my hand against them.
>
> (Zechariah 2:8 NIV)

The real problem

If we are to understand the will of the Lord, we will see the Middle East not merely as some huge political crisis, but rather as a battle of light against darkness, of right against wrong – the greatest such battle since Satan unleashed his fury against Israel's Messiah and now against Messiah's own people and land.

The core of the "problem" lies not in the territory that Israel holds, whether more or less, but *in her very existence*.

The threat to Satan's kingdom of a spiritually restored Israel, at present heralded by its physical restoration, is something Satan is resisting with all the ferocity he can muster. The future event of Messiah's return, and His world rule from Jerusalem (Jeremiah 3:17), are equally unpalatable. The Church, including us as individuals, needs to be aware of this and of what the Bible tells us: nations are to be judged at Messiah's return by their attitude to Israel and the Jews – God's touchstone. Many will be surprisingly shattered:

> The LORD's indignation is against all the nations …
> For the LORD has a day of vengeance,
> A year of recompense for the cause of Zion.
>
> (Isaiah 34:2, 8 NASB)

At the very beginning of His ministry, Jesus briefly referred to this much later "day of vengeance" (see Isaiah 61:2b). Bearing in mind the Lord's own Jewish brethren, it is fascinating and rewarding to study what He shares – just before His crucifixion – on this subject. He calls us to care, not only for believers, but also for His "brothers:"

> "Lord, when did we see you hungry and feed you, or thirsty and give you something to drink? When did we see you a stranger and invite you in, or needing clothes and clothe you?" ...
> The King will reply, "I tell you the truth, *whatever you did for one of the least of these brothers of mine, you did for me.*"
>
> (Matthew 25:37–40 NIV, emphasis added)

If we are considering the shortcomings of the Jewish people, we might remember that Jesus does not refer to what great acts we do for great people but rather to little acts for the least of his brethren. In other words, our smallest deeds are noted, let alone the great ones. This is particularly applicable to the attitudes of nations towards Israel, as well as those of individuals.

International law

1. That the victim of aggression should restore the means of aggression is not only preposterous but immoral. It is a game in which the aggressor cannot lose and the victim cannot win. Such a game can only encourage the wicked. Yet no Israeli leader has insisted in any international forum that what the nations expect or demand of Israel – withdrawal to the 1949/67 Armistice lines – not only violates simple justice, but is contrary to international practice.[5]
2. The facts of the June 1967 Six-Day War demonstrate that Israel acted defensively against the threat and use of force against her by her Arab neighbours ... The facts of the 1948 hostilities between the Arab invaders of Palestine and the nascent state of Israel, further demonstrate that Egypt's seizure of the Gaza Strip, and Jordan's seizure and subsequent annexation of the West Bank and the Old City of Jerusalem, were unlawful ... It follows that the Egyptian occupation of Gaza, and the Jordanian annexation of the West Bank and Jerusalem, could not vest in Egypt and Jordan lawful, indefinite control, whether as occupying power or as sovereign. *Ex injuria jus non oritur.*[6]

3. The only two nations that recognized Jordan's annexation of Judea and Samaria in 1950 were Pakistan and Great Britain. (Britain did not recognize Jordan's seizure of East Jerusalem which had been earmarked by the UN to become an international city in 1948.) Since Jordan never had legal title to Judea and Samaria, the Geneva Convention governing this subject contains no restriction on the freedom of persons taking up residence in such areas in question. This means that Israel has a perfect legal right to establish settlements in Judea and Samaria without prejudging the positioning of final borders.

Israel's "withdrawal policy"

The withdrawal policy followed repeatedly by Israel since 1949 has never led to peace, but rather to renewed and heightened attacks. There is no indication of a change of heart in her foes to suggest that the future could ever be different.

1. The 1949 Armistice lines represented withdrawal by Israel on all fronts after the 1948–49 war.
2. Israel's withdrawal from the Sinai in 1957 left the way open for Egypt's second attack in 1967.
3. Withdrawal to the 1967 lines in central Israel would leave her with a narrow strip of land on the west coast that could be severed in two in a matter of minutes by any force stationed in the West Bank.
4. Withdrawal from the 1973 Yom Kippur War limits did not bring true peace either.
5. The Camp David "peace" agreement, marking Israel's withdrawal yet again from the Sinai, led only to deteriorating relationships with Israel's neighbors, not to improvement.

The declared Arab aim

Notwithstanding the Camp David Peace Treaty signed by President Anwar Sadat of Egypt in September 1978, a few weeks later (4 December) Sadat's Deputy Prime Minister, Fakhri Makram Abid, declared:

> The Peace Treaty with Israel is not the end but only a framework realising the aims of the Arabs ... In the future we shall demand of Israel

to relinquish its Zionist goals – to abolish its law of return, to abandon the idea of its historical rights to the land of Israel and ... to stop the immigration of Jews to Israel.[7]

Thus, apart from requiring Israel to abandon any sovereign rights, this demand also requires Israel to throw overboard any hope or trust in the Holy Scriptures that are her very birthright.

The Sinai withdrawal (April 1982)

Just as the 1957 withdrawal of the Israeli forces from Sinai brought no long-lasting results, the UN forces obligingly vacating at President Nasser's request in May 1957, one cannot avoid some serious misgivings today over the outcome of the Camp David Peace Agreement, whether it be that of September 1978 or the later agreement of 1993.

An indication of the media's total lack of appreciation and understanding of just what Israel has sacrificed is given by the incredible suggestion that the assassination of Anwar Sadat was due not to Egyptian terrorists, but to the lack of "give" by the Israeli government![8]

1. During the withdrawal, apart from an enormous increase in security risks, Israel met a bill of over £5,250,000,000 ($9 billion) for the cost of relocating its roads, warning systems, armed forces, etc., in the Negev, coupled with the almost complete loss of £10 billion ($17 billion) invested in the Sinai from 1968–78.
2. Egypt received, practically free, several million pounds worth of modern buildings and modern towns – Israel's earlier investment.
3. In return Israel received a piece of paper termed a "peace agreement."

Even an international force that would fulfil its function conscientiously will be of little value for keeping the peace when Egypt decides together with other Arab states to launch war on Israel!

When President Sadat signed the peace treaty and agreed to the stationing of a multi-national force in Sinai, he also launched Egypt on an arms-purchasing spree, substantially strengthening her tank and air forces, and ordered the digging of a tunnel under the Suez Canal.

There can have been no doubt in his mind that, faced by Egyptian determination to go to war, such a multi-national force would be no obstacle. Which government – British or Italian, French or Dutch – would risk the storm of public protest and obloquy at the hazards to which its sons would be exposed in protecting the State of Israel against attack? If the Egyptian government orders them out they will leave with alacrity.[9]

As we look back, it becomes plain that the Arab government regarded the 1957 arrangements merely as a breathing space, enabling them to gather strength for a new assault.[10]

That assault came in 1967. Egyptian forces moved into Sinai on 14 May. The Tiran Straits were blocked to Israeli ships and on 18 May Nasser ordered the removal of the UN Emergency Forces. The UN Secretary General, ignoring all the procedures and safeguards laid down for their force and, indeed, the very reason for its existence, acceded instantly to this order!

Israel's attitude to the peacekeeping functions of the UN has been traumatically affected by its experience. What is the use of a fire brigade which vanishes from the scene as soon as the first smoke and flames appear?[11]

What happened in 1967? Then Israel, still believing in the validity of international assurances, turned to the Security Council for action against Egypt's flagrant violation of the 1957 undertakings and of the UN Charter. Then, all that happened was, in Abba Eban's words, a "desultory debate which sometimes reached a point of levity."

As in 1948 – and again subsequently in 1973 – the UN did not lift a finger while all the world waited, in agony or hope, for the Arabs to destroy Israel.

Now, in 1982, the European governments to be represented were not even formally neutral. They were all on the side of the Arabs, accepting the guidance of Saudi Arabia. [12]

They were all parties to the Venice Declaration which called at the time for Israeli surrender of Judea, Samaria and Gaza. They consequently saw a just cause in a renewed Arab effort to force Israel out of these areas.

Who are the PLO?

Originally claiming to be the mouthpiece for the many thousands of "refugees" who left Israel at the call of their Arab brothers in May 1948, the Palestine Liberation Organization was funded and founded by Egypt in 1964 in the Gaza Strip. Since then, its emphasis has shifted from the "refugee" problem to the national struggle for self-determination.

While Yasser Arafat headed the PLO, there were a number of competing organizations from Palestinians in various Arab states and this is still the case.

The problem of refugees was directly the result of the 1948 conflict, and not the cause of it, and even then (to take the words of an Arab spokesman at the time), the result of Arab pressure, *not* Israeli attack. "The fact that there are these refugees is the direct consequence of the act of the Arab states in opposing partition and the Jewish State."

The PLO voice

It is perhaps superfluous today to say that the PLO has been a fully armed, well-financed and well-trained terrorist organization, formerly given full diplomatic status by Russia, where most of its training took place. Although it claimed for many years claimed to be the one legitimate voice for the combined Arab states and for the Palestinian Arabs of Israel, this was not, in fact, the case. While all Arab states have been united against Israel, there has been considerable dissension from time to time between competing Palestinian "liberation" groups, and between these and the various Arab states. Further, the PLO is not an authorized voice for all the Arabs in Israel. Many Arabs there are content under Israeli rule, even within the disputed areas of Judea and Samaria.

The West has come to regard the PLO, whose avowed and published main aim is the destruction of Israel, as a legal entity. It has been allowed to set up offices in many European cities, including the British capital. From these centers, attacks have been made on all sorts of Jewish targets in many places. They include the total destruction of a school bus and its children in Maalot in 1981, and attacks on a Jewish children's holiday bus in Antwerp in July 1980, on synagogues in Paris and Austria in September 1980 and August 1981,and on a gathering outside a synagogue in Antwerp in October 1981. These unreproved, unchecked examples have paved the way for the world terrorism now prevailing. In 1980 the target was children's buses, but two decades later, with the PLO rejoicing in the background in Israel, it was the twin towers of the World Trade Center in New York on 11 September 2001.

The British, American and other governments consider the PLO to be a moderate organization which should be brought into peace talks. The statement "recognition of Israel is unthinkable," made by a high official of the PLO, is symbolic of its general statements and outlook.

Hamas, the more recent and even more violent "offshoot" of the PLO, now vying for sole control of the Arab factions in Israel, and fully backed by Iran and Syria, is far more vocal regarding its aim to annihilate Israel. But again, even here, Britain and the other Western nations are beginning to turn to consider its evil claims. How true it is that "justice is turned back, and righteousness stands afar off, for truth is fallen in the street ... and he who departs from evil makes himself a prey" (Isaiah 59:14–15 NKJV).

Lebanon

Although it has suffered intense inner conflict through Islamic interference from abroad, Lebanon has been the only Arab state with a basically friendly attitude to Israel. However, it also became the home of PLO forces after their expulsion from Jordan by King Hussein in 1970.

Since then, in addition to attacks on northern Israel, the PLO waged an appalling onslaught against the Christian Arabs of Lebanon, who once constituted 40 percent of the population. Having been thus decimated, their numbers are vastly less. Since the late 1980s the PLO has been displaced by the more violent Hezbollah forces, again backed by Iran and Syria.

The world is hardly aware of what has been happening. Lebanon is the only Arab country in the Middle East where Christians have had constitutional rights in the government. The murder of the pro-Israel Lebanese Prime Minister in 2005 (reportedly with Syrian complicity) still awaits international investigation. The serious question arises as to the eventual fate of Arab Christians throughout the Middle East, given the mounting fervor of Islam and hatred of Christians.

In 1980 there was an incursion of Syrian forces into Lebanon, at first supporting the PLO and Muslim factions, but later assuming an independent role. There then developed the bizarre situation in which the PLO was in one sector, the Syrian forces in another, the Christian militia in another, and the UN peacekeeping forces in another! The latter were neither able to protect the Arab Christians, nor to prevent the sixty-nine successful PLO infiltrations into Israel between June and December 1980, all of violent intent.

The situation in 2008 was not dissimilar. The six weeks of murderous Hezbollah rocket attacks on Israel in the summer of 2006 were in no way hampered or held back by the UN forces. In fact there were reports of UN co-operation. The eventual suspension of those attacks will only last for a season, and their resumption is almost certain to lead into a fierce conflict that will seriously affect the whole region and many countries, particularly Syria.

Summary

Watchman, what of the night?

(Isaiah 21:11 NKJV)

We see a tiny land of some 8,000 square miles surrounded by foes holding 660 times that area (5,280,000 square miles), with comparative populations of some six million Jews and 240 million Arabs – a 1:40

ratio. Even were these ratios reduced, the enormous odds can still be gauged.

> The night cometh, when no man can work.
>
> > (John 9:4 KJV)

But we are not praying for superiority for Israel militarily, numerically, or in any other way – other than that she might know the God of Israel, the Holy One of Israel in her midst, as in days of old.

The people of Israel were never delivered from their foes because of their mighty army, their own strength or their wisdom. Time after time, God took pains to ensure that when he delivered his people, their boast would be of Him, not of themselves nor of their strength. He teaches us the same lesson.

> No king is saved by the size of his army.
>
> > (Psalm 33:16 NIV)

The greatest and classic example of this was when Israel had not one single weapon against the pursuing hordes of Pharaoh's army and chariots. It was not a case of "less of self and more of thee" but "none of self and all of thee!" The only "defense" that Moses had was in the rod of authority that he could raise in the name of the Lord.

The very first song in the Bible comes out of that greatest trial and greatest victory: the deliverance of Israel from Egypt. This is why the songs of Israel touch a different note from ours in the West. They are born out of the deepest experiences: from night to day, sorrow to joy, war to peace. They are songs composed not in the parlor, but on the battlefield.

> Then Moses and the Israelites sang this song to the LORD:
>
> I will sing to the LORD,
> > for He is highly exalted.
> The horse and its rider
> > he has hurled into the sea.

The LORD is my strength and my song;
>   he has become my salvation.
He is my God, and I will praise Him,
>   my father's God, and I will exalt him.

(Exodus 15:1–2 NIV)

Moses found salvation in the person of God, not in his own deeds. Every household had sprinkled the blood of an unblemished lamb on its doorposts and lintels before the Israelites' exodus and deliverance. In the same event and chapter, we find the first dance and a further song by Miriam, Aaron's sister, with "all the women" following her, complete with tambourines, singing and dancing:

Sing to the LORD,
>   for he is highly exalted.

(Exodus 15:21 NIV)

Deborah brought a further song when Sisera, who had oppressed Israel for twenty years, was slain by a woman – Jael, Heber's wife (Judges 5:17–21, 24–27).

Before the Lord delivered Israel from the Midianites, Gideon had to destroy his father's altar to Baal, and then reduce his army from 32,000 to 300 men, so that, in the words of the Lord, "Israel may not boast against me that her own strength has saved her" (Judges 7:2 NIV).

Other than calling a fast for the whole nation and earnestly seeking the Lord, King Jehosophat had no idea whatever of how to deal with a huge, threatening army. He cried out to God:

We do not know what to do, but our eyes are upon you.

(2 Chronicles 20:12 NIV)

And he was assured:

Do not be afraid or discouraged because of this vast army. For the battle is not yours, but God's.

(2 Chronicles 20:15 NIV)

Here we also find a song *before* the victory, not just after it:

> Give thanks to the Lord,
>   for his love endures for ever.
>
> (2 Chronicles 20:21 NIV)

In the context of the coming war with Syria (and maybe other factions), Isaiah 17 reveals that the self-sufficient Jacob is going to disappear.

> It shall come to pass
> That the glory of Jacob will wane.
>
> (Isaiah 17:4 NKJV)

Jacob's glory is his self-strength, that which vanished in his all-night struggle with the Angel of the Lord (Genesis 32:22–32). It was only after this that the Angel renamed him "Israel" (Prince with God" or "Overcomer with God"). What happened in that all-night struggle? His thigh muscle (the strongest part of any human body) was dislocated! In the "Hebrew Art Gallery," his "picture" is found as he blesses his sons, "leaning on the top of his staff" (Hebrews 11:21 KJV).

Something is going to happen shortly to the Jewish nation, through the terrible conflict that is on the horizon, whereby they will suddenly begin to turn to their Maker and realize their need of the Holy One of Israel (Isaiah 17:7).

God-chosen

> Blessed is the nation whose God is the Lord,
>   the people he chose for His inheritance.
> From heaven the Lord looks down
>   and sees all mankind;
> from his dwelling-place he watches
>   all who live on earth –
> he who forms the hearts of all,
>   who considers everything they do.
>
> (Psalm 33:12–15 NIV)

God-dependent

> No king is saved by the size of his army;
>> no warrior escapes by his great strength.
> A horse is a vain hope for deliverance;
>> despite all its great strength it cannot save.

(Psalm 33:16–17 NIV)

God-fearing

> But the eyes of the LORD are on those who fear him,
>> on those whose hope is in his unfailing love,
> to deliver them from death
>> and keep them alive in famine.

(Psalm 33:18–19 NIV)

God-trusting

> We wait in hope for the LORD;
>> he is our help and our shield.
> In him our hearts rejoice,
>> for we trust in his holy name.
> May your unfailing love rest upon us, O LORD,
>> even as we put our hope in you.

(Psalm 33:20–22 NIV)

Notes

1. *New Horizon*, vol. 6, 3 December 1979.
2. *Jerusalem Post* (International Edition), 14 March 1982.
3. *ibid.*
4. Henry Kissinger, quoted in *The Times*, 4 March 1982.
5. Paul Eidelberg, *Sadat's Strategy* (Dawn Publishing Co., 1979), 17 Anselme Blvd., Dollard des Ormeaux, Canada, p. 84.
6. Dr Stephen F. Schwebel, Legal Advisor of the State Department, in an editorial for the *American Journal of International Law* (vol. 64, 1970), p. 346.
7. *Ha'Aretz*, 5 December 1978, p. 1.

8. Michael Fidler, JP, CFI, Blackpool, 15 October 1981.

9. Shmuel Katz, "Sinai Illusion of Security," *Jerusalem Post* (International Edition), 7 February 1982, p. 14.

10. Abba Eban quoted by Shmuel Katz in "Sinai Illusion of Security."

11. *ibid.*

12. Shmuel Katz, *op. cit.*

CHAPTER 10

Lebanon and Media Manipulation

Turn ... and go to ... Lebanon, as far as the great river, the River Euphrates.

(Deuteronomy 1:7 NKJV)

Truth is fallen in the street ...
And he who departs from evil makes himself a prey.

(Isaiah 59:14–15 NKJV)

The glory of Lebanon shall come to you ...
To beautify the place of My Sanctuary.

(Isaiah 60:13 NKJV)

Lebanon: a Biblical viewpoint

With Lebanon so much in the news, it is a very sobering thought that, in an ancient covenant which has *not* been revoked, the Lord long ago assigned to Israel territory which included Lebanon. At the time, this included the land eastward of it as far as the River Euphrates – *that is as far as Baghdad!* This will be as fuel to the active flames of worldwide anti-Zionism and anti-Semitism, some of which is from Christian sources. However, it is most appropriate for us to remember that

Lebanon was never fully conquered, although it was included in that of
which the Lord spoke to Joshua:

> You are old and advanced in years, and very much of the land remains
> to be possessed.
>
> (Joshua 13:1 NASB)

Joshua 13:5–6 outlines the Lebanon area which (together with other
areas) the Lord allowed to remain unconquered in order to prove and
test Joshua's successors (Judges 3:3–11). In order to promote moral and
spiritual discipline, the inroads and the effect of Israel's enemies within
these regions were permitted – sometimes involving actual war! *There
are tremendous spiritual lessons and parallels here for Christians today* (see
Exodus 23:29–30 and 1 Corinthians 10:6, 11).

As the July–September 2006 war with the Hezbollah forces in Lebanon revealed, Israel certainly has not the slightest desire to conquer
and hold any part of Lebanon, especially given the huge costs of main-
taining an army there. Nothing is further from her economic reach,
nor from the hearts of her people and government. Israel's sole reason
for entrance into Lebanon in 1982 and in 2006 was merely the need of
self-preservation. The major function and responsibility of any government is the safety of its people.

Bible-believing Christians who have a problem in seeing some
future long-term Israeli presence or control over Lebanon will be in
for a far bigger headache when it comes to the Bashan, Gilead and
Amorite territories. All of these are *east* of the Jordan, and all were
originally occupied by the tribes of Manasseh, Gad and Reuben.

Whatever impression is given by the world media, it is significant
that every one of the six wars in which Israel has been involved since its
birth in 1948 has been for the purpose of self-preservation. This is true,
even though in half of them (1956, 1967 and 1982), Israel made a pre-
emptive strike. While Scripture abounds in spiritual superlatives for
Lebanon's distant future, there is also much to indicate *fierce opposition
to any and every eventual physical or spiritual alignment with Israel* (Isaiah
10:34; Zechariah 11:1).

While greater insights will be gained from records of the 1982 war, let us look firstly at the Israel–Hezbollah War that broke out on 12 July 2006. While attacking two Israeli armored patrol vehicles near the Israeli side of the northern border, Hezbollah militants fired rockets also at Israeli border towns. Of the seven Israeli soldiers in the vehicles, three were killed, two injured, and two (aged 26 and 31) taken captive into Lebanon. Five more were killed in an unsuccessful Israeli rescue attempt.

In response, Israel carried out massive airstrikes (over 12,000 combat missions) and directed artillery fire on targets in Lebanon. There was also a naval and an aerial blockade. Prime Minister Ehud Olmert challenged the Lebanese government over their responsibility for the Hezbollah raid. Surprisingly, Hezbollah's leader (Hasan Nasrullah) said, "Had we known that the capture of the soldiers would have led to this, we would definitely not have done it."

In the early days of the war, strategic, long-range Hezbollah missiles were destroyed, although the militants still fired over 100 rockets daily for the first month. Major targets included Haifa, Kiryat Shmona, Nazareth, Nahariya, Tiberias and Afula. Disruption and fear were widespread. However, it was significant that in more than one of these cities, the combined, authoritative and early morning prayer of some Messianic leaders and their followers saw remarkabe results in preserving life and avoiding or reducing damage.

Nonetheless, at least 1,000 people were killed, mostly in Lebanon – where the militants were targeted. Because of Hezbollah strategy, some of the Lebanese civilians "chosen" to be a protective shield were amongst those killed or injured. The United Nations Security Council eventually (11 August) passed a resolution (1701) calling for the disarmament of Hezbollah, for Israeli withdrawal, and for the deployment of a large UN force (UNIFIL) in southern Lebanon. This managed to preserve peace for the three following years.

Amongst world repercussions, the British Labour government was criticized by its own backbenchers for not backing an earlier ceasefire. This led, at least in part, to the resignation of Tony Blair, then Prime Minister.

The US President (George W. Bush) blamed the suffering of the Lebanese people on Iran and Syria, both of which still support Hezbollah to this day. But in Israel also, there was wide spread criticism, from the media and the families of the reservist soldiers, of the IDF performance – often focusing on the Prime Minister.

The bodies of the kidnapped Israeli soldiers were returned after two years, in exchange for the release of an imprisoned murderer (Samir Kuntar), four Hezbollah militants, and the bodies of Lebanese prisoners captured in the war.

In spite of all the exposure, it is well known today that the stock of Hezbollah rocket missiles in Lebanon was hastily and immediately attended to. By late 2007 to early 2008 the figure of 4,000 rockets was reported, many being longer range than before, thereby bringing all of Israel within range. We are therefore turned again to:

> My help comes from the LORD
>   Who made heaven and earth …
> Behold, He who keeps Israel
>   Will neither slumber nor sleep.
>
> (Psalm 121:2, 4 NASB)

In partial contrast, but adding more to our understanding, the entry of Israel's Defense Forces into southern Lebanon on 6 June 1982 – then termed an "invasion" by the Western media, yet at the time so joyfully welcomed by the Lebanese people as a "liberation" – well warrants our study. This kind of issue, more than any other of the last sixty years, is crystallizing into a determining factor to show on which side of the fence nations, Christians and individuals stand in regard to Israel.

The Christian standpoint – whether for or against Israel – is going to be costly. If we stand *for* and with Israel (which is rejected by the world and increasingly rejected by many within the Church), sooner or later we shall also be rejected. If we stand *against* Israel – seen, as the writer contends, as being in the process of restoration by God – we run the risk of God's displeasure, as outlined in Romans 11:18–22.

Do not be arrogant [towards] the natural branches ... Otherwise, you also will be cut off.

(Romans 11:20–22 NIV)

The Holy Spirit and the Word tell us that our attitude to His brethren reflects our attitude to Him:

Truly I say to you, to the extent that you did it to one of these brothers of Mine, even the least of them, you did it to Me.

(Matthew 25:40 NASB)

While this does not indicate that we approve every Israeli action, nor that we are sentimental and silly over the nation, it does mean that we must get through the dense smokescreen of the world media to real truth, and to the real truth of the Word of God. If we fail to perceive that the most intense spiritual warfare surrounds this whole matter, we shall be blinkered and blinded to the real cause and effect, and left ignorant of God's purposes. Further, our love and prayers for Israel (or any other country) are not based upon her necessarily behaving in the way that we would like, any more than are the love and prayers of a mother for her child.

We must remember that, just as we have been saved by grace, not by works, so will it be for Israel (Romans 11:6; Ephesians 2:8). When Saul of Tarsus, who is embryonic of Israel's coming salvation, met the Lord on the road to Damascus, he had done nothing whatever to "justify" his salvation. In fact, he was on his way at that very moment to further persecute the believers in Damascus.

The Lebanese smokescreen: media manipulation

The following profile of Israel's conflict in 1982 with PLO forces in Lebanon is given to "uncover" the conspiratorial forces (particularly allied with the news media) that *continue at work in Lebanon today*, with the destruction of Israel as their goal. The vicious, shorter and more recent war (12 July – 14 September 2006) involving the Hezbollah forces, and their raining of thousands of rockets on Israel, foreshadows a far more intense confrontation in the near future.

To repeat what has earlier been said in this book, world Islamic policy in regard to the media was clearly revealed long ago in the statement in the Islamic journal *New Horizon* of 3 December 1979. While it is difficult to quantify the effect of this threat on the world press and media, the subsequent and ongoing misreporting and disinformation strongly indicate the result of Islamic intimidation. (Note that while there are over forty-two Muslim countries, there is but one Jewish State in the world.)

> The Islamic Press Union has decided to monitor the Western Press and identify and name the papers which persistently indulge in malicious and mischievous propaganda against Islam and the Muslim World.
>
> The IPU shall communicate every month the names of such papers to the Information Ministries of the 42 Muslim countries besides the airlines, banks, insurance corporations, shipping lines and other major institutions of the Muslim World and recommend them to withhold patronage from such papers.
>
> It would also request news agencies of the Muslim countries to circulate in their news bulletins the name of such papers for the information of the Muslim masses.[1]

This policy of coercion and manipulation was evidenced in the journalism and reporting from Lebanon concerning both the 1982 and 2006 wars. In adopting the "big lie" policy (i.e. if the lie is big enough, said loudly enough and for long enough, people will believe it), the Islamists, the PLO and Hamas are in line with one of the greatest propagandists of all time, i.e. the Nazi Goebbels who did so much to further Hitler's policies.

Other than its ordinary, low-key information briefing, Israel has little propaganda machinery to counter this. She has won many military battles in the past, but frequently loses the political war of words. (Christians can better keep abreast of actual facts through regular update tapes or resources available through Christian resource agencies.[2])

How was an organized group such as the PLO able to impose such a reign of terror and silence on all of Lebanon for more than nine years (1973–82) and yet, when the Lebanese were liberated by the Israelis, the Jewish State – instead of being thankfully approved by the world – was accused of aggression? *Why?*

A history of the Palestine Liberation Organization (PLO)

The PLO was created specifically as an instrument of belligerence against Israel at an Arab Summit meeting in Cairo in January 1964. Its charter includes the following three points:

1. "The partition of Palestine in 1947 and the establishment of the State of Israel are entirely illegal" (Article 9). (This in spite of the UN resolution in November 1947 to establish and recognize the State of Israel.)
2. "Armed struggle is the only way to liberate Palestine" (Article 9).
3. "Nor do Jews constitute a single nation with an identity of its own" (Article 20).

In November 1969 the Lebanese government recognized the "PLO's right" to strike at Israel from Lebanese territory, but only after co-ordination with the Lebanese. However, the PLO's first major base was in Jordan from where it launched many terrorist attacks on Israel. King Hussein began to realize that the PLO threatened his own regime and in September 1970 ("Black September"), he sent his own army to drive the PLO out. Some 20,000 PLO people were killed, and the rest fled. Then, even as until this day, all Arab states were reluctant to receive the PLO but the weakest of them – Lebanon – was forced to allow them in.

In 1973, the PLO signed the Melcart Agreement with the Lebanese, specifying from which areas the PLO was allowed to operate against Israel, what forces could be maintained in southern Lebanon, and what types of weapons were permissible. Heavy weapons were forbidden; only small arms were to be carried by the PLO in the refugee camps and in the towns; some medium-sized weapons were allowed in parts of the south.

The PLO then began to set up a "state within a state," representing no government but heading up a number of affiliated, splinter movements – all for crime on an international scale. Although outwardly existing to attain the "rights" of the Palestinian peoples, the huge finances which the PLO later received annually from the Arab regimes (and more recently from Europe) have been used not for refugee aid, but for military and terrorist projects.

Claiming concern for the Palestinian refugees, the PLO have been allowed offices in Western capitals such as London, Paris and Vienna, and from these, over the years, attacks (referred to in Chapter 9) have been planned and launched on Jewish targets, diplomats, synagogues – and even children. It has been said that if Yasser Arafat, former leader of the PLO, were to have sold all of his massive quantities of arms, ammunition, tanks, troop carriers and the like, *he could have built a villa for every Palestinian living in Lebanon.*

The PLO and the United Nations

The then-President of Lebanon, Suleiman Franijeh, made an historic blunder on 14 December 1973 when he paved the way for Arafat's show at the United Nations General Assembly. With an olive branch in one hand and a gun in the other, Arafat was received with a standing ovation as he addressed the representatives of civilized world governments. Yasser Arafat was thereby turned into an international figure, crowned with victory and prestige, and he returned to Beirut as to his capital.

Then there began the "conspiracy of silence" as his armed bands were let loose. Four months later, the carnage erroneously called the "civil war" began; this was, in effect, a deliberate effort to remove whatever remained of Lebanon's independence.

In the dismantling that followed in Lebanon (then the only Arab Christian country in the world), the most serious inroads were simultaneously made into hindering Arabic gospel work. Beirut had formerly been its center. But today all of this is now buried – lost and forgotten – because of the slant imposed since then on news reporting from and about the Middle East.

Terror stricken but tongue-tied

An "Album of Atrocities" was published in Lebanon in 1978 depicting years of suffering as a result of the PLO, but heavy bribes stemmed distribution abroad. Most copies were destroyed. Journalists, many of whom through fear remain anonymous to this day, explain the silence on the years of terror. There were three categories of journalist, foreign and local:

1. Those who sold out their consciences for bribes, paying either with silence or with sympathetic articles about the Palestinian struggle.
2. Those who went underground, surfacing occasionally, only to find an impenetrable wall of frightened or bribed publishers and editors. Most left journalism in despair.
3. Those who were frightened into silence without bribing – by menacing letters, telephone threats, attacks and attempted attacks, or by the execution of their senior colleagues who had tried to be truthful.

    Said the colleague of the economic editor of one of the daily newspapers: "I can only say that very few will come out with a clean bill of health and those who do will not include the BBC, Radio Monte Carlo, and various British, French and even American journalists."

This campaign to take over the media began after Arafat's triumphant return from the UN.

In July 1978, at fifty years old, Lebanese patriot Salim Lawzi was assassinated. He owned and ran an influential Muslim weekly and had begun warning his countrymen in the early 1970s against the Palestinian organizations. After himself receiving threats and hiding away from his opponents, he was caught, tortured and murdered after trying secretly to visit his family in 1978. Horrible pictures of his dismembered body brought fear to other journalists in Beirut.

This policy of eliminating any voice (particularly Arab) raised in favor of Israel can be traced back to its beginning in the days of the Grand Mufti of Jerusalem in the 1920s. Today this policy is of mushrooming, worldwide proportions. Let us be reminded that the Revelation 12:15 verse refers basically to the flood of water proceeding from the serpent's mouth being aimed to destroy the "woman" – which is firstly Israel, but also the Church.

Of Beirut, which was once a fine and leading Christian center, it was reported (22 February 1982):

> In this battered city there are bombings, kidnappings and political murders every day. To work here as a journalist is to carry fear with you as faithfully as your notebook ... there is nothing you can do to protect yourself and ... nothing has ever happened to any assassin.
>
> (John Kifner, *New York Times*)

The British Guardian newspaper defined the atmosphere in Beirut as "censorship by terrorism." There were endless other news reports, too many to mention here, which bring the same grief and horror. How about those same newspapers which so often focused on the Israeli "invasion" of Lebanon, but never reported a single word on the 20,000 men, women and children who were mercilessly slaughtered in the city of Hama, Syria, in February 1982. Why? Because they had then opposed the then-President Assad. Syrian soldiers blew up whole neighborhoods – but without a murmur from the West. Could it be because of the strong, and growing, Islamic influence upon the West and its whole media?

Inaccurate though it sounds, the Arab is more free and better cared for in Israel than in any other country of the Middle East. In spite of this, there is a widespread current move from within to stir them into discontent and hostility. Pray for the Arab folk, especially for the believers amongst them.

How did Syria get involved in Lebanon?

Syria has always regarded Lebanon as a part of its own country ("Greater Syria"), never accepting its sovereignty, nor having diplomatic relations with it.

In early 1976, under the guise of being a "peacekeeping force," Syria entered Lebanon to quell the PLO domination. At first, Syria intervened on behalf of the Christian community, killing many PLO people. But in securing its grip over the country, these roles were later reversed, as Syria co-operated with the PLO against the Christian communities.

By late 1976 the PLO-Syrian occupation was so extensive, the killing and destruction so wanton, that Lebanon virtually ceased to exist as an independent country. World silence from both the UN and the Church was tragic. And the silence continued until Israel's liberating action in June 1982.

(However, the lifting of that silence lasted only until about 1986, when Israeli forces ended their attempts to deal with the threats on their northern border from within Lebanon.)

By 2008, the Syrian grip on Lebanon, although disguised and now strongly backed by Iranian input, was greater than ever.

Summary

The so-called "civil war" of the 1970s in Lebanon was really a Lebanese versus Palestinian confrontation. Even Muslim sympathies with the PLO waned as they seized land, and turned homes, schools, churches and hospitals into armed fortresses. The Lebanese were subject to curfews and great fear. Women were constantly accosted and raped. Teenagers were dismembered and actually pulled apart by being tied to cars driven simultaneously in different directions. Many who resisted were murdered in the most brutal fashion.

Why did Israel enter Lebanon in 1982?

1. There had been fourteen years of PLO terrorist attacks, especially on northern Israel.
2. During that time, with massive backing from the Soviet Union, Lebanon was turned into a training ground for international terrorism, with huge amounts of advanced weaponry for 15,000 PLO terrorists.
3. Between 1968 and 1982, in Israel and throughout the world, over 1,000 civilians were murdered and 4,250 were wounded through PLO terrorist attacks. These are not just statistics – these are people! Israeli townspeople, diplomats, worshippers in synagogues, tourists, schoolchildren and airplane hostages were amongst the victims. Not all, by any means, were Jewish.
4. As a warning, both in 1978 and 1981, Israel struck against terrorist encampments and munitions depots in southern Lebanon.
5. Constant appeals to the international community to oust the PLO and Syrian forces had gone unheeded.
6. The United Nations (UNIFIL) forces placed there proved ineffective and there was even some indication of collaboration between them and the PLO.
7. After the July 1981 ceasefire, there were 290 attacks or attempted attacks along Israel's borders, on UNIFIL soldiers in Major Haddad's Christian enclave, or in Israel itself and abroad. From these, twenty-nine deaths and 271 injuries resulted. Again, these are people, not mere statistics.
8. The culminating factor occurred in London on 3 June 1982 when the Israeli Ambassador, Shlomo Argov, was gunned down and almost fatally wounded as he left the Dorchester Hotel. He was permanently paralyzed. It is believed this attack had been planned in London's PLO office.
9. The Israeli air force struck back at two known terrorist bases in Lebanon, and the PLO began a seventy-two-hour bombardment of civilian targets in northern Galilee. Hundreds of Katyusha rockets and over 1,000 shells were fired at twenty-three settlements in Israel, including the towns of Kiryat Shmona and Netanya. A whole forest of trees was set ablaze. Only then and with great reluctance was "Operation Peace for Galilee" launched.

In comparison, in 1982, while Britain fought to regain the almost worthless Falkland Islands some 8,000 miles away from her shores, Israel's total existence was at stake with an implacable foe on her very doorstep! Because of their efficiency, we must not overlook the fact that Israel's forces are, and always have been, heavily outnumbered by those of her Arab neighbors. Israel has but to lose one war and she will have lost her life and her land. The only nation appreciating this is Israel herself! She fights to survive. She does not fight for territory.

What did Israel find in Lebanon in 1982?

1. Weapons: A massive, far greater military infrastructure of the PLO was found than had ever been expected. It necessitated the pursuit of the terrorists beyond the boundaries planned, in order to avert what was virtually a premature "Armageddon!"

   Weapons sufficient for an army of 150,000 were uncovered from almost every arms-dealing country in the world, including China, Sweden, Vietnam, UK, USA, France, Germany, Japan, Libya and, of course, the USSR – enough to equip seven brigades.[3] The following were the statistics as at 13 October 1982 (figures in brackets represent the proportion found in West Beirut):[4]
   (a) 540 weapons depots discovered (140). It took 4,330 truckloads to transport the captured material back to Israel.
   (b) 5,610 tons of ammunition (960)
   (c) 1,310 combat and other vehicles (243) including several hundred T-34, T-55 and T-63 tanks.
   (d) 33,303 small arms (4,999)
   (e) 1,532 anti-tank weapons (159)
   (f) 215 mortars (from 60 to160 mm)
   (g) 62 Katyusha rocket launchers (6)
   (h) 87 field artillery pieces (12)
   (i) 198 anti-aircraft weapons (38)
       and much else.
2. Subterranean vaults: Much of the above was discovered in enormous air-conditioned tunnels dug out of hillsides. The machine used to make these was of Soviet manufacture, more massive

than anything ever seen in the West. One of the largest of these vaults had an entrance on the Mediterranean coast of Lebanon, facilitating the concealed arrival of army advisors or leaders from countries abroad.

Due to the storage also of large quantities of food within the tunnels, the impression was gained that a huge army could have been swiftly landed, fed and equipped for a war against Israel launched from Lebanon.

The questions arose:

(a) Did Russia plan to send troops to Lebanon?

(b) Did Israel unwittingly prevent a premature Armageddon being launched against her?

3. Huge numbers of files on people abroad, sympathetic to the PLO cause, were found.

4. Beirut had become the center from which satellite training schools for terrorists were set up in southern Lebanon in Palestinian refugee camps. One of these was found *within* a United Nations vocational school north of Sidon.[5]

5. Terrorists from all over the world – and the Soviet connection: Of the 9,000 terrorists captured, almost one-sixth were non-Palestinian, coming from forty different countries, including Bangladesh, Yemen, Syria, Egypt, Turkey, Pakistan, India, Iraq and Jordan.

Documents proved conclusively that the PLO training personnel were trained ideologically and militarily behind the Iron Curtain and in certain Arab countries. This training included the field of chemical warfare.[6]

6. Several hundred young children using weapons were captured along with the terrorists. In some cases, in a moment of severe moral hesitation, Israeli soldiers risked their lives when confronted by such youngsters carrying rocket-propelled grenades. (These were called the "RPG kids.")

7. Amongst almost 1,000 people under arrest by the official Lebanese Armed Forces (14 October 1982), terrorists from twenty-one different countries were found.[7]

8. The Lebanese crisis clearly showed that the Arab world was not prepared to go to war for the PLO. Nor to this very day are Arab governments willingly prepared to receive them as terrorists into their own lands.

9. The Soviet aid was mainly channeled through the Eastern Europe satellite countries, so that the Soviets were not seen as the chief suppliers to the PLO, or as a major partner in international terror.

Temporary gains from this operation

1. Peace was restored for Israel's northern population.
2. There was the prospect of restored sovereignty for Lebanon.
3. The world center for training in terrorism at that time was dismantled.
4. At least for the time being, the strategic spearhead of the whole Soviet war machine (its SAM missile anti-aircraft system) was made virtually useless. Through Israeli electronic technology, twenty-three of the most sophisticated anti-aircraft batteries in the world, manned by the Syrians in the Beqa'a Valley, were destroyed by Israel without the loss of a single plane. Although the Russians may well find an answer to this, it did, in the meantime, prejudice also the whole of their defense / attack strategy in Europe.
5. The rate of loss for Syrian versus Israeli aircraft was something like 80:1 in favor of the Israelis. It was not surprising, therefore, that the Syrians quickly agreed to a ceasefire on 11 June 1982.

Some media discrepancies

With the foregoing as a background, we can take most reports stemming from what have formerly been thought to be reliable sources with more than a grain of salt. We would do well in future to compare them with reports, for example, from Jewish sources.

Civilian casualties

Any war must produce some casualties, and even a few are too many. But initial figures for South Lebanon from "reliable sources" were ludicrous. The Palestinian Red Crescent (Red Cross) claimed 600,000 as homeless – more than the population of South Lebanon (510,000).

The International Red Cross halved this figure and later reduced it still further to 70,000.

British Foreign Secretary, Francis Pym, on the British television program *Newsnight* (16 June 1982) said the figure was 500,000. Douglas Hurd, of the same Foreign Office, the next day said it was 200,000! The true figure was between 20,000 and 30,000.

Comparative facts and figures not reported

At least 180,000 southern Lebanese had fled north since 1975 to escape PLO terror. Traffic jams occurred in South Lebanon, after the Israeli "invasion," caused by these homeless people swarming back.

In the years 1975–82, 100,000 civilians were killed and over 250,000 wounded in Lebanon, out of a total population of three million. It is estimated that some 40,000 children were orphaned. While the cameras of the world portrayed destroyed and damaged buildings in South Lebanon, no reference was made to the fact that most of this damage had occurred in the preceding seven years through PLO-Syrian action.

A survey of West Beirut which, according to the media, had been turned into a "holocaust," showed 347 buildings damaged out of a total of 25,000 – and most of this had occurred before June 1982.

Towns that were said to have been flattened by the Israelis (e.g. Damour) had but a fraction (10 percent) of the buildings touched through their action, and were back to a flow of life soon after the Israelis had entered.

For media purposes, almost every class of person was interviewed in Lebanon – PLO leaders, Red Cross workers, visiting politicians and Israelis – but not the Lebanese people themselves! Their undisguised joy at being set free, their embracing of the Israelis, their showering them with rice and flowers, their inviting them in for coffee … this was *never* portrayed on television or in newspapers.

Although there was some inevitable damage to property, the very absence of resentment from the Lebanese reflected their thankfulness at having a normal pattern of life restored.

In direct contrast to the news media claims of "indiscriminate Israeli destruction of civilian life and property," the exact opposite occurred. Areas were often leafleted beforehand (as in the 2006 war) to warn civilians to clear out, preparatory to the Israeli army or air force attack aimed at dealing with the PLO. This humane action, contrary to all normal military strategy, cost the Israelis many more dead and wounded, since it gave warning to the PLO.

To avoid civilian casualties, there was often pinpoint bombing. One could compare this with World War Two, when the Allied armies were not so particular and whole cities in Germany were flattened inclusively with the SS command centers and Nazi apartments that they contained. Israel's action in clearing out the PLO from Lebanon was met with the approval of both the Lebanese and American governments, although neither of them had the courage to say so openly! Many Muslims in Lebanon actually helped the Israelis to expel the PLO.

Although the PLO often operated from homes, hospitals and schools (as did the Hezbollah in 2006), one command given to the Israelis was that they were not to fire on civilian targets unless first fired upon. This cost the Israelis much in casualties. The PLO used civilians as shields and hostages around their weapon sites. By this action they gained a propaganda victory in the West amongst both Jews and Gentiles, and even in Israel. (Exactly the same occurred in 2006.)

During the fighting, water, food, shelter and medical care were fully provided by the Israeli army to civilians affected by the hostilities. Women and girls later said that for the first time in eight years they were free to walk the streets without purposely making themselves unattractive.

What needs remained?

1. A strong Lebanese army and government able to bring peace and harmony between its various communities – Muslim, Christian and Druze – and with a desire to be at peace also with Israel. (In 2008–09, Syrian and Iranian forces continued to seek forcefully to

dislodge the existing Lebanese government in order to install an anti-Israel leadership.)

2. The removal of foreign forces from the soil of Lebanon, including all PLO, Syrians and Israelis – of necessity, probably in that order. Syria still occupied 40 percent of Lebanon.

3. A solution to the needs (housing and employment) of the Palestinian refugees still in Lebanon. They do not want to go to the "West Bank" in Israel, but would like Lebanese citizenship.

4. The vigilance of other nations against PLO activities within their own lands and the closure of all their offices.

5. The curtailment of PLO and Moscow-backed training of other terrorists for worldwide activities.

The enormous cost to Israel

1. By November 1982 the cost to Israel was 368 dead (317 officers and 51 privates) and 2,600 wounded. (Israeli officers go into battle at the head of their troops.) In population-proportions for the UK, these figures would have been 6,000 dead and 41,600 wounded – quite enormous numbers. Twenty percent of Israeli army casualties were caused by the *children and teenagers* trained by the PLO in the use of machine-guns, rifles and anti-tank rocket-propelled grenades.

2. Many soldiers, wives and relatives were badly affected, some mentally, by the stress and bereavement.

3. Israel was almost totally isolated and endured large-scale rejection by an uncaring, misinformed world.

4. The Israeli economy, already suffering, was strained to the limit by having to maintain an army at such a distance from its borders.

5. Although at the time a potential Armageddon was averted, conflicting factors and stresses increased within Israel, which raises the question of what hope there can be for the future.

The Middle East: a bird's-eye view

It is customary to depict Israel as the cause of all the unrest in the Middle East, as authorities claim that the Arab–Israeli dispute would end if only the PLO were given a state west of the River Jordan. Such statements take no account of the following facts:

1. Only with reluctance has the PLO been received out of Lebanon into even Arab countries.
2. The PLO's very existence is for the purpose of destroying Israel. (See its Covenant Charter.) Hamas is even more vociferous on this goal.
3. Although all Arab countries are hostile to Israel, their own disunity and warring amongst themselves restrain their combined effort to remove or destroy Israel. With the disagreement amongst themselves, it is hard to imagine them ever allowing Israel to dwell in peace. The history of successful, or even attempted, revolutions in Arab lands since 1948 is in itself phenomenal. The numbers of Arab heads of state and prime ministers who have been assassinated, alongside political murders, are also incredible. Lebanon itself has been a major "victim" in all of this.

Gaza

Before considering the recent conflict (2008–09) within and around Gaza, it is helpful to realize that this area is mentioned nineteen times in the Bible. Joshua, Judah, Samson and even the Egyptian Pharaoh were amongst those found in conflict there. The fact that, to this very day, there have been strong spiritual forces over the region is confirmed as Zechariah proclaims:

> Gaza too will writhe in great pain …
> Moreover, the king will perish from Gaza.
>
> (Zechariah 9:5 NASB)

The Hebrew root of the term "Gaza" is "strong, vehement, harsh, fierce, greedy, mighty." *Nonetheless, Zechariah 9:6–7 also refers to "a remnant for our God" who will seemingly be "Palestinians"*! This should help us in seeking the Lord and having faith as we pray. (At present, some

3,000 Christians live in Gaza, but they, and even the unbelievers, dare not speak out against Islamic terrorism.)

From the 1980s, intense turmoil and conflict has flared up over the Israelis dwelling in Gaza, overshadowed as they were by Israeli soldiers. Consequently, in August 2005, through even more intense tears and confusion, all the Jewish settlers left – quite a few being "forced" to do so by Israeli soldiers, who acted unwillingly under orders! They left behind one of the finest sources of agricultural income for Israel, the produce being of such supreme quality. Yet, in spite of their anguish, many of these Israelis are still without their own homes.

"Officially," this withdrawal from Gaza was to lead to peace with the Palestinians. But, as is well known, the situation got far worse. The number of rockets and mortars that had been fired from Gaza into Israel since 2001 greatly escalated, hitting mainly Sderot and the western Negev. Up to the end of 2008, the total reached over 8,000.

With Hamas in control, nearly 3,000 of these rockets and missiles were fired in just the first half of 2008! Then Hamas agreed to a ceasefire, and the number of rocket attacks was reduced to about twenty from July to October 2008. However, ignoring warnings from other Arab leaders, Hamas then poured over 600 missiles into Israel in December 2008 alone!

In spite of Israel's unilateral disengagement from Gaza, the international community took no action – even though Israel protested against the daily terror.

With the intention of halting these rockets *and* blocking their ceaseless supply through the hundreds of hidden tunnels from Egypt, Israel launched her "surprise" air and ground attack into Gaza on 27 December 2008. The rockets had been fired from crowded civilian areas adjacent to UN compounds, and from disguised places – at times from Gaza school grounds. Schools in Beersheva had to close; Ashkelon and Gedera were hit; an Israeli in Netivot was killed. The years of missile attacks have caused trauma to children and adults. The "multi-supply" tunnels have run under residential areas in Gaza, with their exit points covered and hidden.

Although the Israelis were obliged to withdraw in January 2009, before completing the clear-up process, the situation still carries the same dangers. Neither the Palestinian nor the Hamas attitude can soften.

Regarding our own viewpoint, we must bear uppermost in mind that, in all of this, the Lord is still waiting for His people, Israel, *to turn to Him*. The *true* peace which the Israelis want and need, and which the Muslims also need – not to mention Britain, the USA and the world – is that "peace ... which surpasses all understanding" (Philippians 4:7 RSV).

Jesus said:

> In Me you ... have peace. In the world you have tribulation, but take courage; I have overcome the world.
>
> (John 16:33 NASB)

The nations

Quite apart from United Nation encouragement, there are European governments elevating and making "respectable" the image of the PLO terrorist groups, thus aiding their attacks on Israel. If these governments, including Britain, would withhold their recognition, and thus the legitimization of the PLO (because of their terrorist activities), while expressing sympathy for the Palestinian Arabs, the whole political situation in the Middle East would be entirely different.

More than a little guilt must be assigned to nations which have financed the appalling murders, and which to this day continue to supply weapons whose purpose is Israel's destruction. When the civilized world turns a blind eye to stockpiles of ammunition kept in Lebanese apartment buildings and in refugee camps (as before and during the 2006 war), we have to ask, "Where we are heading?"

Truth has indeed fallen in the street

When a country called Israel, after enduring fourteen years of unprovoked shelling, rocket attacks, plane hijacking, bus bombing, diplomat killings and child murders, moves in to deal with such devilish lawlessness, and then the very group set up by the world to preserve international law and order (i.e. the United Nations' peacekeeping force) *objects*, then it is surely time for politicians, Christians and all people to query the role of this world band of political experts.

When self-defense is termed "aggression," and vicious, incessant aggression becomes as acceptable as the milk upon our doorstep, something is wrong – radically wrong.

Truth has indeed fallen in the street, and whoever is prepared to speak out the truth endangers his own life.

It is time that the Church and the world realized that we are facing the invading and pervading force of Islam. We see it in its adherents and in its takeover bid in Europe, in the USA, and especially in Britain. We see its escalating inroads into British schools, British economy, British towns and cities, British culture.

We all know of the threat that Iran, with its inflexible nuclear ambitions, poses to Israel and the rest of the world – the West in particular.

How should Christians pray?

1. For the deep, inward healing of the people of Lebanon; that they will be free from the Hezbollah (who by 2009 have more or less replaced the PLO) and their enormous repression, especially of the Christians.
2. For the safety and the strengthening of the Christians who have been crushed in spirit within Lebanon. Remember the country as the former center of Arabic gospel work, and the going forth of the Word to Arab and "Christian" alike (Isaiah 29:17–21).
3. For the preservation of the Lebanese government. There were repeated strenuous attempts (initiated from abroad) to topple the Christian Prime Minister, who was still in office after the 2006 conflict within Lebanon.

4. For the government of Israel: for God to provide a leader and other officials of high moral integrity and courage who can hold the nation together, and who fear God.

5. For the boosting of Israeli army morale; for provision of inspired leadership for the days ahead, remembering the probability of renewed attacks from the north.

6. For the people of Israel in their great weariness and isolation from other nations (Numbers 23:9); for the healing and coming together of the land and its peoples in a serious quest for their God (Jeremiah 29:13).

7. For restraint of the intense spiritual powers and principalities so active in the Middle East; for Iran with its nuclear power program under President Ahmadinejad. The controversy over the re-election of the President (June 2009) merely emphasizes the threat looming to Israel, but extending also to elsewhere.

8. For the salvation of Arab peoples in the Middle East, many of whom have indeed been seeking, and finding, His peace.

The glory of Lebanon will come to you,
    the pine, the fir and the cypress together,
to adorn the place of my sanctuary;
    and I will glorify the place of my feet.

        (Isaiah 60:13 NIV)

In His own inimitable way, God, the Master-Weaver, will interweave into his pattern for good all the traumatic events of the Lebanese affair.

We know that in all things God works for the good of those who love him, and who have been called according to his purpose (Romans. 8:28).

Israel, sold like Joseph into the pit of world hostility, will one day be saying, just like Joseph:

Don't be afraid ... You intended to harm me, but God meant it for good to accomplish what is now being done, the saving of many lives.

        (Genesis 50:19–20 NIV)

Those sturdy Lebanese people will figure amongst those saved lives, as the prophet Hosea beautifully describes:

> They will send down deep roots ...
>> their fragrance like a cedar of Lebanon ...
> And their fame and fertility
>> like the wine of Lebanon.
>
> (Hosea 14:5–7, paraphrased)

Notes

1. *New Horizon*, vol. 6, 3 December 1979.
2. For Christian resources and prayer update information (including Lance Lambert Middle East update tapes or CDs), write to PFI, PO Box 328, Bromley, Kent BR1 2ZS, UK; or to CFI, PO Box 2687, Eastbourne, East Sussex BN22 7LZ, UK.
3. "Lebanon – The Facts," British Israel Public Affairs Committee, BM Box 391, London WC1B 6XX.
4. Israel Defense Forces spokesman, 21 October 1982.
5. Robert Fisk, *The Times*, 30 October 1982.
6. Israel Ministry of Foreign Affairs Briefing 412/3.10.82/3.09.074.
7. *An Nahar* and *Al Baraq*, 15 October 1982.

CHAPTER 11

The Isolation of Israel

Then Jacob was left alone, and a man wrestled with him until daybreak.

(Genesis 32:24 NASB)

For the LORD has chosen Jacob for Himself,
Israel for His own possession.

(Psalm 135:4 NASB)

In the divine plan of the Lord's "Get out!" to Abraham in Genesis 12, right up to His dealing with Jacob in Genesis 32, we can catch something of His amazing purpose in His election. The content of Genesis 32 lays a foundation for so much of the rest of the Bible.

For those of us who will meditate on the Genesis 32 passage, we find the Lord is wrestling with Jacob more than Jacob is wrestling with Him! It is the Son of Man, the Angel of the Covenant, God in human form, who is pressing down and pressing out the old Jacob life (Genesis 32:28). What a moment this was, both in Jacob's life – in his desperation crying, "I will not let you go unless you bless me" (Genesis 32:26 NIV) – and for the Lord Himself who had been preparing Jacob for this moment for twenty-one years!

Before the morning dawned and light broke, God had prevailed: Jacob had fallen – with his thigh dislocated (Genesis 32:32)! The strongest muscle in his body (his thigh) had been broken, and from that moment on, Jacob "leaned on the top of his staff." Thus he is pictured at the close of his life, and thereby able to bless his twelve sons through the strength that God provided within him (Hebrews 11:21 NIV).

As Jacob fell, he fell into the arms of God. There he clung and wrestled, until both the blessing and the dawn came. The new life was born in him; he arose from the earthly to the heavenly, from the natural to the supernatural. Going forth that morning, he was a weak and broken man. But God was there instead, and the heavenly voice proclaimed:

> Your name will no longer be Jacob, but Israel, because you have struggled with God and with men and have overcome.
>
> (Genesis 32:28 NIV)

Let us note that as the Lord prevailed and had His way with Jacob (Genesis 32:25), we are told that *Jacob* overcame (or "prevailed")! While inwardly and outwardly in brokenness, at this lowest point in his life, Jacob is also at the culminating point and climax to which the Angel of the Lord had been leading him, ever since he had fled from his twin brother, Esau. Reflecting on the Lord's earlier promise, he is at the fulfillment of God's purposes:

> I will not leave you until I have done what I have promised you.
>
> (Genesis 28:15 NIV)

Jacob was at the foot of the proverbial ladder to heaven, where God's angels were ascending and descending. (See also John 1:51.)

Jacob, father of the twelve tribes of Israel, is in the hands of the great Potter. He is on the Potter's wheel, being molded into shape – into the very likeness of the Angel of the Lord Himself, did he but know it. It had been painful and awesome in the extreme! Yet, approaching with 400 armed men, Esau had been but God's servant to bring Jacob to desperation. In this way, the Lord deals with so many of us in our lives.

Even so, the Genesis picture is incomplete without the fuller perspective Hosea brings:

> In the womb [Jacob] took his brother by the heel,
>> And [or But] in his maturity he contended with God.
> Yes, he wrestled with the angel and prevailed;
>> *He wept* and sought His favor [grace].
>> (Hosea 12:2–4 NASB, emphasis added)

Hosea is virtually saying that from before his birth, Jacob had been doing things "his way" – particularly with regard to Esau! It was not until he came to spiritual maturity (in effect, brokenness and weakness) that he turned to God for help. Hosea shows us that in the struggle with the Angel in Genesis, Jacob had actually come to tears. The wrestling was far more excruciating than Genesis had revealed.

Jacob came to the end of himself, where God had been waiting for so long – the point where He still waits for you, for me, for all of us, but, in particular, the point for which God yet waits for Israel, His people. This is aptly, movingly, and breathtakingly described in the center of the book of Isaiah:

> Therefore the LORD longs [waits] to be gracious to you,
>> And therefore He waits on high to have compassion on you …
> How blessed are all those who long [wait] for Him.

> O people in Zion, inhabitant in Jerusalem, you will weep no longer. He will surely be gracious to you at the sound of your cry; when He hears it, He will answer you.

> Although the Lord has given you bread of privation and water of oppression, He, your Teacher will no longer hide Himself, but your eyes will behold your Teacher.

> Your ears will hear a word behind you, "This is the way, walk in it,"
> whenever you turn to the right or to the left.
>
> (Isaiah 30:18–21 NASB)

Israel in embryo

Without parallel amongst all other nations, Israel has the essence of her future prophetically condensed into her name: "Israel." While she has not yet fully prevailed "as a prince with God and with men," that is her destiny, and it is strongly opposed by other forces and nations. Is God dealing with you on a similar basis? Are you looking for that weakness, of which the apostle Paul says, "When I am weak, then I am strong" (2 Corinthians 12:10 NIV)?

Satan knows the Bible better than we Christians: he knows that one day Israel will be "the head, and not the tail" (Deuteronomy 28:13 KJV); the "chief of the nations" (Jeremiah 31:7 KJV); the place to which "all nations will stream" (Isaiah 2:2 NIV); and that the earthly Jerusalem will be called "the throne of the LORD" (Jeremiah 3:17 KJV).

The Gospel of Matthew prophetically adds what we presently see in process:

> You will be hated by all nations because of My name.
>
> (Matthew 24:9 NASB)

While we know this has an application to the Church also, it is vital to see its specific application to the Jewish people, particularly as the Olivet discourse in Matthew quotes the parable of the fig tree (which is Israel) as being *the* sign of the Lord's near return. "Learn this lesson *from* the fig-tree," says the Lord, not "*of* it" or "*about* it" (Matthew 24:32 NIV, emphasis added).

What happened to Jacob (recorded of him as he comes to and crosses the River Jabbok) encapsulates the present and future experiences of his offspring – the people of Israel. It is a miniature picture of God bringing this nation into isolation from all others, and into dependence upon no one but Him. This is God's aim, of course, for each of us, but Israel is the only people He thus deals with on a *national* basis (Psalm 147:20).

Led by God's call to return to his homeland (Genesis 31:3), Jacob is full of fear and greatly distressed (32:7) when told that his brother, whom he cheated and fled from years before, is coming to meet him with 400 men! It is this fear which drives Jacob to his prayer of confession:

> I am unworthy of all the … faithfulness which You have shown to Your servant.
>
> (Genesis 32:10 NASB)

At the end of his tether, at his wits' end, Jacob sends on a lavish gift to appease his brother, Esau (Genesis 32:13–21).

The river which Jacob had to cross, "Jabbok" (Hebrew root: "to empty"), is symbolic. Beforehand, Jacob poured himself out before God at this crossing. When the simple but piercing question came from the Angel, "What is your name?" Jacob had but one answer: "Jacob," meaning "the supplanter," "the deceiver," "the cheat"…

The Lord had seen the pouring out of Jacob, had heard the confession of his nature and, at that point, renamed Jacob with a name that was to be as illustrious as his old name had been ignominious! There is no other nation on the face of the earth that has such a glorious future before her as Israel. But the pathway of furnace and affliction lies in between. "Israel" itself is a prophetic name: she will eventually prevail and overcome! May the Lord give us faith, purity and perseverance in prayer!

The "arise" and "shine," the "light" and "glory" of the unfading passage in Isaiah 60 are promises which we love to appropriate for ourselves, but the first and fullest application is to the nation placed at the navel of the earth: Israel. It amounts to stealing if we fail to apply it in this way. It is a clear and exciting prediction of Israel's future:

> Arise, shine; for thy light is come, and the glory of the LORD is risen upon thee.
>
> For, behold, the darkness shall cover the earth, and gross darkness the people: but the LORD shall arise upon thee, and His glory shall be seen upon thee.

> And the Gentiles shall come to thy light, and kings to the brightness
> of thy rising.
>
> (Isaiah 60:1–3 KJV)

This stores up, for Jacob and his descendants, something for which we must pray: that the blessing through them to the world will not be hindered, and will be no longer delayed.

In Genesis 32 Jacob did not call the place where he met the Lord, "the place of my protection or preservation," but rather he called it Peniel, meaning "the place of God's presence." He was not changed by an ecstatic experience but by his persevering struggle with God.

In the growing isolation of Israel, God Himself is today at work in His sovereignty. Psalm 135:4, the second of the two opening texts to this chapter, highlights God's sovereignty in election. In his prophecy of 3,500 years ago, even Balaam said:

> How shall I curse whom God has not cursed? ...
>> Behold, a people who dwells apart,
>> And will not be reckoned among the nations.
>
> (Numbers 23:8–9 NASB)

However, in the New Testament, there is a clear warning over Balaam, who did eventually cause Israel to stumble (Numbers 31:16). The reproof and warning are addressed to the Pergamum church (Revelation 2:14) for *harboring those who kept teaching others to put a stumbling block before the children of Israel.* It is indisputable that the Church in the West, with its distorted teaching of the prophetic word, has placed huge obstacles and stumbling blocks across the pathway of Israel's restoration and salvation. There is much to give account for, and chapters 9 to 11 of Romans outline this.

The God of Jacob

While we may generally think that we "know" Jacob (a not-too-nice character, someone whom the Lord might "have difficulty in saving"), we should note that, however we like it, we are all "Jacobs" at heart! There are no exceptions. Why? Jeremiah tells us that "the heart is more deceitful [the Hebrew means "more jacobed"] than all else" (Jeremiah 17:9 NASB). This supports the words of the apostle Paul:

> Now these things [in the Old Testament] happened as examples for us, so that we should not crave evil things as they also craved.
>
> (1 Corinthians 10:6 NASB)

However, we should take great encouragement from the fact that, of all the names that God chooses to apply to Himself, the one used more than any other is "the God of Jacob!" This is a stimulant when considering the nation of Israel itself, other people, and ourselves. God could have written, "The God of Israel is our refuge," but no! He reminds us that it is "the God of Jacob" who is our refuge (Psalm 46:7, 11 KJV) – the God of the cheat, swindler, self-willed, scheming, self-confident individual!

God is seeking through this name to remind us constantly not merely of Jacob, nor of our own earthly background, but rather of His endless mercy to the ungodly.

> To the one who does not work, but believes in Him who justifies the ungodly, his faith is credited as righteousness.
>
> (Romans 4:5 NASB)

Jacob in a real sense is the spearhead emerging from Genesis, the character which God is to further purify and sanctify in shaping Jacob's descendants, later to become Israel.

In Genesis, fourteen chapters are given to the story of Abraham, two to Isaac, but twenty are given to Jacob! God is "the God of Abraham" some 340 times in the Word of God, but He is "the God of Jacob" about 400 times! The millennial reign of Christ begins in Isaiah 2 with "Come, let us go up to … the house of the God of Jacob" (Isaiah 2:3 NASB). With colorful Jacob at the center of these considerations, we must conclude that God cares for us, the outcasts of this globe, whether we be Jew or Gentile, but particularly the former who yet remains as the prototype, the marred vessel *still* on the wheel of the Potter.

> Can I not, O house of Israel, deal with you as this potter does? Behold, like the clay in the potter's hand, so are you in My hand, O house of Israel.
>
> (Jeremiah 18:6 NASB)

Let this faith-building picture of our omniscient God be a bright beam of hope to every reader! If He can make the "Jacob" of Genesis, Rebecca's son, into an "Israel," can He not and will He not also reshape and remake you, and me?

To repeat yet again, it is fascinating to realize that, after all the huge conflicts and battles which we know will occur in the future (i.e. after the wars of Gog and Magog and then Armageddon), at the very beginning of the Millennium, the Lord chooses to call Himself "the God of Jacob," and not "the God of Israel"!

> The mountain of the house of the LORD
>> Will be established as the chief of the mountains ...
> And many peoples will come and say,
>> "Come, let us go up to the mountain of the LORD
>> To the house of *the God of Jacob*."
>
> (Isaiah 2:2–3 NASB, emphasis added)

Why will the nations use that term: "the house of the God of Jacob"? Why not just "the house of the LORD"? It will be because of His awesome intervention on behalf of what will be a defenseless Israel (Ezekiel 38:18–23). The things God will do on behalf of His prodigal son, Jacob!

> My dwelling place also will be with them; and I will be their God, and they [Jacob/Israel] will be My people. And the nations will *know* that I am the LORD who sanctifies Israel, when My sanctuary is in their midst forever.
>
> (Ezekiel 37:28 NASB, emphasis added)

Just as God promised the land unconditionally to Abraham after putting him into a deep sleep, so we shall find the renewal of that promise, given to Jacob while he was fast asleep at the foot of ladder to heaven (Genesis 28:13–16).

As eloquently said elsewhere by Lance Lambert, "Jacob's problem was not Esau, nor Laban, nor even Leah. Jacob's problem was Jacob!" When his self-strength had been dealt with, and he had laid it down, then immediately and with no striving whatever, there was reconciliation with Esau (Genesis 33:4). This is one of the most remarkable transformations in the whole Word of God. Instead of fear on the one hand, and belligerence on the other, Jacob and Esau are found falling over one another with affection and respect, and Jacob lavishes his prepared gifts on his brother. But note that to bring this about, God's dealings were almost entirely with Jacob.

> There will be tribulation and distress for every soul of man who does evil, of the Jew *first* and also of the Greek.
>
> > (Romans 2:9 NASB, emphasis added)

Similarly, when the Lord has fully dealt with "Jacob" in this sense, they (the Jewish people) will be the channels for the release of His blessing to the four corners of this earth:

> Then the remnant of Jacob
> > Will be among many peoples
> > Like dew from the LORD,
> > Like showers on vegetation.
>
> > (Micah 5:7 NASB)

The forerunner

The Jacob of Genesis is therefore the cameo of what God plans to do and to be to the rest of the world. The peoples and areas spoken of in the "Arise and shine" passage of Isaiah 60 – in verses 6 and 7 – live east of Israel today. This speaks of a huge response to the Lord from Arab

Muslim people, after the glory of the Lord has been seen upon the beleaguered Jewish nation.

Rabbi Saul of Tarsus presents a similar embryonic picture of what Israel will one day be. He learned the hard way that God's strength is made perfect in weakness. He came to the position of being "well content with weaknesses, with insults, with distresses, with persecutions, with difficulties for Christ's sake; for when I am weak, then I am strong" (2 Corinthians 12:10 NASB). It took Jacob twenty-one years to learn that same lesson!

And it did not sink in until Jacob was alone with God, until he was isolated! On that fateful night, he began what he thought was a struggle with a man. It was not until halfway through the night that he realized he was struggling, not merely with an "angel," but with the Angel of the Lord – God Himself! This was the Messiah in person, and Jacob was amazed that he saw Him – that he saw God and lived!

Uppermost in God's heart today is His desire to meet with His people, Israel – the many "Jacobs" of this day and age. And in a real sense He desires to meet with each person on a one-to-one basis, in the place where individual transactions can be made. He wants to meet with the Nicodemus who asks, "How can these things be?"(John 3:9 NASB); with the Saul who asks, "Who art thou, Lord? ... What wilt thou have me to do?" (Acts 9:5–6 KJV), and with those who are saying, "Lord, evermore give us this bread" (John 6:34 KJV). Hunger for God and openness to the gospel have been slowly but steadily on the increase ever since the Six-Day War. But this received a marked boost during the unexpected and frightening Lebanese conflict of 2006, and it continued into 2009.

In the days ahead

Let us pause here and, as it were, "go up to the top of Mount Pisgah" (Deuteronomy 3:27 NASB) from which the Lord showed Moses all the land that He had sworn to give to Abraham, Isaac and Jacob. Let us pause for that preview, though we may not ourselves fully see it all under the feet of the Israelis in our lifetime.

In the days to come Jacob will take root,
>Israel will blossom and sprout,
>And they will fill the whole world with fruit.

(Isaiah 27:6 NASB)

1. In this prophecy it is Jacob that takes root, but Israel produces the fruit. The transformed Israel is spoken of as "life from the dead" to the world (Romans 11:15 NIV). "The years that the locust hath eaten" are restored, and the shame is removed (Joel 2:25–26 KJV).
2. But it begins with the isolation of Israel, where she will seek God and not her human helpers.

Therefore, behold, I will allure her,
>Bring her into the wilderness
>And speak kindly to her.

(Hosea 2:14 NASB)

I will bring you into the wilderness of the people, and there will I plead with you face to face.

(Ezekiel 20:35 KJV)

Moses prophesies of this:

From the hills I behold him; lo, the people shall dwell alone, and shall not be reckoned among the nations.

(Numbers 23:9 KJV)

3. The Old Testament closes with a stark reminder of God's prerogative in election.

I have loved Jacob, but Esau I have hated.

(Malachi 1:2–3 NIV; see also Romans 9:13)

The Lord is re-affirming here that before either of them had been born, and before either had done good or bad, He had chosen Jacob as the son of promise (Genesis 25:23; Psalm 135:4; Romans 9:11).

God's prerogative in election is difficult to understand. It is partly explained in 1 Corinthians where we read:

God has chosen the foolish things of the world to shame the wise, and ... the weak things ... to shame the things which are strong, and the base things ... and the despised God has chosen ... so that no man may boast before God.

(1 Corinthians 1:27–28 NASB)

4. The four psalms 45, 46, 47 and 48 are an interlinked and progressive quartet. But Psalm 46 has the *rhema* word of the hour for us just now. It speaks of unimaginable trouble worldwide, but, in its finality, it speaks of the preservation and salvation of the tiny nation of Israel, the butt of world hatred and oppression:

God is our refuge and strength, a tested help in times of trouble.
    And so *we* need not fear even if the world blows up, and the mountains crumble into the heart of the sea ...
    There is a river of joy flowing through the City of our God ... God himself is living in that City ... The nations rant and rave in anger – but when God speaks, the earth melts in submission and kingdoms totter into ruin ...
    He, the God of Jacob, has come to rescue *us* ... "Stand silent! Know that I am God! I will be honored by every nation in the world!"

(Psalm 46 TLB, emphasis added)

This is Israel's history written in advance, in a psalm already with many fulfillments in our lives and that of Israel. But the full fulfillment is yet to come in the time ahead: "Jacob's tribulation" (Jeremiah 30:6–7). A clear picture of this period (Jacob's all-night struggle with the Lord) is found by carefully collating together pieces from various prophets of the Bible (these are too detailed to list here, but will be outlined in a later book). Sufficient to say that not only is Israel to be physically preserved, but the Lord pours out His Spirit upon her people (Ezekiel 39:28–29).

    This will excite and thrill us all, as it takes us back to the twelfth of the Thirteen Principles of Faith found in the *Siddur*, the Jewish book of daily prayer: "I believe with perfect faith in the coming of the Messiah, and though He tarry, yet I will wait daily for His coming." (See also Habakkuk 2:3; Hebrews 10:37.)

This, therefore, is the "land" that lies before us, which we are to possess by faith and prayer. Let us therefore cross the raging Jordan of unbelief and bring death to doubt and confusion, and resurrection life to our prayers and proclamations for the salvation of Israel!

> Israel will be saved by the LORD
> with an everlasting salvation;
> you will never be put to shame or disgraced
> to ages everlasting.

> (Isaiah 45:17 NIV)

> Truly you are a God who hides himself,
> O God and Savior of Israel.

> (Isaiah 45:15 NIV)

Just a few comments before closing this chapter: In the writer's opinion, backed by several scriptures, the "time of Jacob's trouble" will be preceded by a period of false peace which will be lengthy enough to cause Israel to feel that safety and peace have finally arrived.

It appears that Israel will be without defense of any kind against a massive, invading northern army, whereby the peace is shattered. But in answer to national prayer and fasting, God will intervene and the invaders will be totally destroyed. Even more importantly, it is in this period – when Israel's life hangs by a thread – that God will pour out His Holy Spirit upon the house of Israel. This is a reproduction on a national scale of Jacob's coming face to face with Esau in Genesis 32. It was during his perilous plight that Jacob came to Peniel.

I trust that through the study of the Scriptures, readers will begin to see the matching threads that run through:

1. the Genesis 32 account;
2. Psalm 46;
3. Saul's meeting with his Master and Savior on the road to Damascus.

Tribulations ahead

What is also important to bear in mind is that "Jacob's tribulation" is followed later by the "great tribulation" (see Revelation 7). Jacob's tribulation is not of itself *the* great tribulation, as is taught in many places.

It is important to bear in mind that these coming periods of intense trouble may be for the Jews *first*, but they are not for the Jews *only* (Romans 2:9–11)! Those who actively and prayerfully identify with Israel will certainly not be without danger and oppression from the enemy. A life of devotion and worship to God is as essential as that of prayer and intercession. May the river of joy that runs through the City of God (Psalm 46:4) have free course in our hearts and lives!

> There is a river that flows from God above,
> There is a fountain that's filled with His great love,
> Come to the river – there is a vast supply!
> There is a river that never will run dry![1]

The sword of Islam: world trends

Ishmael versus Isaac

It is sobering to reflect that the present Middle East problem did not begin in 1967, nor in 1948, nor in 1917 – indeed not in this century. Smoldering beneath the surface since the time of Abram has been the hostility between the two Abrahamic sons – Ishmael and Isaac – and their offspring.

We can praise God for the fact that once we are found "in the Messiah," imbued with life by Him whom the Bible calls "the last Adam" (1 Corinthians 15:45 KJV), we can be freed and delivered from the unwelcome traits of our family line – the carnal attributes that do not please God, ourselves, nor our fellow human beings.

> With God all things are possible!

(Matthew 19:26 KJV)

Abraham, the patriarch, both then and now, must have wished that he had never listened to the advice of his wife, Sarah! How easy it is to accept a promise of God – how hard to wait years and years for its fulfillment. Humanly speaking, we would not wonder at the incredulity of the couple faced with the idea of bearing a child, since Abram was eighty-five and Sarai seventy-five. But because of his wife's barrenness until that time, Abram did listen to Sarai, took the Egyptian handmaid Hagar, and Ishmael was born. He had "helped" God fulfill His promise of a son (Genesis 15:4).

However, God later told Abraham that the child of promise would not be by Hagar, but by his true wife Sarah, and the Lord would grant the miracle needed. While the miracle of that birth and the preservation of the nation of Israel throughout history defy human explanation, Abraham's earlier carnal judgment and alliance have taken their toll.

> "Woe to the obstinate children," declares the LORD,
>   "to those who carry out plans that are not mine,
>   forming an alliance, but not by my Spirit,
>   heaping sin upon sin;
> who go down to Egypt
>   without consulting me;
> who look for help to Pharaoh's protection,
>   to Egypt's shade for refuge."
>
> > (Isaiah 30:1–2 NIV)

After Isaac's birth and growth, the same arrogance that Hagar had developed towards her mistress was found in Ishmael:

> Sarah saw that the son whom Hagar the Egyptian had borne to Abraham was mocking, and she said to Abraham, "Get rid of that slave woman and her son, for that slave woman's son will never share in the inheritance with my son Isaac."
>
> > (Genesis 21:9–10 NIV)

Though Abraham pleaded with God, "Oh, that Ishmael might live …!" (Genesis 17:18 KJV), God underlined that his covenant was to be with the child of His promise. Therein would lie the inheritance, although Ishmael would also be the fruitful father of twelve tribes.

Ishmael and Islam

"Ishmael" (the Arab people) has never been reconciled to the fact that "Isaac" (the Jews) is the chosen child of inheritance and promise, through whom would come the Messiah.

This explains why the Koran seeks to affirm the reverse – that Ishmael was the child of promise and that no friendship must develop between Muslims and Jews, or Muslims and Christians. It explains also the Arab practice of centuries of keeping Jews in Arab lands as second-class citizens. Throughout history, the classic example of the difference between human efforts and God's provision lies in Ishmael versus Isaac (see Galatians 4:21–31).

This is a clash which not only runs throughout the Bible but is also increasingly evident in the religious, political and economic worlds today. Although Christianity has many foes, the Christians in Muslim lands display a spiritual resistance higher than anywhere else.

All the oppression and harshness of Russia did not prevent the growth of one of the healthiest and largest churches in the world, even though it went partly underground. Before the present resurgence of Islam, Christians were in fractional minorities in Muslim lands, and in some cases entirely secreted from public knowledge. In several strongly Muslim countries today, hundreds of Muslims are coming to faith in Christ – an inexplicable phenomenon!

In the book of Daniel, Babylon and Assyria cover the same Asian territory as modern-day Iraq. Iraq, whose alleged potential to build a nuclear bomb was destroyed by Israel in June 1981, is one of Israel's most implacable foes. In his book on Daniel, G.H. Lang writes:

> Assyria was the first empire to devour Israel and drive him out of his land (2 Kings 17) ... It is when anti-Christ shall have made Babylon its centre of universal government that the empire will become what is so vividly and minutely portrayed in prophetic

Scripture – *Babylon* is Satan's original and final earth centre, just as Jerusalem is the divine centre. And modern world movements tend unceasingly to the Near East.

Islam and Christianity

The people of Israel were very sternly warned by Joshua on no account to associate with the nations that remained among them.

> Do not invoke the names of their gods or swear by them. You must not serve them or bow down to them ...
>
> If you turn away and ally yourselves with the survivors of these nations that remain among you and if you intermarry with them and associate with them, then you may be sure that the LORD your God will no longer drive out these nations before you. Instead, they will become snares and traps for you, whips on your backs and thorns in your eyes, until you perish from this good land, which the LORD your God has given you.
>
> (Joshua 23:7, 12–13 NIV)

Christians need to heed these words today because a marriage is under way between Islam (which denies Christ's deity outright and also the place of Christians) and Christianity. There is no cause for complacency, even though this may be happening in some corner of the world or the Church that appears remote from us. Israel's command was to clean up and possess the land; many of her sons were killed by their brethren for "marrying out."

While we pray for the Muslims, we can have no association, no dialogue, with a faith that proclaims such as the following in its creed:

> The punishment of those who wage war against Allah and his apostle [Muhammad] and strive to make mischief in the land is this, that they should be killed or crucified or that their hands and feet should be cut off on opposite sides or they should be exiled from the land.
>
> (The Table Spread, Sura 5:33)

Make war upon those who believe not ... even if they be People of the Book [i.e. Christians and Jews] until they have willingly agreed to pay the Jizya [tax] in recognition of their submissive state.

(Repentance, Sura 9:29)

You are the noblest nation that has ever been raised up for mankind.

(The Imrans, Sura 3:110)

Islam and Britain

The following accounts highlight the appalling snares that we are running into in Britain – snares which Joshua says will turn into "whips on your backs and thorns in your eyes." Britain is being mercilessly driven into the camp of Islam and we cannot see where we are going. For example, if the Arab nations removed their huge sums of invested wealth from Britain we would be bankrupt; if they withheld their import orders, our commerce and industry would collapse. Increasingly, they are in a position to call the tune in the UK, and when we as Christians feel that Islam is simply another road to God, we are responsible for what follows.

1. Dr Coggan, as the former Archbishop of Canterbury, said in March 1979: "It is essential for the two religions to understand each other better, and I pray for a closer relationship." The Muslims will not share in that ambition.
2. Dr Coggan's successor, Dr Runcie, boldly made a similar statement at his induction a short time afterwards.
3. The nerve center for Islamic evangelism is based in London. It was opened in 1973 and runs a wealth of glossy literature and other teaching aids for doctrinal propagation. In 1976, at an international Islamic conference in London, it was said, "If we can win London for Islam, it will not be hard to win the whole Western world."
4. At a further international three-day seminar held in London in December 1979, Professor Ismail al-Faruqi said, "It is nonsense to speak of Islam in opposition to Christianity or Judaism. There are some domestic disputes only. [We share] belief in one God who has

given the Psalms to David, the heavens to Jesus, and his angels to all. We invite Jews and Christians to co-operate with us."

5. In 1945 there was one mosque in England, in 1950 there were twenty-five, in 1960 there were eighty, in 1976 200, and in 1979 300 (a 50 percent increase in three years). In 2009, it would be unwise to consider the figure as being anything less than several thousands.

6. The largest and grandest mosque in Europe, along with its Islamic university, is in the heart of London, in Regent's Park; it was built by a Christian firm of builders and opened by the Queen.

   But, as this book goes to press, a far, far larger mosque – bigger and "better" than anything yet built anywhere in the world (and funded, as all the others have been, from abroad) – is in the planning stages for central London! *Who ever heard of such a thing – to outdo St Paul's Cathedral and Westminster Abbey?*

7. In England only a few years ago, and in France and Sweden, the Muslims were the second largest religious body. By 2008 their numbers were equal to or exceeded those of Christians.

8. The trend for Muslim–Christian "marriage" advocated by our prelates was seen to be developing in a shared seminar given in the University of London premises on 27 March 1982. The seminar's title, "Revelation and Authority in Christianity and Islam," at once indicates or implies an equally given divine stamp on each religion.

   A Christian speaker is Director of the Centre for the Study of Islam and Christian–Muslim Relations at a very prominent college based in the English Midlands. Their syllabus reads:

The study ... is a joint venture of Christians and Muslims who, in obedience to their respective faiths and in a spirit of openness and trust, wish to explore the living traditions and mutual relations of Islam and Christianity and to prepare for sensitive responses to their personal and varied vocations.

Notes for the Christian
1. What fellowship can light have with darkness?
2. What does a believer have in common with an unbeliever?
3. What agreement is there between the Temple of God and idols? (cf. 2 Corinthians 6:14–17)

"Therefore come out from them and be separate," says the Lord.

(2 Corinthians 6:17 NIV)

Islam and Europe

1. At the dedication of a mosque in Paris, the Second Vatican Council declared: "[The Church] looks with respect upon Mohammedans, since they believe in God."
2. In Belgium, Islam is officially recognized as a religious denomination. The cantor is paid by the state and the mosques will be maintained at the expense of provincial governments.
3. The Roman Catholics have made particularly compromising statements on Islamic and Christian co-operation. St Peter's Square, Rome, is now overlooked by a large mosque and Islamic university.
4. Islam is making vast inroads into European cities, at the same time as Christians and Christian workers are being forced out of Muslim countries.

Muslims do not respect Christians for their tolerance, but rather will take advantage of it. Clearly there is a Muslim bid for the Western world, and for Britain. *It is high time to awaken out of our slumber.*

Ishmael has grown no fonder of Isaac over the years, and Jews and Christians are called to have no part in worshiping the gods of the people around us:

You must not serve them or bow down to them.

(Joshua 23:7 NIV)

There is no doubt that Britain and Europe are bowing down to Islam, and the whips on our backs are already being felt. We are being driven in the direction that both opposes God (and Israel) and aligns with Islam. The Church is sleeping as our countries cradle Islam, Ishmael's offspring, the foe of both Jews and Christians.

The gospel of violence and anti-Semitism

> Mark this: There will be terrible times in the last days. People will be lovers of themselves, lovers of money, boastful, proud, abusive, disobedient to their parents ... without love ... without self-control, brutal ... treacherous ...
>
> (2 Timothy 3:1–4 NIV)

> But you, dear friends, build yourselves up in your most holy faith and pray in the Holy Spirit. Keep yourselves in God's love as you wait for the mercy of our Lord Jesus Christ to bring you to eternal life.
>
> Be merciful to those who doubt; snatch others from the fire and save them; to others show mercy, mixed with fear – hating even the clothing stained by corrupted flesh.
>
> (Jude 20–23 NIV)

Simultaneously with mounting world opposition to Israel, and the Arabs' rejection of the Jewish State, we see an unimaginable escalation in international terrorism. Between 1965 and 1978, the number of annual terrorist incidents increased by fifteen times. There were twenty such incidents in 1965 and 300 in 1978. As long ago as 1980, Paul Johnson, at a conference in Jerusalem on international terrorism, said that terrorism is the greatest evil of our age, a "more serious threat to our culture and survival than the possibility of nuclear war."

The trumpet has sounded

Undoubtedly, the above statement by Paul Johnson was epitomized in what has so far been the most spectacular, appalling and symbolic example of that terrorism – the destruction on 11 September 2001 of the twin towers of the World Trade Center in New York, when some 3,000 people died.

The world and the Church turned a corner at that moment and a warning was given – a trumpet was sounded – which has been heard by neither! Rev. David Wilkerson, whose renowned church at Times Square is just around the corner from the former location of those towers said: "The trumpet has sounded and we have not heard."

As a warning to the world, the disaster occurred at "the heart of Babylon" – the World Trade Center. As a warning to the Jews, it occurred in New York, the city that is home to two million of the seven million Jews still living in the USA. As a warning to the Church and Israel, it occurred at a particular time relative to the Biblical festivals – in this case, the Feast of Trumpets.

The next of the seven Biblical feasts to be fulfilled is the fifth one – the fourth having been the Feast of Weeks (Pentecost), which was followed by a long gap of some 1,970 years till the present day. While the next feast (the fifth, held on the first day of Tishri, the seventh month in the Jewish calendar) has been mistakenly called and celebrated as *Rosh Hashana* (New Year), it is of course *nothing of the kind.* The Biblical (i.e. Jewish) new year has always begun in the month of Nissan (see Exodus 12:2), the fourteenth day of which is Passover.

The New York disaster occurred towards the end of the sixth month (Elul) at the very time when a *shofar* is traditionally sounded to herald and prepare for the Day of Trumpets (*Yom Truah*), the first day of Tishri. This marks the first of the ten Days of Awe when Jews are meant to seek God in preparation for the tenth day of Tishri: *Yom Kippur*, the Day of Atonement. This is the most serious and sobering of all the Biblical festivals; it is a day of fasting, when all activity ceases, when there are five successive and separate services in the synagogues, when the shofar warningly calls us all to repentance, when we are hopefully "inscribed in the book of Life."

The period at the end of the month of Elul, when the shofar is traditionally sounded daily for seven days, is called *Selichot*. It was at the beginning of that period in 2001 when the twin towers fell. It was God's warning to us all, but no one has taken note at all (awful terror though it was) that God was and is speaking to us, seeking to wake us (both the Church and Israel) from our slumber.

What happened on "9/11" seems to be a forerunner and type of what is predicted in the book of Revelation, chapter 18, where we read:

> Babylon the great is fallen, is fallen ... in one hour so great riches is come to nought.
>
> (Revelation 18:2, 17 KJV)

(The time that elapsed, from the point at which the aircraft flew into the towers until the buildings burned and collapsed, was fifty minutes!)

> But all these things are merely the beginning of birth pangs.
>
> (Matthew 24:8 NASB)

Jesus spoke these words 2,000 years ago, directly referring to what is happening today. He saw down the tunnel of world history; He saw the end-time build-up of resistance to His return. And, just as Herod was moved upon by the god of this world to oppose the birth of the Son of God, the King of kings, so today the whole empire of the powers of darkness is in an increasing frenzy to block the coming reign on earth of the Lord Jesus Christ, and the spiritual restoration of His firstborn son, Israel (Exodus 4:22–23).

> But when these things *begin* to take place, straighten up and lift up your heads, because your redemption is drawing near.
>
> (Luke 21:28 NASB, emphasis added)

"All these things" are the wars, the famines, the earthquakes, the iniquity and the lawlessness, and even the deceptions of Matthew 24 that are among the twelve signs therein of the Lord's return. Amazingly, He tells us not to be "troubled: for all these things *must* come to pass [!] but the end is not yet" (Matthew 24:6 KJV, emphasis added).

In these upheavals, the apostle Paul bids us not to sleep as others do, but to watch and be sober. When (not "If") they come, we are not to be surprised as though we were children of darkness, but (as children of light) to put on the breastplate of faith and love, and to edify and comfort one another. It is in this same context that he goes on to exhort us to rejoice evermore, pray without ceasing, and constantly give thanks! He assures us that it is the very God of peace who waits to sanctify us wholly, spirit, soul and body (1 Thessalonians 5:23–24).

> Faithful is He that calleth you, who will also do it.
>
> (1 Thessalonians 5:24 KJV)

In the mounting world lawlessness, whether of Islamic or some other source, let us take adequate "comfort" from the fact that God, the Lord, has warned in many ways and words that the end days would be characterized by one thing – trouble! That is the theme of many psalms; while King David personalized them, they have a real *national* application to Israel – and often we also need to appropriate them as referring to the Church.

> There is a river whose streams make glad the city of God,
>   The holy dwelling places of the Most High ...
> The LORD of hosts is with us:
>   the God of Jacob is our stronghold.
>
> (Psalm 46:4, 7 NASB)

Christian Zionism

The Ishmael-versus-Isaac dispute spills over into the Church with the rise of what is called "Christian Zionism," that is, Christian vision and support for the restoration of Israel, which includes her coming spiritual restoration. Of course, the Father of this vision, the greatest "Christian Zionist" of all time, is the One who declares:

> The LORD has chosen Zion.
>   *He* has desired it for His habitation.
>
> (Psalm 132:13 NASB, emphasis added)

His plans to be enthroned in Jerusalem do not make him anti-Palestinian!

Anti-Christian Zionism

This is becoming much stronger, marked by a growing alliance between professing Christendom and Islam itself, through "Sabeel" conferences which have been held in Jerusalem in recent years. It is the growth and ripening of the errors of replacement theology which is driving both nominal and born-again Christians into an anti-Semitic stance, involving support of the false claims and "rights" of the Palestinians.

The respective positions are likely to harden and polarize in the days ahead, resulting in the bulk of the church being anti-Zionist. This foreshadows what is already on the horizon: the ostracism of those Christians who see and stand for the restoration and salvation of Israel in accordance with God's Word, and all that is written in this book.

So while we speak about the isolation of Israel, we should bear in mind that there is a remnant within the Church, as we know it, that has God's heart and vision for Israel. We also may well know "isolation" in the days ahead. It is nothing new for the Lord to work through a remnant. In fact, it is the far more normal pathway – so let us take heart! And let us continue to pray, especially for Britain, that He will open the eyes of more and more church leaders to the light and truth of His Word. Remember:

> The prophetic word ... [is] as ... a lamp shining in a dark place.
> (2 Peter 1:19 NASB)

The following extracts from a document published by the Church of Scotland give some idea of the general trend within the Church in non-Third World countries. It is part of a "Statement by the [Anglican] Patriarch and Local Heads of Churches in Jerusalem."

The Jerusalem Declaration on Christian Zionism
August 22, 2006

"Blessed are the peacemakers for they shall be called the children of God."

(Matthew 5:9)

Christian Zionism is a modern theological and political movement that embraces the most extreme theological positions of Zionism, thereby becoming detrimental to a just peace within Palestine and Israel. The Christian Zionist programme provides a worldview where the Gospel is identified with the ideology of empire, colonialism and militarism. In its extreme form, it places an emphasis on apocalyptic events leading to the end of history rather than living Christ's love and justice today.

We categorically reject Christian Zionist doctrines as false teaching that corrupts the biblical message of love, justice and reconciliation.

We further reject the contemporary alliance of Christian Zionist leaders and organisations with elements in the governments of Israel and the United States that are presently imposing their unilateral pre-emptive borders and domination over Palestine. This inevitably leads to unending cycles of violence that undermine the security of all peoples of the Middle East and the rest of the world.

We reject the teachings of Christian Zionism that facilitate and support these policies as they advance racial exclusivity and perpetual war rather than the gospel of universal love, redemption and reconciliation taught by Jesus Christ. Rather than condemn the world to the doom of Armageddon we call upon everyone to liberate themselves from the ideologies of militarism and occupation. Instead, let them pursue the healing of the nations!

We call upon Christians in Churches on every continent to pray for the Palestinian and Israeli people, both of whom are suffering as victims of occupation and militarism. These discriminative actions are turning Palestine into impoverished ghettos surrounded by exclusive Israeli settlements. The establishment of the illegal settlements and the construction of the Separation Wall on confiscated Palestinian land undermine the viability of a Palestinian state as well as peace and security in the entire region ...

With urgency we warn that Christian Zionism and its alliances are justifying colonization, apartheid and empire-building.

The best, most authentic comment on the above (which consists only of extracts from the fuller document) is found in the Book of Life:

> The Lord spoke to Jeremiah again and said:
> Have you heard what people are saying? – that the Lord chose Judah and Israel and then abandoned them! They are sneering and saying that Israel isn't worthy to be counted as a nation. But this is the Lord's reply: I would no more reject my people than I would change my laws of night and day, of earth and sky. I will never abandon the Jews, or David my servant, or change the plan that his Child will some day rule over these descendants of Abraham, Isaac and Jacob. Instead I will restore their prosperity and have mercy on them.
>
> (Jeremiah 33:24–26 TLB)

Whatever trouble lies ahead for the nation of Israel, the book of Revelation in several places assures us of God's continuing care and preservation.

Before the adverse winds of Revelation 7 are released upon the world, the four angels are bidden to seal the remnant of Israel (the 144,000) on their foreheads ("bringing into captivity every thought to the obedience of Christ [the Messiah]" – 2 Corinthians 10:5 KJV). In Revelation 14, we find the Lamb standing specifically on Mount Zion with the remnant of 144,000.

There is some (presently concealed) spiritual victory that He is taking them through, probably to do with the fall of Babylon (14:8), but the "new song" which is sung is something *only they experience* (15:3). Probably the words of that song are those recorded in Revelation 15:3–4.

The point is that the Lord (as a Lamb) is with them on Mount Zion, they follow Him (lamb-like) wherever He goes, and they sing. They represent the twelve tribes of Israel and they have therefore not lost their identity, even as they follow the Lamb on Mount Zion.

I am so glad that, in spite of the sinfulness, obstinacy, unworthiness and carnality of the Jewish race (my kinspeople), the blood of the Lord Jesus, the Messiah and the Lamb of God, cleanses us from all sin. And those redeemed, 12,000 out of each of the twelve tribes, will be able to sing and shout:

> Great and marvellous are thy works, Lord God Almighty ...
> All nations shall come and worship before Thee.
>
> (Revelation 15:3, 4 KJV)

Notes

1. Words and music by Max and David Sapp ©1969.

CHAPTER 12

How Should We Pray for Israel?

On your walls, O Jerusalem, I have appointed watchmen;
    All day and all night they will never keep silent.
    You who remind the Lord, take no rest for yourselves;
And give Him no rest until He establishes
    And makes Jerusalem a praise in the earth.

(Isaiah 62:6–7 NASB)

Introduction

Hopefully, the leading question "Why pray for Israel?" has been largely answered. But before addressing the thorny question of "How should we pray?" let us look at the imperishable text above, which comes from the lips of *the* great Watchman and King of the Holy City Jerusalem: the Lord Himself.

While His word focuses upon the city itself, let us bear in mind that it is the capital, and that what He says concerns and covers *the whole land*.

It is captivating to realize that He opens this passage, not by speaking only to us as His watchmen, but also to the city itself. He brings assurance to the inhabitants of Jerusalem that *He Himself* is raising unceasing day-and-night prayer for the city and all that it stands for!

The great Watchman, the Lord Jesus, who "ever liveth to make intercession" for us and His people (Hebrews 7:25 KJV), has taken it upon Himself to oversee the continuance of ceaseless prayer throughout the centuries for the Royal City. It is as if He knows in advance that the inhabitants will at times be in despair – and He lays before them this unfading reminder of His nearness and involvement.

It indicates that when things were at their lowest ebb – in, say, the Middle Ages – when Jerusalem was under the heel either of the Crusaders or the Muslims, He had not dozed off, and He had His intercessors at hand at every point. They were at work during World War One, and paved the way for General Allenby's humble but triumphant entry on the first day of Hanukkah, 9 December 1917. The Holy Spirit had engineered and overseen events that led to that sudden and unexpected return of the city into the hands of the leading Christian nation of the day – Britain!

It was no less so in 1967 when, again, quite suddenly and unexpectedly, the city fell back into Jewish hands after some 1,900 years. *What a landmark, and what an historic day that was!* And He assures the city to this very day, and proclaims to all His adversaries, that *He* has appointed, *He* has set, *He* has positioned His watchmen. The root meaning here of the Hebrew word translated "appointed" is not merely "to be given a task to do," but "to tend with care." That is important!

It is interesting to note that in Ezekiel 33, the chapter immediately preceding those that deal with the restoration of Israel (chapters 34–39), the Holy Spirit repeats His call: "I have appointed you a watchman for the house of Israel" (Ezekiel 33:7 NASB), as was previously recorded in Ezekiel 3:17.

If you, dear reader, are feeling His nudge here, do not look at your weaknesses, your inadequacies, your poverty – all of which may well be valid. Consider only His strength and His faithfulness, and that His power is only made perfect in our weakness. Constantly, He reminds us that His grace is sufficient. Very often, our "confidence" is actually a hindrance.

Just as a journey of 1,000 miles begins with one step, so have prayer movements been raised that began with no more than a single whisper of a prayer, which later grew into an avalanche of prayer warriors! We must walk by faith, not by feeling – nor by sight!

As watchmen

If you have heard something of that call of God in your heart and soul, let it be tempered with faith. We do not always experience great depth of feeling or of faith, especially when we first begin. But pray using God's Word, and the more you pray, the more you will want to pray. Ask Him to put His burden and His thoughts into you, and to take away anything that is just of your flesh.

God will answer you – and I speak from experience. Feeling is not faith!

If you happen to be on your own in the early days, do not let the enemy discourage you. Recognize that even if in your locality the Church is ignorant or silent, or even hostile to these issues, God is in control. He can cause flowers to grow out of the top of icy mountains, and put a "bell" of ice over them to protect them!

Let us, with the Holy Spirit as our Teacher, take some pointers from watchmen and the walls of Jerusalem:

1. Watchmen have but one main task: to remain awake and alert when everyone else is asleep or otherwise occupied.
2. They are there to guard and to warn against approaching danger, the stealth of the stranger, and the thief.
3. They must be weaned from the many "good" things that could distract them or divert attention into other activities which might interest them, or even into other areas to watch. They are to stay where they are appointed.
4. They must guard against side issues which a foe might engineer or devise.
5. Watchmen do not get drunk or go to night-time revelries. They are to remain sober and alert. Their task is to outwit the enemy and to forewarn the city of any hostile approach (1 Thessalonians 5:7; Mark 13:33–37).

(a) Spiritual "highs" are rampant in the Christian world today, with deception at their very roots. Many of us (the so-called elect) overlook the fact that we can be deceived, failing to remember that the devil disguises himself as "an angel of light" – so attractive, so genuine-looking (2 Corinthians 11:14 KJV).

(b) The New Testament contains some eighteen verses on the subject of remaining sober, not for the purpose of being dull, but for the purpose of *prayer* (see 1 Peter 4:7). We are told to "test everything" or to "examine everything carefully" (1 Thessalonians 5:21 KJV, NASB).

(c) Proper testing takes time, and we need to start from the perspective with which Jesus began his Olivet discourse: "Take heed that no man deceive you" (Matthew 24:4 KJV) i.e. individual responsibility is important. This does not mean us to be legalistic or imprisoned, but to gain the sensitivity of the Holy Spirit in the general matter of prayer.

6. The watchmen are set. God does that. This alludes to perseverance, amongst other things. They are not to wander off into other activities which might interest them. Or even into other areas to watch. They are to stay where their master has placed them: constant, untiring, attentive and single-eyed.

   In Isaiah's day, Jerusalem had guards on regular four-hour shifts, night and day. These guards were not silent, but called to each other every few minutes, especially in times of danger, and the cry would pass from one to another, right around the city. They could see "eye to eye" and "lift up the voice" of warning or of cheer (Isaiah 52:8). This speaks to us of being called into prayer cells or prayer chains, and thereby relating to one another.

7. Although normally facing *outwards*, the watchmen could also see *into* the city. We are to be vigilant not only against known foes, but against subtle infiltration into the ranks of the Church, and also against our personal carnality and tendency to allow wrong attitudes within our minds and hearts. This is especially so when we begin to pray for Israel. We must never assume that we are "better" than someone else who has not had this revelation concerning Israel.

   Humility and gentleness are necessary and essential ingredients.

8. Jerusalem's walls were (and are) high, strong and massive – thick enough for a person to walk comfortably upon them.

   This speaks to us of being raised by the Spirit, with ample provision for us to walk and be in the Spirit, able to see things which those at lower level would not see or understand. In addition, we are to be strengthened with His power by His Spirit in the "inner man"!

   While needing to remain truly humble, it is also true that Biblical revelation on Israel, in God's time and way, brings revelation on other matters of spiritual warfare that are not otherwise evident to other believers.

9. Take encouragement from the fact that one stone remaining in the Western Wall today is thirty-seven feet in length, and others lower down are forty feet in length!

You are ... built on the foundation of the apostles and prophets, with [Messiah] Jesus himself as the chief cornerstone.

(Ephesians 2:20 NIV)

Faithful is He that calleth you, who will also do it.

(1 Thessalonians 5:24 KJV)

Will not God bring about justice for His elect who cry to Him day and night?

(Luke 18:7 NASB)

10. But there is another, happier function of the watchmen: to detect the messenger of God.

While David was sitting between the inner and outer gates, the watchmen went up to the roof of the gateway by the wall. As he looked out, he saw a man running alone. The watchman called out to the king and reported it.

The king said, "If he is alone, he must have good news." And the man came closer and closer.

(2 Samuel 18:24–25 NIV)

This idea is beautifully reflected in Isaiah:

How beautiful on the mountains
    are the feet of those who bring good news,
who proclaim peace,
    who bring good tidings,
    who proclaim salvation,
who say to Zion,
    "Your God reigns!"
Listen! Your watchmen lift up their voices;
    together they shout for joy.
When the LORD returns to Zion,
    they will see it with their own eyes.

                            (Isaiah 52:7–8 NIV)

Not only do we look expectantly for the return of the Lord, the Messiah, but one of the eight commands to the watchmen of Isaiah 62 is:

Say to the Daughter of Zion,
    "See, your Savior comes!
See, his reward is with him,
    and his recompense accompanies him."

                            (Isaiah 62:11 NIV)

This had a partial fulfillment when Jesus rode into Jerusalem on a donkey on what is now called Palm Sunday (Zechariah 9:9; John 12:12–15). But what a day it will be when He is revealed and fully received as both the King of kings and the Lamb of God that takes away the sin of the world!

There is no other nation under the sun that lives and waits in expectancy for its Messiah and Savior, even though this is only partially true of Israel at this moment, as some of her people hold viewpoints that do not tally with Holy Writ.

Israel's national anthem, *Hatikvah*, means "The Hope," and the hope of Israel for 2,000 years (only fully understood by born-again Jews or Gentiles) remains the coming of her Messiah.

O the Hope of Israel, his Savior in time of trouble,
Why should You be like a stranger in the land,
And like a traveler who turns aside to tarry for a night?

(Jeremiah 14:8 NKJV)

Even in their dispersion, many Jews have been prisoners of this hope – prisoners perhaps in a subconscious way, but held there by the God of Israel Himself – even as the *Siddur* (the Jewish daily prayer book) indicates in the twelfth of its Thirteen Principles of Faith: "I believe with perfect faith in the coming of the Messiah and, though He tarry, I will wait daily for His coming."

It is significant that the Zechariah passage exhorting the Jew to behold the lowly and victorious coming of his King is followed by:

As for you also, because of the blood of My covenant with you,
　　I have set your prisoners free from the waterless pit.
Return to the stronghold, O prisoners who have the hope;
　　This very day I am declaring that I will restore double to you.

(Zechariah 9:11–12 NASB)

The prophet Jeremiah addresses his God thus:

O LORD, my strength and my *stronghold*,
　　And my refuge in the day of distress [i.e. tribulation],
　　To You the nations will come
　　From the ends of the earth.

(Jeremiah 16:19 NASB, emphasis added)

In the work that the Holy Spirit is accomplishing today in Israel, our prayer should not only cover the growth of this hope within the hearts of the Jewish people, but also that it might be seen in our own lives, in our own love, in a selflessness that would point and draw them to that wonderful Hope.

11. As for reaching Jewish people, the above is not a *carte blanche* to start preaching who Jesus is. Instead it is a pointer to wisdom and the prompting of the Holy Spirit. A great pioneer in Jewish evangelism said some forty years ago, in regard to "fishing:" "You keep out

of sight, and you do not expose the hook before the fish start nibbling!"

Study the other seven commands in Isaiah 62 and note that they all precede this eighth one. One of the earlier commands tells us to "gather out the stones" (Isaiah 62:10 KJV). As Christians, we need to remove the boulders and barriers of centuries, caused by Christian persecution and vilification of the Jews. We cannot simply relegate this task to others. The Church as a whole, of which we are part, has a history of "planting" these stones – for example, many people have blamed the Jewish people for the crucifixion, whereas Jesus came to die for *us all* (John 12:27).

Here is an area, as many will well know, for repentance of the deepest kind – perhaps putting something into writing – if we expect God to act to bless both Israel and Britain. Most Christians do not realize that as a country, as a Church, as an area, or even as a family, we can suffer and continue to suffer through the sins of our forebears and predecessors, until repentance, renunciation and perhaps also restitution, and *then* authoritative prayer, are made.

Let us then gather out the stones! Prejudice and persecution, misunderstanding and injustice have no place in the life of a Christian whose main guide is the Bible and the Holy Spirit – not television, radio, newspapers, or even popular thinking. One of the most prestigious broadcasting organizations in the world, the BBC – in earlier years hailed as the most reliable and illustrious – today has an anti-Israel bias.

While simultaneously promoting Islam at every turn, its inaccurate, misleading and distorted daily reports on Israel open the door widely for God's displeasure and judgment on our country. Our government agrees and consents through its silence, while the poison spews out via the media continuously. Today, it is the "waves" that "rule Britannia," not "Britannia" that "rules the waves."

12. Yet the Lord is omniscient and omnipotent, and one day "the sons of those who afflicted you [Israel] will come bowing to you ... And they will call you the city of the LORD, The Zion of the Holy One of Israel" (Isaiah 60:14 NASB). Amazing!

As God's watchmen, we can share in His joy, knowing that one day the people of Jerusalem will be called "Sought After, the City No Longer Deserted" (Isaiah 62:12 NIV).

What a day that will be for Israel and for the God of Israel! How great will be God's joy and ours in the practical fulfillment of these prophetic passages, which will include:

The King of Israel, the LORD, is in your midst;
    you shall fear evil no more.
On that day it shall be said to Jerusalem:
"Do not fear, O Zion ...
The LORD, your God, is in your midst,
    a warrior who gives victory;
he will rejoice over you with gladness,
    he will renew you in his love;
he will exult over you with loud singing
    as on a day of festival.

(Zephaniah 3:15–18 RSV)

The watchman's brief

It is important to dispel some of the queer and nebulous ideas that many have on the subject of praying for Israel.

1. As with all prayer, we need factual information. If possible, we need to be able to assess the reliability of that information. We need to ascertain God's will as to how to pray. We may not have to work out how God is going to answer, but we do need at least some appreciation of the facts.
2. We must be careful not to allow the information or facts fed to us to so overshadow our thinking that there is no room for faith, or for things God may want to show us.
3. At times, the Spirit may guide us without our minds having previously had any factual information. In group situations, after waiting upon the Lord, someone may have an impression or a word which, after testing, needs to be prayed through.

Someone may stand up and pray with a heart of love "for the peace of Jerusalem." This may be a fine, lovely, well-intentioned prayer. But if we are watchmen, we will know that a lot of things have got to happen before that peace comes. It will accompany the reign of the Prince of Peace, and it is not going to happen at the press of a button. The Lord wants us to travail with Him in prayer, step by step, until that day (John 16:21).

4. Of course, *the* major thing to pray for is the growth and maturing of the Messianic Body of believers in the land of Israel today. These represent the "remnant" in the land, about which the Old Testament prophets have much to say and of whom the Lord says He will make them into "a strong nation" (see Micah 4:6–7; 5:7; 7:18).

Try to obtain reliable, regular and not too lengthy information here – Arab believers form part of the spiritual remnant, and God is wonderfully and miraculously revealing Himself to many of these also.

5. While it is necessary to pray for God's mercy and protection of Israel in and through the incessant terrorism, and the many military conflicts, it is not an easy and straightforward thing so to do. Appalling though these are, the Lord is allowing such excessive trials! This is with the purpose of bringing Israel into a situation from which the only escape will be into the arms of God, exactly like Jacob in his all-night struggle with the Angel of the Lord in Genesis 32.

As with Jacob, so with Israel, His firstborn son (Exodus 4:22), of whom God says:

Behold, I will hedge up her way with thorns,
    And I will build a wall against her so that she *cannot* find her paths.
She will pursue her lovers ... but will not find them.
    Then she will say, "I will go back to my first husband!"
                                            (Hosea 2:6–7 NASB)

For further guidance in prayer on this aspect, carefully study Hosea 5:15–6:3, which begins with "In their affliction [i.e. tribulation] they will earnestly seek Me" (Hosea 5:15b NASB).

6. Pray for stamina and strength for the nation:

> I have called you by name; you are Mine!
> When you pass through the waters, I will be with you;
> And through the rivers, they will not overflow you.
> When you walk through the fire, you will not be scorched,
> Nor will the flame burn you.
>
> (Isaiah 43:1–2 NASB)

The watchman's wisdom

1. As with everything else, there is much to pray for in regard to Israel. It is good to wait upon the Lord and then to focus and pray regularly and more specifically for certain topics, towns, people, projects or fellowships that He puts on your heart.

> He who is faithful in a very little thing is faithful also in much.
>
> (Luke 16:10 NASB)

2. This is where the value of group prayer cannot be overestimated. The spiritual warfare involved in praying for Israel needs teamship. God's way is through His "army." So ask Him to bring you into contact with others who are similarly motivated – where possible, of course, within your own fellowship or church. Remember, though, that while "two are better than one" (Ecclesiastes 4:9 NKJV), He is "able to do exceedingly abundantly above all that we ask or think, according to the power that works in us" (Ephesians 3:20 NKJV).

3. It is better by far (where possible) to meet specifically to pray for Israel and the Jewish people, rather than to include them only in general prayer times. This is what is meant by being "single-eyed" over a subject so crucial to the world and so close to the heart of God at this hour.

    The rebirth of Israel on and into the world scene in May 1948 introduced the countdown to the Lord's return. He cannot and will not return until Israel is saved.

You will not see me again *until* you say, "Blessed is he who comes in the name of the Lord."

(Matthew 23:39 NIV)

So salvation must occur beforehand!

4. Remember not only to pray for the "ministry" but also for the ministers, the servants of God – that they will resist the evil powers that oppose both the work and the workers of God in Israel, and bring the latter by faith into the fullness of God. Pray for His blessing, His strengthening and equipping, and for the families and marriages of those thus involved.

5. It is helpful to have access to at least one secular Jewish or Jerusalem news report (weekly or monthly, regularly and consistently), by internet, news, radio, newspaper, or other means. The reporting and the facts are likely to be far more accurate and nearer the truth than any Western reporting..

For instance, the grossly slanted reporting in the Lebanese conflict of July–Septermber 2006 portrayed Israel as the aggressor, indiscriminately destroying thousands of homes in Lebanon, whereas she was rooting out Hezbollah militants who deliberately established their firing lines and headquarters within the civilian population.

While the world condemned Israel for its bombing of Iraq's atomic reactor in June 1981, few facts were given to inform the public of Iraq's nuclear-bomb potential and intentions. Instead of portraying Israel's act as one of self-defense, she was made to appear as the aggressor. No coverage was given to President Reagan's later radio statement that it was indeed an act of self-defense, and that in any case, Iraq was still officially in a state of war with Israel, no peace pact having been signed since the fighting in 1948–49.

6. Hidden Islamic pressure upon all aspects of the media has soared totally beyond measure in the last thirty years.

Truth has stumbled in the streets,
   honesty cannot enter.

Truth is nowhere to be found,
and whoever shuns evil becomes a prey ...
The LORD looked ...
he was appalled that there was no-one to intervene.

(Isaiah 59:14–16 NIV, emphasis added)

7. Do not share confidential information with people who are ignorant on the delicate issues of the Middle East. Jesus had His inner few. We need the same.

8. Jesus did not save the world by interceding for it while in glory. He gave Himself. He made Himself of no reputation and became a Servant, His humility extending to the point of self-sacrifice and death.

We need this attitude in our living and praying if we are to follow in the Master's footsteps and to stand in the gap for Israel. The Church on the whole in Britain has become even more hardened against and ignorant of God's purposes for His people in these end-time days.

We have yet to learn what the apostle Paul meant when he said:

I ... fill up ... what is lacking in the afflictions of Christ, for the sake of His body, which is the church.

(Colossians 1:24 NKJV)

Carrying this burden for Israel can be quite lonesome and demanding, but inwardly, initiated and kept by the Holy Spirit, we are accomplishing something in the unseen realm of intercession that is recorded. It is of infinite and intricate worth in heaven!

There is a priceless role for us to play on behalf of the Church in this matter of Israel's salvation.

9. There is a sowing in tears and a reaping in joy, but the tears come first. There is mourning and there is dancing, but the mourning comes first. There is sackcloth and there is gladness, but the sackcloth precedes the gladness (Psalms 30; 126).

God's greatest gifts come through travail, which is born of the Spirit in us as we open our hearts to God.

Hear [our] prayer, O LORD, and let [our] cry come unto thee.

(Psalm 102:1 KJV)

May our prayer have that ring about it that is hallmarked in the courts of heaven!

10. Paul concludes his theological treatise on Israel (Romans 9–11) with the following words:

I beseech you therefore, brethren, by the mercies of God, that ye present your bodies a living sacrifice, holy, acceptable unto God, which is your reasonable service.

(Romans 12:1 KJV)

He is telling us that it is rational – reasonable – for us to yield to God on this matter and in this way. After Paul came to Rome, where he was imprisoned and eventually executed, he declared to his own brethren, the Jews:

For the hope of Israel I am bound with this chain.

(Acts 28:20 NKJV)

Are you chained or bound by the hope of Israel? Is it also your "heart's desire and prayer to God … that they might be saved"? (Romans 10:1 KJV). The Holy Spirit waits to thus "imprison" you!

Make me a captive, Lord,
and then I shall be free;
Force me to render up my sword,
and I shall conqueror be.

I sink in life's alarms
when by myself I stand;
Imprison me within thine arms,
and strong shall be my hand.

(George Matheson 1842–1906)

CHAPTER 13

Jerusalem: Quintessence of Jewish History

By the rivers of Babylon –
    there we sat down and there we wept
    when we remembered Zion ...
If I forget you, O Jerusalem,
    let my right hand wither!
Let my tongue cling to the roof of my mouth
    if I do not remember you,
if I do not set Jerusalem
    above my highest joy.

(Psalm 137:1, 5–6 NRSV)

Lament and remembrance

Compressed into the above few words we have the lament, history, heartbeat and untold sufferings of a whole nation over 2,600 years. The tears and anguish of the Jewish people since 606 BC have ebbed and flowed (mainly flowed) down to this very day. It is an awesome thing to be chosen by God!

Streaming from the loss of Jerusalem and its magnificent first Temple in the sixth century BC, there comes this poignant cry of lament. It is a cry from the heart of the Jewish people, putting remembrance of the Holy City far above everything else. From many other passages sprinkled throughout the Word of God, we see that these inspired words of the psalmist reflect far more than the heart of God's people, the Jews.

They reflect the heart of God Himself, words from the One who one day had wept and prayed, "O Jerusalem, Jerusalem, who kills the prophets and stones those who are sent to her!" (Matthew 23:37 NASB), and yet who also declared, "For Zion's sake I will not keep silent, and for Jerusalem's sake I will not rest, until her vindication" (Isaiah 62:1 RSV).

The engraving of Jerusalem on the memory of the Jewish people has had expression on Jewish lips century by century. This has been symbolized in the utterance at every Passover celebration in every country where Jews have been found: "Next year in Jerusalem."

This has been their prayer, a work of the Spirit, the unseen travail of centuries. *No other people have been so drawn to a particular place in the world than the Jews to Jerusalem.* To assign this desire to human sources devalues the beauty and portent, sorrow and joy of Holy Scripture.

> Every word of God is pure.
>
> (Proverbs 30:5 NKJV)

Who else but the Jew covenants to remember his capital city forever against the cost of both manual skill and vocal ability? Who else wants to lose the use of his right hand or his capacity to speak rather than forget a particular spot on earth? None but the Jew for Jerusalem, and none but his God, who Himself says of Zion:

> Can a woman forget her sucking child? ... yea, they may forget, yet will I not forget thee. Behold, I have graven thee on the palms of My hands.
>
> (Isaiah 49:15–16 KJV)

With God's command here to "behold," we recall the literal fulfillment of the words, as the Messiah, with His arms outstretched at Calvary, on the very outskirts of Jerusalem, displayed undying love for His people and their city, as well as His love for all humanity.

Joy restrained

As is well known, Jewish love for Jerusalem is portrayed at every Jewish wedding. Although the bride and bridegroom have a glass of wine under the *hoopah* (canopy), at each synagogue marriage service the wine glass is crushed at once under the foot of the bridegroom. The reason? It is a reminder to subdue joy until the full restoration of Jerusalem. It is not merely the city, but also *the Messiah's presence* there that will give the release to a full joy.

Jewish music, so much of which is in a minor key, also re-echoes the Jewish sorrow over Jerusalem. Nowhere is this depicted more clearly than in the synagogue itself where, in remembrance of Jerusalem, there are no musical instruments whatever. For a people with such a love and skill in music, this is a sacrifice indeed – a poignant reminder, in laying aside manual and vocal skills, that Jerusalem is so engraved on their hearts.

Election

How is Jerusalem the quintessence of Jewish history? The answer is that in the history, events and characteristics of the one, we find the reflection of the other.

At the time of their election, the Jews were no more than a dejected, ragged band of slaves, with virtually no possessions up until the time of their being called and led out of Egypt to be formed into a nation for the Lord.

In a similar way, Jerusalem bore no earthly reason to be chosen. It did not (and it does not) have any great wealth, mineral resources or industry. It has never stood geographically on a useful trade route or river. However, as declared elsewhere within these pages, Jerusalem has been the bridge by which Jesus, the Messiah and Savior, the King of all kings, entered into and made Himself known to His nation and to this world.

Of no other city in the world is it said:

> The LORD has chosen Zion,
>> he has desired it for his dwelling:
> This is my resting place for ever and ever;
>> here I will sit enthroned, for I have desired it –
> I will bless her with abundant provisions;
>> her poor will I satisfy with food.
> I will clothe her priests with salvation,
>> and her saints shall ever sing for joy.

(Psalm 132:13–16 NIV)

And of no other nation in the world does the Lord say:

> I will dwell in your midst.

(Zechariah 2:10 NKJV)

Two other scriptures echo each other and harmonize to affirm God's election of Jerusalem as "the city of the great King" (Psalm 48:2 and Matthew 5:35 NKJV). The psalm also prophetically adds that Jerusalem is "the joy of the whole earth."

Born into a nation out of the travail and tears of Egyptian slavery, the Jewish people reflect Jerusalem's afflictions and sorrows over the years.

The crossroads of history meet at Jerusalem

The crucifixion in Jerusalem divided history, the calendar, and humankind into two parts. The latter is mirrored in the two criminals on the two crosses, one on either side of the Lord Jesus. Each is equally guilty, but one rants and raves at Jesus, while the other repentantly and remorsefully beseeches the Messiah, "Remember me when you come with your kingly power" (Luke 23:42 NIV, alternative reading).

Jerusalem was the city which first saw humankind divided into two camps: those who recognized divinity in the death of the Lord Jesus, and those who merely saw another man die. It is not by chance that our Western calendar is marked into two: BC or AD – before Christ or *anno domini* (in the year of our Lord).

In the cross at Jerusalem we see simultaneously not only human sinfulness but God's absolute holiness, human hatred and God's love, human pride and God's humility, human degradation and God's glory. With our desire to look into God's character, the events of Jerusalem are a stark backcloth from which the divine traits shine forth.

Was the crucifixion an appalling tragedy that should have been avoided? Those of us thinking this way should remember the words of Jesus:

> ... for this cause came I unto this hour.
>
> (John 12:27 KJV)

In other words, "I came to this world and this city for the express purpose of this moment. I came not only to live but to die."

Which of us would ever have imagined the Father calling this event the one by which he would bring glory to His name? Yet Jesus continued:

> Father, glorify Thy name [in and through my death].
>
> (John 12:28 KJV)

> "For My thoughts are not your thoughts,
>   Nor are your ways My ways," declares the LORD.
>
> (Isaiah 55:8 NASB)

At Jerusalem, the stark contrasts between God's thoughts and ways, and ours, were first highlighted. And, instead of rejecting the Jewish people, as almost all theologians would have it, we see the Holy Spirit, in all His power and liberating influence, first being poured out here on humankind – on those 120 Jewish people in the upper room! The city of His crucifixion became the city of His resurrection and ascension, and the place yet to be known as "The Throne of the LORD" (Jeremiah 3:17 NIV).

There at "Jerusalem, Jews, devout men out of every nation under heaven" (Acts 2:5 KJV) heard the gospel preached for the very first time – and what a response there was, resulting in the salvation of 3,000 souls that very first day of Pentecost (Acts 2:41)!

Jerusalem saw the first persecution against the gospel, and the first martyr, Stephen, giving his lifeblood as the heavens opened to reveal the Savior standing to receive him (Acts 7:56). Here also, the first Jewish council was held to decide how Gentile believers should be received into the general body of believers (then almost entirely Jewish), and what burdens should or should not be laid upon them through Jewish law and tradition (Acts 15:22–30). The worldwide Church to this day benefits from and acts upon those early decisions by the Jewish apostles.

Temple site reflections

Nothing matches Jerusalem in historical significance and world-changing events. Solomon "in all his glory" built the first structured building, the ornate first Temple in which to worship God our Creator. The Queen of Sheba, Pompey, Pilate and Herod all strode across Jerusalem's stage. Titus, in all his blazing fury, razed the city to the ground, sealing the scattering of God's people until this very day.

But, above all, the King of kings entered the world there via a stable, and He left via a skull-shaped mountain and a sepulchre!

From the Temple site, where there now stands the Mosque of Omar (the Dome of the Rock) – the Islamic fruit of Ishmael, built over the spot where Abraham originally offered up Isaac – one looks across the Kidron Valley to discern the history of a bygone age.

From the Garden of Gethsemane, one's eyes are lifted to the Mount of Olives, from which our Lord was taken up into heaven, and to which He is due to return one day (Zechariah 14:4; Acts 1:11; 3:20–21). In the very last "picture" of Jesus on earth, He is described ascending from the Mount of Olives, raising His nail-pierced hands, and blessing the very people of the city that had crucified Him (Luke 24:50–51). What compassion and condescension combine in this last portrait of Messiah Jesus!

We now see why the disciples "returned to Jerusalem with great joy and were continually in the temple praising God" (Luke 24:52–53 NASB). Wonderful!

> The love of God is greater far
> Than tongue or pen can ever tell;
> It goes beyond the highest star
> And reaches to the lowest hell ...
>
> Oh, love of God – how rich and pure!
> How measureless and strong;
> It shall forevermore endure –
> The saints' and angels' song ...
>
> Could we with ink the ocean fill,
> And were the sky of parchment made,
> Were every stalk on earth a quill,
> And every man a scribe by trade,
>
> To write the love of God above
> Would drain the ocean dry;
> Nor could the scroll contain the whole
> Though stretched from sky to sky.
>
> (Frederick M. Lehmann 1868–1953)

When Jesus does return, it will not be just a return to the Mount of Olives but a fabulous return, in love and compassion, to His people (Isaiah 54;8, 10). There is no more moving part in the whole of the Bible than the reconciliation of Joseph (then "ruler" over Egypt) with his eleven brothers. That is a pale reflection of what the return of Jesus will mean to Him Himself, quite apart from His brethren. Before the revelation in Genesis, Joseph is found weeping no fewer than seven times for his brothers and his father.

Contesting that awaited return of Jesus, will be the false messiah (anti-Christ) who will have deceived most people and eventually taken his seat in the Temple (Daniel 9:27; 11:31; 12:11; Matthew 24:15; 2 Thessalonians 2:4). This false messiah will come in his own name and will be received, unlike the One who came in His Father's name and was not received or recognized (John 1:11; 5:23).

What is today being seen as a conflict between peoples over Jerusalem, between one nation and many others, is actually *the outward manifestation of the opposition of spiritual powers of wickedness.* These are battling relentlessly against the God of righteousness in order to prevent the establishment of His throne and will.

We wrestle not against flesh and blood, but against the spiritual hosts of wickedness in the heavenly places. Wrestling is an all-in, close-quarters, personal affair. Nowhere on earth has this conflict been greater than in, and over, Jerusalem. It has yet to grow far more intense than we may dream possible. And there, also, will the *last* battle be fought against Satan (2 Thessalonians 2:8).

Geography

Along the winding road climbing eastwards to Zion for thirty-two miles from the Mediterranean seaboard, we suddenly gain a glorious view of Jerusalem, initially hidden by the seven hills around her which are higher than the one on which the city itself stands.

> As the mountains are round about Jerusalem, so the LORD is round about his people from henceforth even for ever.
>
> (Psalm 125:2 KJV)

One day, at the coming of the Lord, these hills will literally melt (as Amos 9:5, Nahum 1:5 and other scriptures show) and then we shall see fulfilled the words of the prophet Isaiah:

> Every valley shall be raised up,
>> every mountain and hill made low ...
> And the glory of the LORD will be revealed,
>> and all mankind together will see it.
> For the mouth of the LORD has spoken.
>
> (Isaiah 40:3–5 NIV)

And this will result in Jerusalem being on the highest hill in the area, the "city set on a hill [that] cannot be hid" (Matthew 5:14 KJV), fulfilling the glorious future for the city:

> In the last days
> the mountain of the LORD's temple will be established
>> as chief among the mountains;
> it will be raised above the hills,
>> and all nations will stream to it.
>
> Many peoples will come and say,
>
> "Come, let us go up to the mountain of the LORD,
>> to the house of the God of Jacob.
> He will teach us his ways,
>> so that we may walk in His paths."
> The law will go out from Zion,
>> the word of the LORD from Jerusalem.
>
> (Isaiah 2:2–3 NIV)

The geographic centrality of Jerusalem will then be demonstrated spiritually. The Word of the Lord will proceed in authority from Jerusalem. From Jerusalem, governments throughout the world will take their cue; essentially, the Word of the Lord will be a spiritual foundation for all decisions. Swords are to be beaten into plowshares, and the Lord "shall rule ... with a rod of iron" (Revelation 2:27 KJV).

Pilgrims will not come simply to see "holy sites" in Israel, but will come up to Jerusalem to really worship the Lord: Jerusalem will be the world's spiritual capital, Messiah's throne.

> My house will be called a house of prayer for all nations.
>
> (Isaiah 56:7; Mark 11:17 NIV)

Jerusalem will move from its stained history into a sanctified eternity. Isaiah writes futuristically and specifically of that period of transition:

> Put on your garments of splendor,
>> O Jerusalem, the holy city ...
> Shake off your dust;
>> rise up, sit enthroned, O Jerusalem.
>
> (Isaiah 52:1 NIV)

In God's Word, amongst many other names for Jerusalem, we find twelve names, twelve good reasons and twelve good ways to pray for the Holy City:

1. "City of the Great King" (Matthew 5:35 NIV)
2. "City of Truth" (Zechariah 8:3 NIV)
3. "City of Righteousness" (Isaiah 1:26 NIV)
4. "Faithful City" (Isaiah 1:26 NIV)
5. "City of the LORD" (Isaiah 60:14 NIV)
6. "Zion of the Holy One of Israel" (Isaiah 60:14 NIV)
7. "City of the LORD of Hosts" (Psalm 48:8 KJV)
8. "Hephzibah" (My Delight is in Her) (Isaiah 62:4 NIV)
9. "Sought out" (Isaiah 62:12 KJV)
10. "City not forsaken" (Isaiah 62:12 KJV)
11. "The Throne of the Lord" (Jeremiah 3:17 NIV)
12. "THE LORD IS THERE" (Jehovah Shamah) (Ezekiel 48:35 NIV)

How good to note in the middle of all of these that she is not only a "city not forsaken," but the city where the Lord is enthroned!

General history

"Foundation (or City) of Peace": 1900 BC

Abraham "looked for a city which hath foundations, whose builder and maker is God" (Hebrews 11:10 KJV). While this refers, of course, to the spiritual realm of our abode in the Messiah – not only our trust being in Him, but, mysteriously, our very being contained in Him – the earthly counterpart is referred to in the person of Melchizedek, who appeared as King of Salem to Abram (Genesis 14:18).

It was from "Jerus [Foundation]-salem [Peace]" (*shalom* is the modern counterpart) that Melchizedek, King of Righteousness, mysteriously appeared as High Priest of God to bless the father of the Jewish race. Ironically, the City of Peace has known less peace than any other on earth.

Conflicts from 1450 BC

In Joshua 10 we find Joshua, also a type of the Messiah and Savior, fighting against the earthly king of Jerusalem, Adonizedek. Significantly, the signs then occurring in the sun and moon are to have a later form of expression in the conflict over Jerusalem (Isaiah 24:23; Joel 2:10; Amos 5:20; Zephaniah 1:15; Matthew 24:29). These, and many other Biblical references, foreshadow the day of conflict beyond which God's foreordained and important plans for Jerusalem will be established. The prophet Zechariah tells us that there will be no day like it: it will be a unique day (Zechariah 14:7).

There have been something like thirty sieges of Jerusalem: ten from the time of Joshua to Nebuchadnezzar, ten from the close of the

Old Testament until AD 70, eight from then until 1917, and then more in 1948–49 and 1967.

In 1048 BC King David captured the city from the Jebusites (2 Samuel 5:6–10) and, thirty years later, purchased the threshing floor of Araunah, the Jebusite, for 600 shekels of gold. God's seal upon this spot, as His altar, came in His answering David's call with fire from heaven, consuming his sacrifice (1 Chronicles 21).

Some sixty-six years later (952 BC), God's further seal on the Temple site again fell in the form of fire, to consume Solomon's offering and sacrifice (2 Chronicles 7:1) at the dedication of the first Temple. Thus we see the continued manifestation of "the God who answers by fire" (1 Kings 18:24 NKJV). At the very beginning of the ministry of Aaron's priests, in the days of the Tabernacle (forerunner of the Temple), the Lord consumed the offering and sacrifice by fire – to the joy of all present. The "betrothal" in the wilderness had its "wedding" in Jerusalem.

The Muslim claim to Jerusalem

Muslims, in all their present claims over Jerusalem, never refer to the following facts:

1. Jerusalem is never mentioned in the Koran – the Muslim "Bible."
2. Muhammad's ministry was in southwest Arabia, not Palestine.
3. Some believe that the story of Muhammad's flight there on a winged horse (Al Buraq) was a fable, and that he was never in Jerusalem – which is, in any case, mentioned only in connection with his supposed later flight to heaven. In the latter, others see that there is no direct flight to heaven *except* via Jerusalem!
4. Islam has two other holy cities: Mecca and Medina. Each is ranked higher in importance than Jerusalem.
5. Jerusalem has never been a religious capital to the Muslims.
6. If the city is of such religious importance to the Muslims, why did no Saudi Arabian king ever travel there when it was easiest for him to do so – in the years 1948 to 1967?

For over 165 years, Jews have been in the majority of the population of Jerusalem. To present the city, or indeed the land, as an Arab city or country "taken by the Jews" is utterly false! Even when Arabs entered the land in the seventh century AD, they called it "the land of the Jews." Just how eroded, wasted and neglected the land and city were prior to the Jewish return (beginning in the nineteenth century) is plain from history books. The memories of many Jews alive even today simply verify the changes that have taken place since the 1920s.

Contrary to the claim that Muslim occupancy is needed in order to "liberate" the holy sites, it is only *since* Jerusalem has been occupied by Jews that the sites have been properly cared for and liberated. This was not so from 1948 to 1967, a period when half the city had been in Arab hands.

The claim at the Islamic International Seminar on Jerusalem (London, 1979) that Jerusalem should be an Arab city, where Jews and Christians could live peaceably with one another, has not been a standard met in other existing Arab capitals. There are *no* known Christians in Saudi Arabia, and no churches. In Iran, both Jews and Christians have had to flee for their lives; in Syria, the 5,000 remaining Jews are virtually prisoners in a ghetto. The amount of liberty granted to any Christian in any Muslim country is well known.

The Christian and the international claim to Jerusalem

Although much talk has been made of Jerusalem as the heart of Christianity, it is significant that no denominational church has sought to make its headquarters there. Even the Roman Catholic Church, sometimes stressing the desirability of making Jerusalem an international city, keeps its seat at the Vatican in Rome.

Plainly, those who make religious claims to Jerusalem have the hidden aim, not of fulfilling any real desire or legitimate claim on their part to Jerusalem, but of negating the historic and Biblical Jewish claim thereto.

The burning issue of Jerusalem

At this point, we may personally feel that neither the government nor the people of Israel could ever negotiate on the question of Jewish sovereignty over Jerusalem. It is too precious, too symbolic of the whole resurrection of Israel, too reminiscent of her centuries of desolation and isolation. This is not simply some form of human obstinacy, but rather *an expression of God's will* in the matter. God Himself has breathed into the heart of Jewish people:

> If I forget you, O Jerusalem,
>   let my right hand wither!
> Let my tongue cleave to the roof of my mouth ...
> if I do not set Jerusalem
>   above my highest joy!
>
> (Psalm 137:5–6 RSV)

At the same time, the battle over the city is relentless. The most contested site on the face of the earth is this – where Abraham offered up Isaac, and where Jesus offered up Himself. This is where the cross and the crown, and death and resurrection, have met each other. This is where the Lord led captivity captive (Ephesians 4:8), and where the pinnacle of history culminates. This is Jerusalem – humanity's worst and God's best in collision!

> Why stand ye gazing up into heaven? This same Jesus who is taken up from you into heaven shall so come again in like manner as ye have seen him go into heaven.
>
> (Acts 1:11 KJV)

Public opinion has already been indoctrinated with the formula of "Arab rights in East Jerusalem." Through Pope John Paul II, the Vatican demand for it to be an international city was voiced (with Yasser Arafat's backing) in 2001. Over the issue of Jerusalem will come the final head-on clash between the forces of anti-Christ (the nations gathered together) and the Lord himself (Zechariah 14; Daniel 2:44).

Over Jerusalem, not merely is the anti-Christ destroyed, but the Gentiles are judged! (If governments only knew this, and if Christians only realized it!) The apathy, indifference and ignorance of the Church over an issue so near to the heart of God is quite incredible (Zechariah 1:14–15; 2:8; 8:2; 14:3; Jeremiah 30:17).

The swiftly growing movement within the Church of anti-Christian Zionism (whose headship includes Spirit-filled, born-again, ordained Christian ministers) is aggressively opposed to any such Christian view of Jerusalem and Israel. The battle is mounting, and we must be grounded more strongly than ever in the Word of God – not opinions, news reports or humanism.

What is the Holy Spirit saying today?

It was no coincidence that the Dead Sea Scrolls, having been hidden for around 1,900 years, were discovered in 1947, at the very time of Israel's restoration.

> A time to tear apart, and a time to sew together,
> A time to be silent, and a time to speak.
>
> (Ecclesiastes 3:7 NASB)

Neither is it a coincidence that the scroll of the prophet Isaiah itself, telling us that the Word of the Lord "will go forth from Jerusalem," was found in its entirety, thus underlining the authenticity of that very book at the time of the rebirth of the nation of Israel.

Still less is it a coincidence that the second "half" of this book, speaking of a change of times, opens at chapter 40 with the counsel of God to His Church to bring words of comfort and tenderness not merely to the Jews, but to the very heart of Jerusalem!

> Comfort, comfort my people, says your God.
> Speak tenderly to Jerusalem,
>   and proclaim to her
> that her hard service has been completed.
>
> (Isaiah 40:1–2 NIV)

The fact that a change in times is involved is emphasized in the period of "hard service" being accomplished. Changes in the course of Israel's history and fortune always affect the rest of the world, even if we are unaware of the fact. Our thoughts inevitably turn to the "appointed time" to "favor" Zion mentioned in Psalm 102:13 and in Chapter 6 of this book.

What is the Christian to make of this passage, this call of God to bring tender comfort to Jerusalem? If Christians spiritualize "Jerusalem" here, they are at once in difficulty over the next line of verse 2: "proclaim to her … that her sin has been paid for" (NIV). The spiritual, heavenly Jerusalem is already aware of that – that her sin is paid for.

There are over 1,000 references to the City of God in the Bible; we Christians dare not continually steal the nice, comforting passages and leave the rest for the Jews.

No! God has been calling his Church, particularly within Britain, to comfort Israel and the Jewish people since 1947 and before! "Jerusalem" is a corporate "body" matter for *the Church*, not a matter simply for thousands of Christians, nor a matter only for Jewish people. It is a matter in which God's army has got to get involved. It is true that due to the apathetic, lethargic attitude of the Church as a whole, the Lord has been raising "para-church organizations" to fill the gap (see Ezekiel 34:10–11).

When Israel needed a king, God first caused Hannah to weep! And later Samuel the prophet, who anointed King David, was born (1 Samuel 1:7). But Hannah's subsequent thanksgiving (1 Samuel 2) actually proved to be the foundation for Mary's "Magnificat" (Luke 1). And this preceded the birth of David's greater son – the Lord Jesus Christ!

Weep with those that weep

This is something we see, but know little about. From the whole of the book of Lamentations – and it is a lamentation over Jerusalem – only two passages are commonly used, and then out of context! The rest of the five chapters, exhorting us, the Church, to have concern over Jerusalem, are ignored.

The first passage is:

> Is it nothing to you, all you who pass by?
> Behold and see if there is any sorrow like my sorrow,
> Which has been brought on me,
> Which the LORD has inflicted
> In the day of his fierce anger.
>
> (Lamentations 1:12 NKJV)

Although we can apply this verse to the Lord at his crucifixion, it should be clearly noted that the sorrow referred to is that of the city of Jerusalem:

> How deserted lies the city,
>   once so full of people!
> How like a widow is she,
>   who once was great amongst the nations! ...
>
> The roads to Zion mourn ...
>
> The Lord has brought her grief ...
>
> In the days of her affliction and wandering
>   Jerusalem remembers all the treasures
>   that were hers in days of old.
>
> (Lamentations 1:1, 4, 5, 7 NIV)

It is a great grief to our Lord today that, in current Christian theology, we completely miss the relevance and importance of God's call to us over Jerusalem.

> Is it nothing to you, all you who pass by?
>
> (Lamentations 1:12 NKJV)

Is it nothing to you, or to me? The tear-stained book of Lamentations mirrors the history of Israel, of Jerusalem. The sob of centuries, the slaughter of people, the bereavement of families, the desolation of cities – all assail our hearts and minds as we read, pause and ponder. And the Holy Spirit waits for a response from us.

Of what melted-heart response do we know in reference to these passages?

> Zion spreads out her hands,
>> but there is no-one to comfort her.
>
> (Lamentations 1:17 NIV)

> Streams of tears flow from my eyes
>> because my people are destroyed.
>
> (Lamentations 3:48 NIV)

God's heart cry

This is what the Lord wants to impart to us by his Holy Spirit. When Jesus last beheld Jerusalem from a distance, approaching it for the last Passover meal, he wept bitterly. The crowd rejoiced when he came into view, desiring there and then to crown him. But Jesus had wept.

As he approached Jerusalem and saw the city, he wept over it and said,

> If you, even you, had only known on this day what would bring you peace – but now it is hidden from your eyes. The days will come upon you when your enemies will build an embankment against you and encircle you and hem you in on every side. They will dash you to the ground, you and the children within your walls. They will not leave one stone on another, because you did not recognize the time of God's coming to you.
>
> (Luke 19:41–42 NIV)

The Greek word for this weeping is not as elsewhere (*dakruo*), but rather *klaio* – hard crying, loud wailing, lamentation. It is the same crying as of the mothers bereaved of their children at the hand of Herod

(Matthew 2:18); the same uncontrolled crying as that of Jairus and the crowd over his deceased daughter; the same wailing as that of the widow of Nain over her son; and the same lament as that of the crowd over the death of Tabitha (or Dorcas) at Joppa.

Such sorrow and tears of our Lord did not end abruptly at His approach to Jerusalem. We are mysteriously but clearly called to share in these "that [we] may know him ... and the fellowship ... of his sufferings" (Philippians 3:10 KJV).

And it is in this way that we also live out something of the mysterious passage where Paul tells us that he "fill[s] up that which is behind of the afflictions of Christ in [his] flesh" (Colossians 1:24 KJV).

Do not think that He accomplished His work in the travail of His soul in order to exempt us from having to do anything or to suffer in His cause. He opened the way that we might follow (Matthew 16:25). Ah! We have yet to learn what it is to travail in birth for souls and for Christ to be formed in others (Galatians 4:19).

Again, remember that it was not by interceding for the world while in glory that Jesus saved it. Rather, *He gave Himself.* "Our prayers for the world are a bitter irony as long as we give out of our superfluity, and draw back the sacrifice of ourselves."[1]

It is not those who sow who reap with shouts of joy, but those who sow in tears.

> He that goeth forth and weepeth, bearing precious seed, shall doubtless come again rejoicing, bringing his sheaves with him.
>
> (Psalm 126:5–6 KJV)

We sow seeds in prayer and this is how we must pray for Jerusalem and for Israel.

The second passage in Lamentations, also usually used out of context is:

> It is of the Lord's mercies that we are not consumed, because his compassions fail not.
>
> They are new every morning: great is thy faithfulness.
>
> (Lamentations 3:22–23 KJV)

From these beautiful verses on the faithfulness of God, instead of ascribing them to His people Israel and the city of Jerusalem, we wrench the mercy, compassion and faithfulness of God and apply them solely (and in most cases exclusively) to the Church. Oh, the shame of it! Oh, the sorrow of it!

At countless Christian meetings and crusades where not a vestige of thought, prayer or cognizance is given to Jerusalem, we hear this chorus sung, based on the passage above:

> Great is Thy faithfulness,
> Great is Thy faithfulness,
> Morning by morning new mercies I see.
> All I have needed Thy hand hath provided,
> Great is Thy faithfulness, Lord, unto me.
>
> (Thomas O. Chisholm 1866–1960)

Nonetheless, we can take heart in the fact that though we, as God's children, may fail him, God is utterly faithful – and faithful to His Word. Jeremiah ends his long lament with:

> You, O LORD, reign for ever …
> Restore us to yourself, O LORD, that we may return;
>   renew our days as of old,
> unless you have utterly rejected us
>   and are angry beyond measure.
>
> (Lamentations 5:19–22 NIV)

This inspired prayer ends the book of Lamentations, and presents a call to the Lord to impart repentance, something which none of us can generate of ourselves. It is the most precious of gifts that comes from God – the key to change within us if we are ever to inbreathe the divine nature, as God intends (2 Peter 1:3–4).

The words "renew" and "restore" conceal the actual Hebrew terms: "Turn us ... and we shall be turned" (Hebrew: *tsuba*). The desire may be within a human being, but the prerogative and initiating are with God. Herein lies a clue and incentive in "praying for the peace of Jerusalem." The "shalom" of "peace" takes in the completeness that has to begin with contrition and repentance over the earthly, and turning and receiving of the heavenly.

The intellect cannot impart this to the Jews, to Israel, Jerusalem or ourselves. It can only be the work of the Holy Spirit, with the emphasis on "Holy." That same Spirit waits to use the altar of your heart to pray for the outcasts of Israel – and to one day soon make their capital city, Jerusalem, the praise of all the earth. What a magnificent goal to set before our mean and humble hearts – something that will bestow blessing in the Millennium, and eternity to this globe.

The mercy and compassion of the Lord could not allow Him to deny Himself and to turn from Zion, His city. In Psalm 132 He made many promises to the city, ending with the following:

> I will clothe her priests with salvation,
> and her saints shall shout aloud for joy.
>
> (Psalm 132:16 NIV)

What has been sown in tears in the prayers of many will then be reaped with endless joy. God's ways are different from ours. His first day began with night and ended with morning. The poignant history of Jerusalem will be crowned with abundance and joy.

> Light after darkness,
> Gain after loss,
> Strength after weariness,
> Crown after cross;
> Sweet after bitter,
> Hope after fears,
> Home after wandering,
> Praise after tears.

Sheaves after sowing,
Sun after rain,
Sight after mystery,
Peace after pain;
Joy after sorrow,
Calm after blast,
Rest after weariness,
Sweet rest at last.

Near after distant,
Gleam after gloom,
Love after loneliness,
Life after tomb;
After long agony,
Rapture of bliss,
Right was the pathway
Leading to this.

(Frances R. Havergal 1836–79)

And he will come to Zion as Redeemer,
    to those in Jacob who turn from transgression, says the LORD.

(Isaiah 59:20 RSV)

Arise, shine:
For your light has come!
And the glory of the LORD is risen upon you.
For behold, the darkness shall cover the earth,
And deep darkness the people;
But the LORD will arise over you,
And His glory will be seen upon you.
The Gentiles shall come to your light
And kings to the brightness of your rising.

(Isaiah 60:1–3 NKJV)

The overcoming, responding Church

Of the seven churches in Revelation, Philadelphia receives an even
higher commendation than Smyrna (the only other church not

reproved), in that she not only endures despite her foes, but actually sees some of them won over to her, in acknowledging God's love.

> To the angel of the church in Philadelphia write:
> These are the words of him who is holy and true, who holds the key of David. What He opens no-one can shut, and what he shuts no-one can open.
>
> (Revelation 3:7 NIV)

The key of David is the key to David's city, Jerusalem. Isaiah 22 fills in the details. In Hezekiah's day, the key had been held by Shebna, who had been in charge of the palace; he had thus been given responsibility for Jerusalem. With Jerusalem and Judah under severe attack (Isaiah 22:4–9), the Lord had looked for tears and intercession (verse 12). Instead He found revelry, pride and luxury (verses 13, 16, 18), and God removed the key holder, Shebna, from office.

His authority was transferred to Eliakim who would be a servant and "a father to those who live in Jerusalem and to the house of Judah. I will place on his shoulder the key to the house of David; what he opens no-one can shut" (Isaiah 22:20–22 NIV). (The transfer parallels the times of Queen Vashti and Queen Esther.)

At the time of this prophecy, Jerusalem was surrounded and sorely threatened by Sennacherib's vast Assyrian army. Hezekiah had spread the whole matter before the Lord. He had no army and no resources by which to defend Jerusalem. We too can take heart when interceding, because the open door to the house of David is promised to those of "little strength," not to those of great might, power or wisdom:

> I know your deeds. See, I have placed before you an open door that no-one can shut. I know that you have little strength, yet you have kept my word and have not denied my name.
>
> (Revelation 3:8 NIV)

There are insuperable odds as we contest world powers and the satanic realm of Islam, but, in the Lord's strength, we can overcome. The church at Philadelphia – which means "brotherly love" – was commended for its obedience and adherence to God's Word, for not denying God's name, and for her endurance through much trial.

"Philadelphia" is a part of God's remnant church today. We may not be popular as we stand for the historic, legal and Biblical rights of the Jewish people over Jerusalem, but God promises to keep those who thus stand "from the hour of trial that is going to come upon the whole world" (Revelation 3:10 NIV). This promise, although often taken out of context, is not made to any of the other six churches in Revelation. That is important, even though we not have full understanding of its promise and meaning.

In the earthquake region of Philadelphia today, five roads meet to make it the gateway and key to the Middle East. How interesting that the church of brotherly love stands at that gateway! Endurance (through the earthquakes) in that church is typified in that, to this day, a Christian witness continues, in spite of Muslim pressure and invasion – the town now being called Allah Shehr (City of God).

There are five churches and six mosques there. It is interesting to realize also that although Philadelphia was constantly shaken and sometimes destroyed by earthquakes, the best soil for fruitful vines – lava (the result of volcanic eruptions!) – is found there! As we endure affliction, as we abide in Christ and His words abide in us, we too shall be more than fruitful. The Lord encourages us:

> I know your deeds. See, I have placed before you an open door that no-one can shut ... Hold on to what you have, so that no-one will take your crown. Him who overcomes I will make a pillar in the temple of my God ... I will write on him the name of my God and the name of the city of my God, the new Jerusalem ... He who has an ear, let him hear what the Spirit says to the churches.
>
> (Revelation 3:8, 11–12, 13 NIV)

Open my ears that I may hear
Voices of truth Thou sendest clear;

And while the wave notes fall on my ear,
Everything false will disappear.

Silently now, I wait for Thee,
Ready, my God, Thy will to see,
Open my ears, illumine me,
Spirit Divine!

(Clara H. Scott 1841–97)

Notes

1. M. François Coillard.

CHAPTER 14

The Jewish Messiah: King of all Kings

Endow the king with your justice, O God,
    the royal son with Your righteousness.
He will judge your people in righteousness,
    your afflicted ones with justice.
The mountains will bring prosperity to the people,
    the hills the fruit of righteousness.
He will defend the afflicted among the people
    and save the children of the needy;
he will crush the oppressor.

He will endure as long as the sun,
    as long as the moon, through all generations …

He will rule from sea to sea
    and from the River to the ends of the earth …

All kings will bow down to him,
    and all nations will serve him …

All nations will be blessed through him,
and they will call him blessed.

Praise be to the Lord God, the God of Israel,
   who alone does marvelous deeds.
Praise be to his glorious name for ever;
     may the whole earth be filled with his glory.
         Amen and Amen.

(Psalm 72:1–5, 8, 11, 17–19 NIV)

The King of God's anointing

Radiant in Messianic glory, this "psalm of Solomon" outshines all
other passages in the Old Testament, giving us a complete vision of
the Messiah's coming reign. It is filled with lines of hope, and passages
of promise, which have been portrayed in the lives of Old Testament
characters.

There are thirty references in this psalm (mainly in the second
person) to a single figure. There can be no question that this figure
is divine, and because of this we can do no other than to hope and
rejoice, and to overflowingly obey its last injunction to "praise ... the
Lord God, the God of Israel."

Were the promises based on some fine "Messianic age" where the
depicted ruler is simply a good human specimen, our hope would be
ill-founded indeed. However, who else but God Himself will endure
(or be feared) "as long as the sun [and] moon, through all generations"
(verse 5)? By what way other than by divine intervention could "all
nations" be "blessed through him" (verse 17)?

What mortal being is there, unstained by sin, who could be relied
upon to judge the world "in righteousness" (verse 2)? We have had
almost 6,000 years of history, latterly with the United Nations, preceded earlier by the League of Nations, each revealing to us our need
of a kingly King – One of truly Royal seed, One above and beyond
human selfishness and sinfulness; One who will not only have compassion on the weak and needy, and who will be unswerving in justice,
but One who will also have divine power to impose His will through
omniscience, omnipotence, omnipresence and holiness.

It does not require a sage to perceive the world's need of such a King, such a Ruler. Our world scene makes it more obvious every day! The difficulty comes with our failure to realize our total dependence upon God, as we try to go it alone, ignoring the injunction:

> Without Me, you can do nothing.
>
> (John 15:5 NKJV)

The King of human choice

The nation by which Messiah was (and is) to be revealed to the world began its era of kings with its own obstinate choice. Israel was set by Jehovah to be "a kingdom of priests and a holy nation" forever (Exodus 19:6 NIV). Its rulers were to be God-appointed to lead them thus. At one point, however, Israel demanded of its God-appointed leader, Samuel (last of the judges and first of its successional prophets):

> We want a king over us. Then we shall be like all the other nations.
>
> (1 Samuel 8:19–20 NIV)

While this was displeasing both to Samuel and to the Lord, Israel was granted its request in the later appointment of King Saul. It is noteworthy that one major factor leading to the choice of Saul – whose reign ended in total disarray and sorrow – was that he was a "head taller than any of the others" (1 Samuel 9:2 NIV). God's later choice was a man after His own *heart*, a stripling shepherd boy. The choice of King David shows us the difference between human ways and God's ways, between human thoughts and God's thoughts. The first requirement for a ruler is not wisdom and intellect, desirable though they may be, but righteousness.

The key word in our Messianic psalm is just that – righteousness. It occurs three times in quick succession, in the first three verses. The same theme is picked up in another psalm, this time addressed to the King.

You love righteousness and hate wickedness;
    therefore God, your God, has set you above your companions
    by anointing you with the oil of joy.

(Psalm 45:7 NIV)

The King of Righteousness as Priest

It is no accident that in the first chapter in the Bible bearing the mention of kings, all of whom are earthly and involved in warfare, there is one exception: the mysterious figure of Melchizedek (Genesis 14).

Melchizedek just "appears" on the scene without explanation of his origin or of his going. "Melchizedek" – the Hebrew term for "King of Righteousness" – conveys the thought of regality in righteousness or character, someone enthroned above the normal concept of righteousness, who could be the source or origin of righteousness for his subjects.

It is more than significant that, again, without any explanation, this King mysteriously produces bread and wine! Emblems used to this very day by Jews to celebrate the (later-introduced) Passover, and by Christians in what is called "the Last Supper" or "Communion." For Abram's benefit, the King brought out bread and wine from somewhere upon or within himself. We all know that unleavened bread and the blood of an unblemished lamb were later to be emblematic of Passover, of deliverance from Egypt. We know, too, that One who was later called both "Lamb of God" and "King of Israel" laid down His life voluntarily for His own people. His name was Jesus. Although then declining (though not denying) His role as King, Jesus could not have stooped lower as priest, nor at the same time could His function have been higher. The parallels in the appearance of the first King of Righteousness unmistakably equate him with the ministry of the Lord Jesus, as he portrays what was to follow some 2,000 years later.

To begin with, Melchizedek, King of Righteousness, is also called "priest of God Most High" (Genesis 14:18 NIV). Normally, in Old Testament typology, a person is either a king or a priest – never both.

In one case where a king (Uzziah) endeavored to perform both functions (he endeavored to burn incense), he was struck with leprosy. In another case, King Saul lost the continuation of his kingly line as a result of trying to take on the priesthood (1 Samuel 13:11–18).

The King of Righteousness as Prince of Peace

In the case of Melchizedek, in addition to his being King of Righteousness, there is reference to a second kind of kingship: he is described as "King of Salem" (Genesis 14:18 NIV) – King (or Prince) of Peace. This also refers to the City of Peace – another term for Jerusalem. We cannot help but turn to a later scriptural reference – to that somewhat possessive passage in Isaiah 9, written by and initially for the Hebrew race.

> To us a child is born,
>   to us a son is given ...
> And he will be called ...
>   Prince of Peace.
>
> (Isaiah 9:6 NIV)

Dr Herbert Lockyer comments: "The child born reveals his humanity; the Son is given His Deity."

Compounded within this mysterious Old Testament figure producing the Passover emblems (wine being included in the Passover service long after the exodus), we see pictured just what the world is today looking for: provision for our needs, and peace. But note his first name: Melchizedek, meaning "King of Righteousness." Most rulers today would vow, "Give us peace and we'll be righteous." But the Lord, through Isaiah, *reverses the order*, to teach us that "the fruit [the effect] of righteousness will be peace" (Isaiah 32:17 NIV).

This Messianic psalm, majoring on righteousness in its early verses, underlines that on which true world blessing depends. It does not depend upon the righteousness of human beings and their good deeds (*mitzvot*), but upon a divine righteousness. A world and a nation

crying out for peace can do no better than to study the figure and
typology of Melchizedek, bearing in mind that the Holy Spirit must
inwardly reveal and confirm these truths. Of all the kings that appear
in Genesis 14, Melchizedek shines forth as *the* King of kings and, in so
doing, he exemplifies that One, later called King of the Jews, who died
on a Roman cross. There, righteousness was truly personified: Pilate
had said, "I find no fault in Him" (John 19:6 NKJV). He was the One
who "opened not His mouth" (Isaiah 53:7 NKJV) as He was led to the
slaughter, displaying a kingliness in manner that is so despised as weakness in the eyes of the world today.

The King of Righteousness: the Blesser of Abram

Melchizedek blesses Abram, saying:

> Blessed be Abram by God Most High,
>   Creator of heaven and earth.
>
>   (Genesis 14:19 NIV)

Note that Abram here is blessed by God. The fulfillment of God's promise
to Abram in Genesis 12, that the whole world would be blessed "through"
him, hinges upon what Melchizedek here pronounces: "Blessed be Abram
by God Most High." This figure, both King and Priest of the God Most
High, is the forerunner of Him who is to be the means of blessing, the
seed of Abraham, the One of whom the apostle John writes:

> The Word became flesh and lived [for a while – "tabernacled"] among us.
>   (John 1:14 NRSV)

Our Messianic psalm says of him:

> All nations will be blessed through him.
>
>   (Psalm 72:11 NIV)

A further sign of the stature of this Messianic figure is revealed in the reverence Abram shows for him. He gives the King of Salem "a tenth of everything" (Genesis 14:20 NIV), introducing, in fact, the later and similar allegiance of all those who descended from Abram, from Isaac and Jacob onwards. So what a figure Melchizedek is! And he is introduced at the very birth of the Hebrew race, to its father, Abram!

Let us not forget that the blessing which Melchizedek brought, and which he pictures, are inextricably linked with the bread and wine he also produced. The Messianic King of the New Covenant said, to the consternation and perplexity of His disciples:

> I am the bread of life ... the living bread that came down from heaven. If anyone eats of this bread, he will live for ever. This bread is my flesh, which I will give for the life of the world ...
>
> Unless you can eat the flesh of the Son of Man and drink his blood, you have no life in you.
>
> (John 6:48–53 NIV)

It was at that exact point that there materialized the bread and the wine which Melchizedek had centuries earlier exemplified for Abram, but it was at this same point that many of Jesus' disciples turned from him (John 6:66).

God's love for the world, and for His people Israel, is nowhere more moving, nor more marvelous and incomprehensible than here. It is here, quite early in his ministry, that the One who is both Priest and King speaks of His forthcoming death, by which Life – spiritual life – would be released to all who would, by faith, both believe and receive.

The King of Righteousness: the Great Physician

Jesus came to identify with the needs of human beings and particularly those of Israel.

In all their affliction He was afflicted.

(Isaiah 63:9 KJV)

Because He became the High Priest of all time, He is also the King of all time, the King of Israel and the King of kings. Jeremiah, prophetically looking ahead, said:

> Is the LORD not in Zion?
>> Is her King no longer there? ...
> Is there no balm in Gilead?
>> Is there no physician there?
> Why then is there no healing
>> for the wound of my people?

(Jeremiah 8:19–22 NIV)

There is an obvious, implied answer in the affirmative to the first four questions, which then gives rise to the fifth question: "Why, then, is there no healing for the wound of my people?"

The resinous gums of Gilead, previously and prominently used in Israel, were even exported to Egypt for the embalming of the dead. The prophet is really asking, "Is there no means of healing; is there no healer to apply these resinous gums, the balm, to the spiritual wounds of my people?"

The word "balm" is a contraction of "balsam," itself derived from the Hebrew *Baal-shemen*, "Lord of oil." This balm was famed as early as Jacob's time as being amongst the best fruit of Canaan. It was exported to Egypt and used to heal wounds (Jeremiah 46:11; 51:8). The tree was cultivated near Jericho and the Dead Sea in the first century, and it still grows in gardens near Tiberias; it is about fourteen feet in height. The resin is fragrant and has been known as the "balm of Mecca."

We should note that this highly valued, greatly beneficial resin is only obtained by making an incision in the bark of the tree.

He was wounded for our transgressions.

(Isaiah 53:5 KJV)

The incision will yield three or four drops a day from each tree, which, when left to stand, take on a clear golden color. The healing properties of the transparent life of the King of kings are known by many. The gold of the Tabernacle in the wilderness speaks of His deity, as does the gold of this precious balsam.

The balm was so scarce in earlier days that it was worth twice its weight in silver! So valuable was it that Titus in the first century had to fight two battles near Jericho to prevent the Jews (in despair) destroying the balsam-tree groves. Through all of this, there shines a merit and a worth which speak to us of the worthiness and preciousness of the King of kings.

This is why Jeremiah, with unwitting prophetic insight, enquires, "Why then is there no healing for the wound of my people?"

Elsewhere he explains why, declaring:

> They dress the wound of my people
> as though it were not serious.
> "Peace, peace," they say,
> when there is no peace.

(Jeremiah 8:11 NIV)

The precious balm needs applying. The Priesthood as well as the Kingship of the figure in our Messianic psalm has to be "applied" and to be received for healing.

The Kingship of Jesus: in humility

An earthly king is protected by his army. He is kept in a palace, waited on hand and foot by a host of servants, and has unlimited wealth. Not so for the King of kings.

His birthplace was a stable; His ministry was as a Servant to the nation. He possessed nothing and died in a borrowed grave. Instead of being protected by the army which He could well have summoned, He laid "down [his] life for the sheep" (John 10:15 NIV). How important it is to recognize His submission to the Father!

> I lay down my life ... No-one takes it from me, but I lay it down of my own accord.
>
> (John 10:17–18 NIV)

No wonder that Abram unhesitatingly pays homage to that mysterious forerunner! No wonder that some closing words of Scripture speak of him as the King of kings and Lord of lords (Revelation 19:16)!

Greatness in the eyes of the world is measured by position or status, but not so in God's eyes. Jesus said:

> Whoever wants to become great among you must be your servant ...
>
> (Matthew 20:26 NIV)

This is taken from the Gospel that focuses on the Kingship of Jesus – Matthew. And Jesus continued:

> ... just as the Son of Man did not come to be served, but to serve, and to give his life as a ransom for many.
>
> (Matthew 20:28 NIV)

God's unique yardstick for greatness, which is the very thing that causes both Jews and Gentiles to stumble, is compressed into a few words:

> God chose what is foolish in the world to shame the wise; God chose what is weak in the world to shame the strong; God chose what is low and despised in the world, things that are not, to bring to nothing things that are.
>
> (1 Corinthians 1:27–28 RSV)

Why?

So that no human being might boast in the presence of God. He is the source of your life in [Messiah] Jesus, whom God made our wisdom, our righteousness and sanctification and redemption.

(1 Corinthians 1:28–30 RSV)

No wonder we are exhorted to boast of the Lord, to boast of the kingly figure who humbled Himself unto death for us! It was out of His death (a life that "was not") that God has brought to nought the life that is – the false values of this materialistic age.

In a similar way, Israel, a nation that was not, has been resurrected in order to one day bring to nought the godless nations of this world (Jeremiah 30:11)! In Jeremiah 51:19–20 Israel is described as God's "battle axe" with which He breaks nations in pieces and destroys kingdoms. One day, Israel, as God's servant nation, will fulfill even this God-appointed role!

Her people will display Messiah's glory, not in political supremacy, but in divine worship. Let us soberly recall that the very first human being to enter God's kingdom through faith in the Messiah was not a doctrinally correct Christian (!), but a Jew who was a criminal on a cross alongside the Savior. How unsearchable are God's ways! How awesome the sum of his thoughts!

From lowliness to loftiness: the exalted King

Jesus was not born into a palatial residence of the world system, nor into the hands of state-qualified midwives, but into a manger that no one else wanted. Although the world needed Him, it did not welcome Him. His home was not a great city, but a place of low repute:

Can anything good come out of Nazareth?

(John 1:46 NIV)

He wore no crown of gold, no diadem inset with ruby and diamonds. His was a crown of thorns which pierced His brow, adding more blood to a face already marred more than that of any other man (Isaiah 52:14). But praise God that today there are many of Abrahamic and Gentile stock who sing:

> The head that once was crowned with thorns
> Is crowned with glory now;
> A royal diadem adorns
> The mighty Victor's brow.
>
> The highest place that heaven affords
> Is His by sovereign right,
> The King of kings, and Lord of lords
> And heaven's eternal light.
>
> (Thomas Kelly 1769–1855)

In the Kingship of Jesus, death was not conquered through some mighty surgical operation, but through death itself.

> He ... shared in their humanity so that by his death he might destroy him who holds the power of death – that is, the devil – and free those who all their lives were held in slavery by their fear of death.
>
> (Hebrews 2:14–15 NIV)

The greatest *descent* of all time – that of the heavenly King to this earth to identify with the needs of humanity and with Israel's need – has led also to the greatest *ascent* of all history.

> Therefore God exalted him to the highest place
>   and gave him the name that is above every name,
> that at the name of Jesus every knee should bow ... and every tongue confess that Jesus [the Messiah] is Lord,
>   to the glory of God the Father.
>
> (Philippians 2:9–11 NIV)

This is foreseen through the wisdom in Proverbs:

Who has ascended to heaven and come down?
Who has gathered the wind in his fists?
Who has wrapped up the waters in a garment?
Who has established all the ends of the earth?
What is his name, and what is his son's name?
Surely you know!

(Proverbs 30:4 RSV)

The King's descent from David

In spite of all the false charges leveled against the Lord Jesus in His days on earth, no one ever questioned His genealogy! While it proved surprising that something good did come forth from Nazareth, no one denied the fact of His descent from the very family line Biblically recorded to be that from which the Messiah was to come.

The Lord's promise to King David had been:

I will raise up your offspring to succeed you ... and I will establish the throne of his kingdom for ever.

(2 Samuel 7:12–13 NIV)

Over a period of 500 years, the prophecy of an eternal King, to arise from David, is repeated over and over again by King David himself (especially in his psalms), by his son Solomon, and by various prophets. In answer to the question from Jesus, "What do you think about the [Messiah]? Whose son is he?" the Pharisees replied, "The son of David" (Matthew 22:42 NIV).

It was known by all Jews that the Messiah would come from the line of David. So when addressed by the Jews, as He often was, as "Son of David," Jesus was really being referred to as the King and Messiah. If Jesus had been falsely claiming His family line, the people of his day would have undoubtedly contested it, because all the genealogical records of families were available to be checked; anyone's claim could be verified.

There are no such genealogical records available today! They were lost with the destruction of Jerusalem and the second Temple.

Other, then, than the Son of David having already come, we have no way today of humanly verifying the claims of any would-be Messiah as coming from the line of David. In the divine prerogative of God, who is the One who gave the record by which to check the Messiah's credentials, we are left to assume that He has already come. The reason why so few accept this is that most people look first for the King who will bring peace. But God has instead first sent the Priest to ordain and to become the Source of righteousness.

The blind men who recognized the King

Just after the bringing back to life of the ruler's daughter, two blind men followed Jesus. They were obviously not led by human eyesight, but by some inward insight. In their cry for mercy and healing, by the very language they used, they both recognized and acknowledged the Messiahship of Jesus:

> Have mercy on us, Son of David!
>
> (Matthew 9:27 NIV)

They also addressed Him as "Lord" and expressed faith in His power to heal. Once healed, they were commanded by Jesus to keep quiet about it. But they disobeyed.

Out of a large crowd following Jesus from Jericho, no one appears to have been touched particularly, apart from two more blind men. These were sitting by the roadside, and they, again in their blindness, acknowledged the Kingship of Jesus in crying:

> Lord, Son of David, have mercy on us!
>
> (Matthew 20:30, 31 NIV)

Jesus stopped, asked them what they wanted, had compassion on them and granted their request – the restoration of their sight! One touch from Him was all that was needed to give them *immediate* vision, and they then followed Him (Matthew 20:30ff). Today, as believers, we need a renewed touch from the Son of David, the Messiah, upon our sight – our spiritual insight – that we may see things clearly and follow Him. Let us not become proud, complacent or self-satisfied! It was for believers that Paul cried:

> I pray … that the eyes of your heart may be enlightened in order that you may know the hope to which he [the Messiah] has called you.
>
> (Ephesians 1:18 NIV)

The King's birth

Although often spoken of as a miraculous birth, the birth of Jesus was in fact quite normal and not unique in any way. The miraculous occurs in the manner of conception, for Jesus was not born of a human father. All the miraculous births of Old Testament women were miraculous in the sense of the women having been barren for years – and only a touch from God could have changed the situation.

In the case of Mary, the miracle was not in relation to barrenness but rather to the implanting of holy seed.

> She was found to be with child through the Holy Spirit.
>
> (Matthew 1:18 NIV)

There is nothing miraculous about a maiden giving birth, but there is everything miraculous about a virgin conceiving! This was the "sign" – the miracle promised by the Lord through the prophet Isaiah:

> Therefore the Lord himself will give you a sign: Behold, a young woman shall conceive, and bear a son, and shall call his name Immanuel.
>
> (Isaiah 7:14 RSV)

The "sign" or miracle here is that the young woman who conceived is in fact a virgin. Otherwise it would not be a "sign."

We must note that whenever the birth of the Messiah is spoken of in Old Testament prophecy, reference is made only to His mother, or to the womb, and never to a human father, which Jesus did not have.

> The LORD ... formed me from the womb to be his servant.
>
> (Isaiah 49:5 KJV)

> The LORD hath created a new thing in the earth, A woman shall compass a man.
>
> (Jeremiah 31:22 KJV)

> Thou art he that took me out of the womb.
>
> (Psalm 22:9 KJV)

Even in the first prophetic reference to the Messiah, and to the putting down of Satan, we find no reference to male seed, but rather to female seed or offspring:

> I will put enmity
> > between you and the woman,
> > and between your offspring [or seed] and hers.
>
> (Genesis 3:15 NIV)

The woman's seed was to be male, as the prophecy continues:

> *He* will crush your head,
> > and you will strike *his* heel.
>
> (Genesis 3:15 NIV, emphasis added)

Who amongst us can even begin to explain not only the miracle of Mary conceiving, but the even greater miracle expressed and contained therein of God's love for humankind?

> For God so loved the world that he gave His only begotten Son, that whosoever believeth in Him should not perish, but have everlasting life.
>
> (John 3:16 KJV)

King of the Jews – at birth

> Behold [i.e. take careful note], wise men ... came to Jerusalem, saying, "Where is He who has been born King of the Jews?"
>
> (Matthew 2:2 NKJV)

The very first question of the New Testament comes from men referred to as "wise." "Where is He who has been born King of the Jews?" Their terminology implies their non-Jewishness. Nathaniel, the Israelite or Jew "in whom [was] no guile," referred to that same One as "the King of Israel" (John 1:49), as did other Jews (Matthew 27:42 KJV).

This One then, for whom the wise men made enquiry, was born King. He did not become King, but was born King of the Jews. *Born King!* How different from the human line of royalty! One may be born a prince or a princess, but never a king. How and why should Jesus have been referred to thus? Again, under Holy Spirit inspiration, these men were simply picking up a truth referred to later in the New Testament:

> Now to the King eternal, immortal, invisible, the only wise God, be honour and glory for ever and ever. Amen.
>
> (1 Timothy 1:17 KJV)

As the King of Creation, the Sovereign Lord, Jesus had been pre-existent before His birth. But at this point, the wise men did not ask for the Great King, nor for the King of kings, nor even for the King of Christianity. Surprisingly, they asked for the King of the race which was at that time under the heel of Roman rule. It was to this One, although He was but an infant, that they paid homage. They did not need to wait until He "became" King. He was already a King! Other men become kings, and they may be born princes, but they await a later crowning. Not so for Messiah Jesus. In fear of His kingly rivalry, King Herod ruthlessly slaughtered all the young male Jewish children that he could lay his hands on.

King of the Jews – at death

For different reasons, but with similar conviction, another Roman ruler, Pilate, thirty-three years later inscribed over the cross of the Jewish King (in three languages – Greek, Latin and Hebrew):

THIS IS THE KING OF THE JEWS.

(Luke 23:39 NIV)

And, against protests from some Jewish people, though not all by any means, he retorted, "What I have written, I have written" (John 19:22 KJV). In other words, "That's it! I will not revoke it!" In this, even Pilate was simply, though unwittingly, expressing God's truth.

King of the Jews – in life

The phrase "King of the Jews" appears nineteen times in the New Testament. Jesus was not only born as, and did not only die as, but also lived as King of the Jews, even though He was much otherwise in appearance to some.

He was recognized at once by Nathaniel. His authority was evident throughout His ministry, although He declined political status at that time (John 6:15).

The crowd who cried "Hosanna to the Son of David!" as Jesus triumphantly entered Jerusalem was, in effect, acknowledging Jesus' Kingship as the offspring of King David (Matthew 21:9 NIV). That term "Hosanna" expresses the hope that the crowd placed in Him, for it means "Save us!"

We read that elsewhere the crowd, taking up the victory note from Psalm 118:26, cried:

Blessed is the king who comes in the name of the Lord!

(Luke 19:38 NIV)

It was at this point that His Kingship, His righteousness, Saviorship, gentleness and humility were all merged together in the precious and indelible words of the prophet Zechariah:

> Rejoice greatly, O Daughter of Zion!
>   Shout, Daughter of Jerusalem!
> See, your king comes to you,
>   righteous and having salvation,
>   gentle and riding on a donkey,
>   on a colt, the foal of a donkey.
>
> (Zechariah 9:9 NIV)

That great multitude, on that "Palm Sunday" at the entry of the Lord into the city of David, obeyed God's Word. They did rejoice – greatly! They did shout "Hosanna" (Save us now!).

They provided the preview of how the whole nation will (once the veil is taken away) receive their King! There can be no doubt whatever about that. But at that time, "They will see the Son of man coming on the clouds of heaven with power and great glory" (Matthew 24:30 NKJV) – not on a colt!

King of the Jews – as prophesied

Although his disciples could not understand the prophetic significance of Jesus' entry into Jerusalem, His coming as "King of the Jews" is alluded to in many Old Testament scriptures. Some of these are:

> I shall see him ... there shall come a Star out of Jacob, and a sceptre shall rise out of Israel.
>
> (Numbers 24:17 KJV)

> Behold, the days are coming, says the LORD, when I will raise up for David a righteous Branch, and he shall reign as king [the term used in the Hebrew Bible] and deal wisely, and shall execute justice and righteousness in the land.
>
> (Jeremiah 23:5–6 RSV)

The emphasis as King of the Jews is underlined by the reference to His rule in "the land," i.e. the land of Israel.

They shall serve the Lord their God and David their king, whom I will
raise up for them.

(Jeremiah 30:9 RSV)

The term "David" here reflects again the line from which Messiah
Jesus descended.

The Jewishness of Jesus – by a Jew

Neither Christian protest nor Jewish lamentation annuls the fact that
Jesus was a Jew, a Hebrew of the Hebrews. Surely it is not wholly unfit
that Jesus be reclaimed by those who have never unitedly or organi-
sationally denied him, though oft denied by his followers? That Jesus
should not so much be appropriated by us but assigned to the place in
Jewish life and history which is rightfully his own? Jesus was not only a
Jew but he was the Jew of Jews, and it is little less than tragic that, with
respect to Jesus, the world imagines that his life belongs to Christianity, while his death was due to Israel.

That Jesus was a Jew is only half-admitted when not wholly
denied; but that Judas was a Jew is always affirmed without doubt
or hesitation. Whatever the death of Jesus may have been, we
believe that his life was Jewish, and we devoutly affirm that his
teaching was Jewish. In that day when history shall be written in
the light of truth, the people of Israel will be known not as Christ-
killers, but as the Christ-bearers; not as the God-slayers, but as the
God-bringers to the world.[1]

The King Eternal as King of the Jews

Although Rabbi Stephen Wise eloquently speaks of Jesus as King of
the Jews, we need to remember that Christians speak of Jesus as "the
same yesterday, today and forever" (Hebrews 13:8 NKJV). He was and
is (humanly speaking) a Jew. He was and is King of the Jews. He has
not forgotten the people amongst whom he lived and died. It was God
who chose the Jews and He will not renege on His promises to the

nation – He will honor these, not only because His name and His righteousness are at stake, but because His nature is love and His character is faithful.

At this late point in time, the Lord still waits to impress this fact upon the Church so that we will really pray, really act and really believe in correct perspective. *The Lord's return to earth will see Him not at Canterbury, Westminster or Rome, but at Jerusalem!*

Have you ever seriously pondered who the "us" is, when reading your many Christmas cards: "Unto *us* a child is born, unto *us* a son is given"? It is, of course, a Jewish scripture taken out of the Jewish Bible, written by a Jewish prophet to the Jewish nation. It goes on to say:

> He will reign on David's throne
> and over his kingdom,
> establishing and upholding it ...
> from that time on and for ever.
>
> (Isaiah 9:7 NIV)

David's kingdom was the nation of Israel. When the King of kings does come to reign on earth, His first major function will be as King of Israel, King of the Jews, whom He will have saved out of the teeth and hatred of the nations.

Let us not, out of our own self-centeredness, rob the Jewish people in thought or prayer of their own King, the One by whom the Church and the world have been blessed, and the One also by whom Israel and Judah will yet be united under God's love.

The vital letter in the New Testament that summarizes the Priesthood of Jesus is addressed to the "Hebrews" (not even to the "Hebrew Christians") and it begins:

> God spoke of old to our fathers by the prophets, but in these last days he has spoken to *us* by a Son.
>
> (Hebrews 1:1–2 RSV, emphasis added)

This is New Testament teaching. Note the possessive, almost worshipful term "us." He has spoken to "us"!

Through the Church becoming largely "Gentilized," it has lost much more than it realizes or admits, by pruning off its Jewishness. One important example of this is the place of the festivals of Israel, which Biblically are actually called the "feasts of the LORD" (Leviticus 23) – not "Jewish" feasts. Much that yet remains to be fulfilled in the world and in the Church is mirrored in these festivals. In our prejudice we remain blinded and hardened to this aspect.

The feasts of Trumpets, Atonement and Harvest Ingathering speak of spiritual topics through which the Holy Spirit has more to say both to Israel and the Church.

Jesus was not ashamed to call Jews His "brethren" (Hebrews 2:11 KJV). This is one factor to bear in mind where Scripture exhorts us, "Prepare ye the way of the Lord" (Matthew 3:3 KJV). The only place in Scripture where Jesus applies the term "King" to Himself is in Matthew 25:34 when depicting the time of His return to His people, of whom He will then, in retrospect, say:

> Inasmuch as ye have done it unto one of the least of these my brethren, ye have done it unto Me.
>
> (Matthew 25:40 KJV)

> All kings will bow down to him
>   and all nations will serve him.
>
> (Psalm 72:11 NIV)

Thus shall the King, who was found lowly, humble and riding upon a donkey, be found as King of kings and Lord of lords. The Gentile domination that has existed since the days of Nebuchadnezzar will then have ended. Looking through the telescope of prophecy, the psalmist explicitly and lucidly proclaimed the Word of the Lord some 3,000 years ago. This is found in the *second* of the 150 psalms, where the Holy Spirit chooses to place this somewhat stark warning:

Why do the nations conspire
>   and the peoples [Gentiles] plot in vain?
> The kings of the earth take their stand
>   and the rulers gather together against the LORD
> and against his Anointed One [Messiah] ...
> "I have installed my King
> on Zion, my holy hill."

(Psalm 2:1–2, 4–6 NIV)

In other words, our God in heaven foresaw 3,000 years ago the kind of controversy and opposition that would come from this world (and the Church) against His Son, His city, His land and His people. And the second psalm ends with the call:

> Do homage to the Son, that He not become angry, and you perish in the way.

(Psalm 2:12 NASB)

Only the King's return will bring with it the elusive peace which the world has been seeking interminably. But the Lord will come, of all places, to Zion!

> He will judge between the nations
>   and will settle disputes for many peoples.
> They will beat their swords into plowshares
>   and their spears into pruning hooks.
> Nation will not take up sword against nation
>   nor will they train for war anymore.

(Isaiah 2:4 NIV)

The King of kings in Joseph

The King of Glory is nowhere pictured more beautifully, more movingly, or more powerfully than in the life of Joseph. There, in him we see Jesus as the Provider, Preserver, Savior and Ruler of his people Israel, but also in those same capacities as Sovereign over the world.

Joseph was sold into slavery by his own brothers. For years he was "missing, presumed dead." It was not until famine forced these brothers to look for food that they, unwittingly, went to Joseph. Although moved by tears, Joseph did not at once reveal his identity to his people. He adopted ruses to persuade them to bring to him the father of his family. Upon his brothers, in an outwardly brusque manner, Joseph lavished love and copious provision, but the moment of the revelation of who he was – the one they had plotted to kill – is one of the most emotional stories in the whole of the Bible.

It is not accidental that the story of Joseph is by far the lengthiest biography in the book of Genesis, and in the whole of the Bible! The apex is reached when he shares with his brothers:

> As for you, you meant evil against me; but God meant it for good, in order to bring it about as it is this day, to save many people alive.
>
> Now therefore, do not be afraid; I will provide for you and your little ones.
>
> (Genesis 50:20–21 NKJV)

Joseph mirrors the Servanthood of Jesus, both in the prison and the palace. He also resists temptation, and is wrongly accused. He is later exalted to be second only to Pharaoh. No flaw whatever is found in the depicted life of Joseph. He reflects more than any other the kingly nature of the Messiah who was later to come. In the final analysis, only the divine Person of the Lord could live perfectly and die, unblemished by sin, in atonement for the human race.

> We do not have a high priest who is unable to sympathize with our weaknesses, but we have one who has been tempted in every way, just as we are – yet was without sin.
>
> (Hebrews 4:15 NIV)

The King of kings: greater than Solomon

> Behold, a greater than Solomon is here.
>
> (Matthew 12:42 KJV)

In spite of all the splendor and magnificence of the reign of Solomon, Jesus, plucking a few lilies from the field around Him, declared,

> Even Solomon in all his glory was not arrayed like one of these.
>
> (Matthew 6:29 KJV)

The beauty of the lily is God-originated from a source unseen and perenially renewed. Solomon's beauty and glory were transient, outward, and prone to human lapse and failure. Within the psalm penned by Solomon that opens this chapter, Psalm 72, we have a picture of the coming universal reign, sovereignty and character of the Messiah.

Nowhere else in the Bible do we see such wealth, such a time of peace, such fame allotted to its ruler, or such homage paid to him as in the references to Solomon and Israel in Psalm 72. Solomon's reign, the most peaceful and glorious of Jewish history, foreshadows that yet-to-be reign of Him who is "greater than Solomon."

The area and extent of Solomon's reign and territory are to be found in 1 Kings:

> Solomon ruled over all the kingdoms from the River [Euphrates] to the land of the Philistines, as far as the border of Egypt.
>
> (1 Kings 4:21 NIV)

These countries brought tribute and were Solomon's subjects all of his life.

This means that Israel's territory, far from being decimated through present-day contention, is going to be expanded many times – right up to the River Euphrates, which runs through Iraq!

So we also fall down and worship the King of kings and Lord of lords. We marvel at His ways which transcend our understanding. And we join in praise:

> Blessed be the LORD God, the God of Israel,
> Who only does wondrous things!
> And blessed be His glorious name forever!
> And let the whole earth be filled with His glory.
> Amen and Amen.
>
> (Psalm 72:18–19 NKJV)

Thus ends this glorious Messianic psalm and the preview of the Lord's coming reign – the Lord by whom all nations will be blessed, and whom all nations shall call "blessed."

> The Lord God will give him the throne of his father David, and he will reign over the house of Jacob for ever; his kingdom will never end.
>
> (Luke 1:33 NIV)

So that Israel may say:

> The King of love my Shepherd is,
> Whose goodness faileth never;
> I nothing lack if I am His
> and He is mine forever.
>
> Where streams of living water flow,
> My ransomed soul He leadeth;
> And where the verdant pastures grow,
> With food celestial feedeth ...
>
> And so, through all the length of days
> Thy goodness faileth never;
> Good Shepherd, may I sing Thy praise
> Within Thy house forever.
>
> (Henry W. Baker 1821–77)

Notes

1. Stephen Wise, quoted in *The Messiahship of Jesus* by Arthur W. Kac (Moody Press USA).

For further information please contact PFI (Prayer For Israel)
at the following address:

PFI UK
PO Box 328
Bromley
Kent BR1 2ZS
United Kingdom

Email: pfi@prayer4i.org
Web: www.prayer4i.org

We hope you enjoyed reading this Sovereign World book.
For more details of other Sovereign World books
and new releases please see our website:
www.sovereignworld.com

If you would like to help us send a copy of this book
and many other titles to needy pastors in developing
countries, please write for further information
or send your gift to:

Sovereign World Trust
PO Box 777
Tonbridge, Kent TN11 0ZS
United Kingdom

You can also visit www.sovereignworldtrust.com.
The Trust is a registered charity.